WorkFiles

FIFTH EDITION

Intercambios

Spanish for Global Communication

Guiomar Borrás Álvarez
Thunderbird—The Garvin School of International Management
Glendale Community College

Michelle Evers
Creighton University

James N. Hendrickson

Australia • Brazil • Canada • Mexico • Singapore • Spain • United Kingdom • United States

Intercambios: Spanish for Global Communication, Fifth Edition, WorkFiles
Borrás A. / Hendrickson / Evers

Executive Editor: Carrie Brandon
Acquisitions Editor: Helen Alejandra Richardson
Development Editor: Heather Bradley
Marketing Manager: Lindsey Richardson
Marketing Assistant: Marla Nasser
Advertising Project Manager: Stacey Purviance
Editorial Production Manager: Michael Burggren
Manufacturing Manager: Marcia Locke
Senior Permissions Editor: Isabel Alves
Senior Art Director: Bruce Bond
Photo Manager: Sheri Blaney
Technology Project Manager: Sacha Laustsen
Media Assistant: Rachel Bairstow
Production Service/Compositor: Pre-Press Company, Inc.
Cover Designer: Linda Beaupre
Text/Cover Printer: West Group

Cover Photos: Clockwise from top left: ©LLC, Fogstock/Index Open; ©Danita Delimont/Alamy, ©Photos.com select/Index Open, ©Kim Karpeles/Alamy; ©Peter Adams/Alamy; ©Getty RF; ©blickwinkel/Alamy; ©J. Marshall/Tribaleye Images/Alamy; ©Corbis RF; ©David Noton/Alamy.

Printed in the United States of America
2 3 4 5 6 7 09 08 07

ISBN-13: 978-1-4130-2016-8
ISBN-10: 1-4130-2016-X

Thomson Higher Education
25 Thomson Place
Boston, MA 02210-1202
USA

Text Credits
Page 159: "La aspirina", Clara, mensual con mil ideas, No. 58, julio de 1997. **Page 161:** "Medico de familia", Clara, mensual con mil ideas, No. 58, julio de 1997. **Page 175:** "Veraneantes solidarios", Clara, mensual con mil ideas, No. 58, julio de 1997. **Page 71:** "El submarinismo", Clara, mensual con mil ideas, No. 44, mayo 1996. **Page 97:** "Cartitas a Santa Claus", por Arturo Olmedo, El Excelsior del Condado de Orange, 22 de diciembre de 1993.

Photo Credits
p. 192 TL: ©Eric Risberg / AP Photo
p. 192 TR: ©Kevork Djansezian / AP Photo
p. 192 BL: ©Christian Charisius / Reuters / AP Photo
p. 192 BR: ©Ann Johansson / AP Photo
p. 371: Diego Rivera: ©Banco de Mexico Trust, *Día de muertos, La ofrenda.* 1923–24. Photo Schalkwiji / Art Resource, NY.

Contents

Preface

The *WorkFiles* for the fifth edition of ***Intercambios: Spanish for Global Communication*** combines the workbook, the laboratory manual, the flex files, and the video manual in order to cohesively practice and reinforce the concepts and skills introduced in the main text. The manual provides additional practice in developing vocabulary and grammar usage, listening comprehension, and reading and writing skills. Furthermore, throughout the *WorkFiles,* students will find numerous suggestions for topics to recall or review, study hints, and glosses for new vocabulary words.

The *WorkFiles* contains three parts—*Lo esencial, Lo suplemental,* and *Realidades en video*—, which are each divided into sixteen lessons *(Lección preliminar* and *Lecciones 1–15).*

In *Lo esencial,* each lesson contains the following sections:

Práctica esencial

- *Vocabulario esencial* provides discrete point exercises and productive activities aimed at vocabulary practice.
- *Gramática esencial* reinforces the two or three major grammatical structures of Spanish that are introduced in the main textbook. These exercises are designed to help students manipulate grammatical structures in written form so that they can visualize how the various structures work within a situational context.
- *Cultura* reinforces the cultural content of the main text by combining a variety of exercise formats with an occasional cultural reading that expands upon the content covered in the chapter.
- *¡A leer!* is designed to practice reading strategies in Spanish using authentic material. The *Antes de leer* activities are designed so that students can benefit from pre-reading activities that focus on the topic of the authentic text. This section includes in-class activities and techniques that make use of students' existing knowledge of the world and allow them to brainstorm and produce ideas that might appear in the authentic text. The *Vamos a leer* section requires the active participation of the students by encouraging them to use their relevant background information to read authentic texts in Spanish. The reading may be an in-class or out-of-class activity; however, it is important that students do not attempt to read word-for-word, but rather utilize the reading techniques suggested in the *¡A leer!* sections in the main textbook. In particular, the skimming and scanning strategies will help students acquire a global view of the text. The *Después de leer* activities allow students to go beyond the factual details of the text. These post-reading activities place students in contact with the material in realistic settings by means of role plays and other activities designed to integrate and personalize information gained from the authentic texts. This final stage links the development of reading skills to development of listening, speaking, and writing skills.
- *¡A escribir!* is divided into three sections. In *Antes de escribir,* students brainstorm ideas about a topic that has been introduced in the lesson from the main textbook. In *Vamos a escribir,* with the support of the ***Atajo 4.0: Writing Assistant for Spanish,*** they write about their own experiences or about a situation in which the characters from the main textbook find themselves. In *Después de escribir,* students reflect, share, and examine what they have written. In several instances, a peer editing activity is included that is designed to be done in class.

Práctica auditiva

- *Pronunciación esencial* appears in the first ten lessons *(Lección preliminar* and *Lecciones 1–9)* to provide practice in pronouncing the Spanish sounds that are the most problematic for native speakers of English. These sounds are integrated into short dialogs based on the characters and situations introduced in the main text. The dialogs provide samples of authentic discourse in Spanish and are designed to develop students' pronunciation in Spanish well enough to be understood by native speakers who have had little or no contact with non-native speakers. Native speakers of Spanish have recorded the dialogs in this section on the Laboratory Audio Program (available on compact disc).
- *En contexto* dialogs give students exposure to aural input that contextualizes new chapter content. Students work with the same story line, structures, vocabulary, and topics found in the main text, and demonstrate mastery over new material by completing questions in a variety of formats: true/false, fill-in-the-blank, multiple-choice.
- *Vocabulario esencial* give students more listening practice using the new vocabulary that was introduced in the main text. Students will demonstrate their understanding in a variety of formats: multiple-choice, short sentences, fill-in-the-blank.

In *Lo supplemental,* students will encounter additional activities that may be used in class or out of class.

Práctica suplemental

- *Vocabulario suplemental* provides more words or phrases for use with each vocabulary theme presented in the main text. Students have the opportunity to practice this new vocabulary through accompanying exercises.
- *Gramática suplemental* allows students to demonstrate their understanding of the grammatical structures presented previously in the textbook through short sentences, fill-in-the-blanks and multiple-choice exercises.

Práctica comunicativa suplemental gives students the opportunity to practice oral communication through different types of pair activities.

The new *Realidades en video* section introduces students to five friends that come to live together in San Juan, Puerto Rico for a month. The section contains pre- and post-viewing activites, plus stills from the video. After watching the video in class (at least twice), students will engage in discussions in small or large groups about the activities of the roommates and what they would or would not do in similar situations.

The *WorkFiles* offers students an abundance of varied practice, which they may adapt to fit their individual needs.

Please note, the authors have deliberately decided to use the 'tú' form of address in the *WorkFiles.* The instructions in the ***Intercambios*** text utilize 'usted'; as such, students are familiar with that form of address. We would like to be certain that they are equally as familiar with the 'tú' form as well.

Lo esencial

Nombre ______________________________ Fecha ______________

LECCIÓN PRELIMINAR

Práctica esencial

VOCABULARIO ESENCIAL

P-1 Meeting and Greeting People in Your Class. Choose the best response for each situation described. Write the letter of that response in the space provided.

a. la mochila
b. Escuche a la profesora.
c. ¡Buenos días! ¿Qué tal?
d. Abran el libro en la página 18.
e. Siéntense, por favor.
f. Muéstreme la tarea, por favor.

1. ______________ You have just arrived at class at 9:00 in the morning. You greet another student.
2. ______________ Your professor is ready to begin the lesson. She wants you to take your seats.
3. ______________ Now your professor wants you to look in your book.
4. ______________ You are talking to your neighbor during class. She asks you to stop talking and listen to your professor.
5. ______________ Your professor wants to see that you have completed the homework.
6. ______________ What do you use to carry your books to class?

P-2 Los números. Write out the following numbers in Spanish.

1. 25 ______________
2. 14 ______________
3. Your telephone number ______________

GRAMÁTICA ESENCIAL

P-3 Indefinite Articles: Personas famosas. Complete the following sentences with the appropriate indefinite article **(un, una)**. Some Spanish nouns always end in **-a**, whether they are referring to a man or a woman. For example: **un artista / una artista.** Pay attention to the gender of the famous people in this activity.

1. Isabel Allende es ______________ autora chilena.
2. Carlos Fuentes es ______________ novelista mexicano.
3. Pedro Almodóvar es ______________ director español.
4. Ronaldo es ______________ futbolista brasileño.
5. Pablo Neruda es ______________ poeta chileno.
6. Shakira es ______________ cantante colombiana.

P-4 Definite and Indefinite Articles: Personas y productos. Complete the following sentences with appropriate definite articles **(el, la, los, las)** or indefinite articles **(un, una, unos, unas).**

1. ____________ líderes *(leaders)* del mundo son responsables.
2. ____________ presidente de Francia es inteligente.
3. ____________ presidente de Colombia es interesante.
4. Costa Rica es ____________ país fascinante.
5. Kiwi es ____________ fruta de Nueva Zelanda.
6. ____________ papaya es ____________ fruta tropical.
7. ____________ teléfonos de Taiwán son fantásticos.
8. ____________ computadoras de los Estados Unidos son excelentes.
9. ____________ autos de Corea son prácticos y buenos.
10. ____________ bicicletas de Italia son maravillosas.

Cultura

P-5 Cultura. Answer the following questions based on the cultural readings in your textbook.

1. Can you name the capitals of the following countries: Mexico, Spain, Argentina, Costa Rica?
____
2. Name three countries in the world where Spanish is the official language.
____
3. Identify some of the ancient languages that have influenced Spanish.
____

¡A leer!: Mercosur

P-6 Skimming and Scanning. Skimming and scanning are important reading techniques used to gather information quickly. Skim the Aerolíneas Sur advertisement to get the gist, or general idea, of its content. Next, scan the advertisement to find the specific information asked of you in the questions below. Finish by reading carefully to fill in the rest of the information.

Antes de leer

P-7 Can you answer these questions even before carefully reading the Aerolíneas Sur advertisement?

Use the information in English in the box on the next page.

1. What does Mercosur mean?
____
2. What countries in Latin America belong to Mercosur?
____
3. What are the goals of this group?
____

Nombre ______________________ Fecha ____________

Mercosur

Mercosur is the name for the Southern Common Market. The countries that belong to this group now are Argentina, Paraguay, Uruguay, and Brazil. Chile, Bolivia, Venezuela, Colombia, and Peru have also shown great interest in joining. The member countries of Mercosur have a combined population of 390 million people living in an area larger than the total surface of the European continent. Some of Mercosur's goals are the free transit of goods, the elimination of customs rights, and open competition among the member countries.

DIARIO AL MERCOSUR Y A

SANTIAGO DE CHILE

Aerolíneas Sur le ofrece la mejor forma de llegar al centro de sus negocios en la capital de Chile, Santiago. Con las ventajas y beneficios de la Clase Club y la comodidad de su nueva generación de asientos. Sume puntos con su tarjeta Aerolíneas Plus. Aerolíneas Sur, su línea directa con el Mercosur. Si desea más información, **consulte en su agencia de viajes** o llame a Aerolíneas Sur: Tel.: (91) 444 47 33, Internet: http://www.aerolineas.sur.com.ar.

P-8 Find this information by scanning the advertisement. Do not read the whole advertisement closely.

1. What is the name of the airline? ______________________
2. What is the Internet address? ______________________
3. What countries does this airline visit? ______________________

Después de leer

P-9 Now that you have read the ad in greater detail, think about what the airline is offering.

1. If you were flying with Aerolíneas Sur, to which city or cities would you like to travel and why? ______________________
2. Why do you think Aerolíneas Sur flies to the countries that belong to Mercosur? ______________________
3. What type of people will go to these countries? ______________________
4. What do you think are the advantages of flying the Club Class? ______________________

Nombre ______________________ Fecha ______________

¡A escribir!

Antes de escribir

P-10 Look at the map and list five countries you would like to visit.

1. ______________
2. ______________
3. ______________
4. ______________
5. ______________

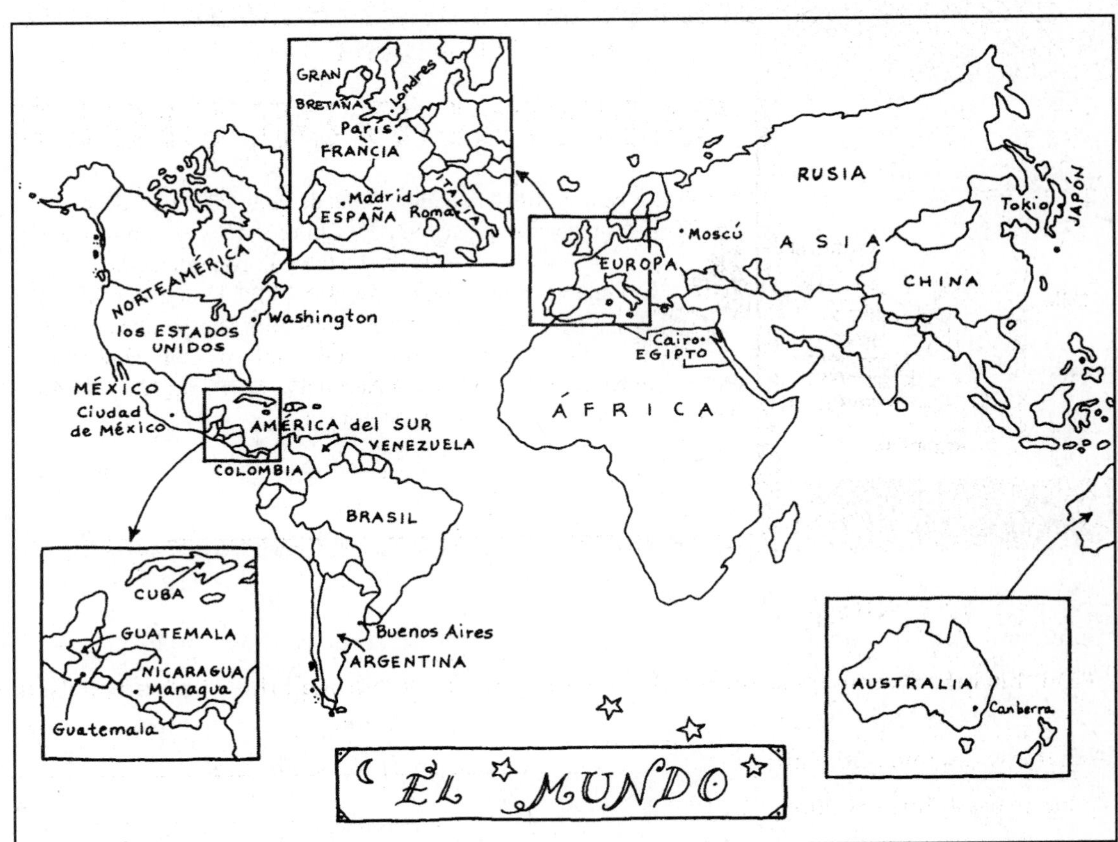

Nombre ________________________ Fecha ____________

Vamos a escribir

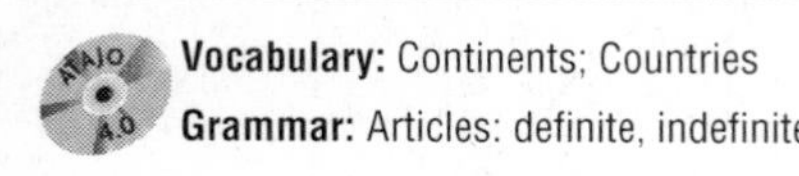

P-11 Use the map to find the capital of each country listed below and write a short sentence for each one.

Modelo: Egipto
La capital de Egipto es el Cairo.

1. México
____
2. España
____
3. Francia
____
4. Costa Rica
____
5. Cuba
____

Después de escribir

P-12 Use the lines provided to write your responses.

1. Select one country from your list in Exercise P-10 and write a short paragraph in English about why you would like to visit that particular country.
____
____
____
2. Read the paragraph you have just written. Do you already know how to write some of the words you used above in Spanish? If so, list them here.
____
____
____
3. Share the **Antes de escribir** and **Después de escribir** exercises with a fellow student. Working together, can you come up with additional Spanish words to add to your lists from item 2 above?
____
____
____

Práctica auditiva

Pronunciación esencial

CD 1-2 **P-13** The alphabet is the best place to start learning the sounds of a new language. It will be helpful to know the alphabet when you need to spell your name or your address in Spanish. It will also help you when you want to know how to spell a word in order to look up its meaning. Listed below are the letters of the Spanish alphabet along with their names. Repeat the letters after they have been modeled.

a	a	j	jota	r	ere
b	be	k	ka	s	ese
c	ce	l	ele	t	te
d	de	m	eme	u	u
e	e	n	ene	v	ve
f	efe	ñ	eñe	w	doble ve
g	ge	o	o	x	equis
h	hache	p	pe	y	i griega
i	i	q	cu	z	zeta

CD 1-3 **P-14** Pronounce these first and last names and then spell them.

Modelo: Robin Morán
ere, o, be, i, ene; eme, o, ere, a, ene

Joe Santiago	Pepe LePeu
Alison Marks	Dolores Friedman
Reed Wynne	Cornelia Zavala
Carmen Miranda	Yuspi Zavarse
Carlos Fuentes	Sonia Morales

P-15 Write your first name, last name, and address. Then practice spelling them aloud.

____

____

En contexo

CD 1-4 **P-16 Saludos.** You will hear a short conversation between two students. Based only on the information you hear, decide whether the statements below are true **(V: verdadero)** or false **(F: falso)**, or whether there is not sufficient information to decide **(N: no hay información suficiente)**. Write the corresponding letter next to each statement.

____ 1. Los estudiantes se llaman Raúl y Ben.

____ 2. Raúl es de Nuevo México.

____ 3. Antonio es de Nueva York.

____ 4. Antonio y Alex son amigos.

____ 5. Ellos son canadienses.

Nombre ______________________ Fecha ______________

Vocabulario esencial

CD 1-5 **P-17 Saludar y conocer a tus compañeros(as) de clase.** You will hear three conversations. Look at the pictures while you listen and consider everything you see and hear. Write the number of the conversation below the picture it matches.

_____

_____

_____

CD 1-6 **P-18 Las nacionalidades.** Listen to the following nationalities and repeat them after the speaker on the CD. Pronunciation takes practice and experience with the language. Try to match your pronunciation of these words as closely as you can to the pronunciation of the native speaker on the CD.

árabe	nicaragüense	boliviana	francesa
chino	cubana	chileno	griego
japonesa	dominicano	colombiano	holandesa
costarricense	puertorriqueña	alemana	inglés
guatemalteca	argentino	español	estadounidense
hondureño			

Nombre ______________________ Fecha ______________

CD 1-7 **P-19 Los países y las nacionalidades.** Listen to the name of each country and circle the corresponding nationality. You will hear the name of the country twice.

Modelo: *You hear:* el Canadá
You circle: canadiense

	(canadiense)	estadounidense	griego
1.	boliviano	cubano	peruano
2.	uruguayo	venezolano	salvadoreño
3.	portugués	argentino	panameño
4.	indú	inglés	mexicano
5.	guatemalteco	ruso	paraguayo
6.	canadiense	mexicano	estadounidense
7.	griego	guatemalteco	colombiano
8.	costarricense	puertorriqueño	ruso
9.	salvadoreño	panameño	hondureño
10.	argentino	español	portugués

CD 1-8 **P-20 ¿Cómo te llamas?** You will hear five questions or phrases. Circle the appropriate answer to each.

Modelo: *You hear:* ¿Cómo te llamas?
You circle: Me llamo Kelly.

	Soy de Minnesota.	(Me llamo Kelly.)	Bien.
1.	Buenas tardes.	Buenas noches.	Buenos días.
2.	Adiós.	Hola.	Gracias.
3.	Bien, gracias.	Soy de Colorado.	Me llamo Sara.
4.	Más o menos, gracias.	Adiós, gracias.	Buenas tardes, gracias.
5.	Muy bien, gracias.	Soy del Canadá.	Me llamo Mary Ellen.

CD 1-9 **P-21 En la clase.** You will hear eight commands. Look at the pictures while you listen and consider everything you see and hear. Write the number of the command below the picture it matches.

Nombre ______________________ Fecha ______________

PASO 1 Nuevos amigos en México

LECCIÓN 1 ¡BIENVENIDA A MONTERREY!

Práctica esencial

VOCABULARIO ESENCIAL

P1-1 Greetings and Good-byes. Fill in the blanks to complete the following conversation. Select from the list of expressions below.

Encantado(a)	Bien, gracias	¿Cómo te llamas?
El gusto es mío	Hasta luego	Me llamo Javier
Hola		

Enrique: Hola, Alicia. Me llamo Enrique González.

Alicia: ¡______________! ¡Mucho gusto!

Enrique: ______________. ¿Qué tal?

Alicia: ______________. ¿Cómo está usted?

Enrique: Bien, gracias. Quiero presentarte a mi hijo.

Alicia: Hola. ¿______________?

Javier: ______________. Hola, Alicia. ______________.

Alicia: Mucho gusto.

Enrique y Javier: Bueno, adiós, y hasta mañana.

Alicia: ¡______________!

P1-2 Personal Titles. Provide the correct title for the following people according to the information given. Select from the list below.

señor señora señorita doctor don doña

1. Alicia Benson, estudiante, 20 años ______________
2. Javier Gómez, profesor, 41 años ______________
3. Ernesto González, padre, 55 años ______________
4. Carmen, abuela *(grandmother)*, 85 años ______________
5. Jorge, abuelo *(grandfather)*, 89 años ______________
6. Emilio Fernández, médico, 42 años ______________
7. Blanca González, madre/esposa, 53 años ______________

Nombre ______________________ Fecha ______________

GRAMÁTICA ESENCIAL

P1-3 Forms of *ser*. Fill in the following blanks with the appropriate form of the verb **ser** according to the subject. Choose your answer from the word list below.

soy eres es somos sois son

1. Patricia y yo ______________ de México.
2. Yo ______________ de Guadalajara.
3. Patricia ______________ de Monterrey.
4. Mis padres ______________ de México, D.F.
5. Vosotros ______________ de Madrid.
6. Tú ______________ de Veracruz.

P1-4 *Ser* with Origin and Nationality. Write sentences stating where the following people are from. Then choose the correct nationality for the same people. Make sure that your adjective matches in gender and number with the person or people described.

Modelo: Rigoberta Menchú: Guatemala
Rigoberta Menchú es de Guatemala. Es guatemalteca.

1. Mel Gibson: Australia
____
2. Sting: Inglaterra
____
3. Vicente Fox: México
____
4. Enrique Gonzáles (jugador de béisbol en Arizona): Venezuela
____
5. Gabriela Sabatini: Argentina
____
6. Shakira: Colombia
____
7. Carlos Fuentes y Octavio Paz: México
____
8. Enrique y Julio Iglesias: España
____
9. Gabriel García Márquez y Juanes: Colombia
____
10. Yo: ¿... ?
____
11. Mi mejor amigo y yo: ¿... ?
____
12. Mi familia: ¿... ?
____
13. Mi profesor(a) de español: ¿... ?
____

Nombre ______________________ Fecha ______________

P1-5 ***Ser*** **and Professions.** Complete the following sentences with the correct form of **ser** and a profession, when necessary.

1. Alicia ______________ estudiante.
2. Ricardo y Alicia ______________ profesores de español.
3. Cristina Aguilera y Gloria Estefan ______________ cantantes.
4. Sammy Sosa ______________ jugador de béisbol.
5. Mi papa ______________ ______________.
6. Mis amigos y yo ______________ ______________.
7. Yo ______________ ______________.

P1-6 ***Ser*** **and Descriptive Adjectives, Adjective Agreement.** Choose from the list of adjectives below to describe the following people in your life. Then, write sentences to describe those people. Be sure to make your adjectives agree in gender and number with the people they describe. Feel free to use other adjectives that you have learned that are not listed below.

generoso(a)	guapo(a)	viejo(a)	trabajador(a)
simpático(a)	moreno(a)	bueno(a)	cortés
interesante	rubio(a)	malo(a)	honesto(a)
débil	pelirrojo(a)	bonito(a)	encantador(a)
grande	fuerte	feo(a)	nuevo(a)
pequeño(a)	perezoso(a)		

1. Yo ______________________________.
2. Mi mejor amigo *(My best friend)* ______________________________.
3. Mis hermanos ______________________________.
4. Mi abuela ______________________________.
5. Mis profesores ______________________________.
6. Mis compañeros de clase y yo ______________________________.

Cultura

P1-7 **¿Abrazos?** Read the following situations and decide which greeting would be more appropriate in the Spanish-speaking world, a handshake or a hug **(abrazo).** Circle your answer.

1. You are introduced to your classmates at the Tecnológico de Monterrey.

2. You run into your best friend downtown.

3. You visit your aunt and uncle during a family reunion.

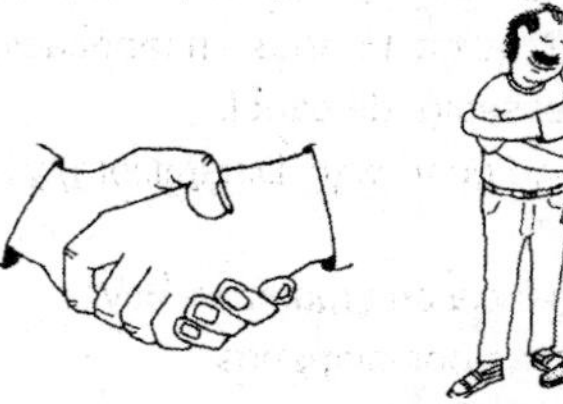

4. You greet a client at your office.

Nombre ______________________ Fecha ______________

P1-8 **¿Tú o usted?** Indicate **tú** or **usted** as the appropriate form of address for the following people.

1. el profesor Gómez ______________________
2. la abuela Carmen ______________________
3. su amiga Carlota ______________________
4. el presidente George Bush ______________________
5. Juan Diego, su compañero de clase ______________________

¡A leer!: Anuncios clasificados

Antes de leer

P1-9 Imagine that you are looking for a job and you want to describe yourself in a classified ad for a magazine or newspaper.

1. Make a list of the words you know in Spanish that describe you.

   ____

2. Now imagine that you've agreed to help one of your friends draft a personal ad. Make a list of the words you know in Spanish that describe your friend.

   ____

   ____

Vamos a leer

P1-10 Look at the classified ads below and on page 14 and complete the following exercise.

Sometimes when you do reading activities, it helps to read through the questions first. That way, you know what information to focus on during your reading. Also, it may help you figure out unfamiliar words. Remember, you need not understand every word when reading. Instead, try to focus on the words that you do recognize so that you can figure out the overall meaning.

SE OFRECE

- Licenciado(a) en Ciencias Químicas.
- Diplomado(a) en Administración de Empresas.
- Experiencia: Más de 15 años en fabricación y dirección en el sector de papel.
- Gran capacidad de trabajo. Dinámico(a) y perseverante.
- Amplia experiencia en organización y motivación de grupos humanos.
- Liderazgo y comunicación.
- Total disponibilidad y dedicación.

Apartado de Correos 11043
50080 Zaragoza

SE OFRECE EJECUTIVO(A) PARA

DIRECTOR(A) COMERCIAL/REGIONAL/MARKETING O JEFE DE VENTAS

- ❑ Experiencia en Sector de Automóviles, Alimentación y Alquiler de Servicios.
- ❑ Idioma: Alemán.
- ❑ Disponibilidad para viajar, así como movilidad geográfica.
- ❑ Responsabilidad demostrada en multinacionales.
- ❑ Con iniciativa, dinámico(a), con experiencia en negociación de grandes cuentas y en dirección, motivación y organización de equipos.

Interesados contactar al teléfono: (91) 351 31 18.

Nombre ______________________ Fecha ______________

1. Examine the ads and write a list of words that you recognize or whose meaning you can guess.

____

____

2. Which classified ad shows a person with responsibility?

____

3. Which ad shows a person who speaks English?

____

4. Which ad shows a person with 15 years of experience?

____

Después de leer

P1-11 Write the adjectives that describe the following.

1. Licenciado(a) en ciencias químicas *(B.S. in chemistry)*

____

2. Ejecutivo *(Executive)*

____

3. Director comercial / Jefe de ventas *(Sales manager)*

____

4. Los mejores *(best)* adjetivos para describir a un(a) ejecutivo(a) son:

____

____

Nombre ______________________ Fecha ______________

¡A escribir!

Antes de escribir

P1-12 Alicia Benson is greeting people first in her host family, then at the university. Complete the conversations, keeping in mind the norms for formal and informal greetings.

1. En la casa de la familia González por la mañana

Alicia: ¡Buenos __________! ¿Cómo __________, abuelita?

Doña Carmen: __________ __________. ¿Y __________, mi hija?

Alicia: __________, gracias.

2. En la universidad

Alicia: ¡Buenas tardes, profesor Gómez! ¿__________ __________ usted?

Profesor Gómez: __________ __________, señorita Benson. ¿Cómo __________ usted?

Alicia: __________ __________, gracias, profesor.

P1-13 Alicia Benson has just introduced you to her host parents, Ernesto and Blanca González. How do you respond to the questions below in Spanish?

1. ¿Cómo te llamas?

____

2. ¿De dónde eres?

____

3. ¿Cómo estás?

____

Vamos a escribir

Phrases: describing people; describing places; introducing; writing a letter (formal); writing a letter (informal)

Vocabulary: nationality; personality; school: studies, university

Grammar: adjective agreement; verbs: present tense, **ser**

Spanish faculty and students are visiting the International Programs Office on your campus. Your Spanish instructor met them at a welcoming reception and invited them to visit your class to converse with the students. The following people are scheduled to attend: Pedro Morales Ramos (a student), Carlota Ramírez Chong (a student), Doctor Germán Pérez Torres (a chemistry professor), and Justina Gonzáles (the coordinator of the exchange program). Your instructor has assigned students to write to the invited guests. Write a letter of introduction to one of them and welcome him or her to your Spanish class.

P1-14 A good way to improve your writing is to organize the ideas you want to express. In the **Lección preliminar** of ***Intercambios***, you read and acted out many conversations with your classmates. You can use the expressions from these conversations to compose your letter of introduction.

- Make a list of the phrases you would use to greet others and to introduce yourself.
- Make a list of expressions you would use to say where people are from and to welcome people to your Spanish class.
- Make a list of any other information you would like to include in your letter.
- Organize your ideas before you begin writing your letter.

1. Expressions you would use to greet others and introduce yourself:

____

____

____

2. Expressions to say where people are from and to welcome them:

____

____

3. Other information:

____

____

P1-15 Use the information below to write your letter in the space provided.

1. Greet the guest **(Estimado[a] señor[a], doctor[a]).**
2. Introduce yourself. State your name, say that you are a student and indicate where you study, and say where you are from. Include additional biographical information.
3. Welcome the guest to the university and to your Spanish class **(Bienvenido[a] a...).**
4. Include a closing **(Cordialmente** or **Sinceramente).**
5. Sign your name.

____

____

____

____

____

____

Después de escribir

P1-16 With a classmate, edit the letter you have written. Look for subject/verb agreement every time the verb **ser** is used. Also watch for adjective agreement with gender and number.

Nombre ______________________________ Fecha ______________

Práctica auditiva

Pronunciación esencial

Spanish *a, o, u*

Spanish vowels are always short, crisp, and tense. They do not have glide sounds as in the English word *go.*

CD 1-10 **P1-17** Spanish **a** is pronounced approximately like the *a* in *father*. Listen to the following sentences and repeat after the speaker.

—¡Hol**a**, **A**licia!
—Buen**a**s t**a**rdes, profesor**a** **A**rbell**a**s.
—¿Cómo est**á** tu **a**buel**a**?
—Ell**a** est**á** muy bien, gr**a**ci**a**s.
—Y tu p**a**p**á**, ¿cómo est**á**?
—Bien. ¡**A**y! ¡Tengo un**a** cl**a**se!
—H**a**st**a** m**a**ñ**a**n**a**, **A**lici**a**.
—H**a**st**a** m**a**ñ**a**n**a**, profesor**a**.

CD 1-11 **P1-18** Spanish **o** is pronounced approximately like the *o* in *hope.* Listen to the following sentences and repeat after the speaker.

—¡H**o**la! Me llam**o** Dieg**o** **O**rduñ**o**.
—Mi n**o**mbre es Alicia Bens**o**n.
—Much**o** gust**o**, Alicia.
—El gust**o** es mí**o**, Dieg**o**.
—¿Cuánt**o**s añ**o**s tienes?
—Veintid**ó**s. ¿Y tú, Dieg**o**?
—Veinti**o**ch**o**. Cha**o**, Alicia.
—Cha**o**. Much**o** gust**o**.

CD 1-12 **P1-19** Spanish **u** is pronounced approximately like the *u* in *tube.* Listen to the following sentences and repeat after the speaker.

—B**u**enos días, profesor Gómez.
—Hola, H**u**mberto.
—¿Cómo está **u**sted?
—M**u**y bien, H**u**mberto. Gracias.
—Quiero presentarle a mi novia, **Ú**rs**u**la.
—M**u**cho g**u**sto, **Ú**rs**u**la.
—Encantada, profesor.

Nombre ______________________ Fecha __________

En contexto

CD 1-13 **P1-20 Bienvenida a México.** Listen to the following conversation. Based only on the information you hear, decide whether the statements below are true **(V: verdadero)** or false **(F: falso)**, or whether there is not sufficient information to decide **(N: No hay información suficiente).** Write the corresponding letter next to each statement.

(Before playing the CD for any listening activity, scan the written portion so you will know beforehand what information to listen for.)

_____ 1. La familia González es la nueva familia de Alicia.

_____ 2. Doña Carmen es la mamá de Alicia.

_____ 3. Ernesto es el esposo de Blanca.

_____ 4. Gerardo tiene 28 años.

_____ 5. Teresa estudia en el TEC.

Vocabulario esencial

CD 1-14 **P1-21 Buenos días.** You will hear three conversations. Look at the pictures before you begin and while you listen, considering everything you see and hear. Write the number of each conversation below the picture it matches.

_______ _______ _______

CD 1-15 **P1-22 Los amigos de Alicia.** You will hear Alicia describe several of her classmates at the TEC. In the space provided, write the letter that corresponds to the country of origin of each student.

1. _____ Gerardo	a. México
2. _____ Adriana	b. Venezuela
3. _____ Mercedes	c. Colombia
4. _____ Arturo	d. Panamá
5. _____ Enrique	e. los Estados Unidos

Nombre ______________________ Fecha ______________

CD 1-16 **P1-23 ¡Mucho gusto!** Alicia has met several people in Monterrey: Blanca, Graciela, and Juan. Listen as the three of them talk about themselves, and fill in the charts below with information about each person. You will hear each description twice.

(Listen to these descriptions carefully. It is not necessary to understand every word in order to comprehend the main ideas of these descriptions. Listen for the gist of the descriptions based on the words you recognize.)

1. **Blanca**	2. **Graciela**	3. **Juan**
Edad: ______	Origen: ______	Origen: ______
Ocupación: ______	Profesión: ______	Ocupación: ______
¿Cómo se llama el hijo? ______	¿Cómo se llama el esposo? ______	Descripción de Juan: ______ ______ ______
Descripción de Blanca: ______	Descripción del esposo: ______	

Nombre ______________________ Fecha ______________

LECCIÓN 2 ¿TE GUSTA ESTUDIAR Y TRABAJAR EN LA UNIVERSIDAD?

Práctica esencial

VOCABULARIO ESENCIAL

P2-1 Describe Your Friends and Classmates. Using the words from the list provided, describe the people below.

aburrido(a)	honesto(a)	trabajador(a)	ambicioso(a)
deshonesto(a)	perezoso(a)	simpático(a)	estudioso(a)
liberal	antipático(a)	extrovertido(a)	cortés
conservador(a)	tímido(a)	descortés	

1. El (La) amigo(a) ideal es ______________. No es ______________.
2. El (La) compañero(a) de clase perfecto(a) es ______________. No es ______________.
3. Mi *(My)* profesor(a) favorito(a) es ______________. No es ______________.

P2-2 Academic Subjects. Match each textbook with the class in which you would use it.

1. _____ *La vida de Frank Lloyd Wright* a. la clase de psicología
2. _____ *Freud y tú* b. la clase de ciencias políticas
3. _____ *El marxismo y el comunismo* c. la clase de ciencia
4. _____ *Don Quixote de la Mancha* d. la clase de arquitectura
5. _____ *Micro y macrobiología* e. la clase de literatura

GRAMÁTICA ESENCIAL

P2-3 ¿Qué tienen? Look at the drawings on page 21 and write sentences in Spanish describing what these people have. Use the correct form of the verb **tener.**

(Remember to match the form of the verb **tener** to the subject of the sentence.)

Modelo: Alicia
Alicia tiene una computadora portátil.

Nombre ______________________________ Fecha ______________

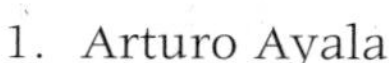

1. Arturo Ayala

____

____

2. Ernesto y Blanca González

____

____

3. Enrique

____

____

4. Trinidad y yo (nosotros[as])

____

____

5. el profesor Gómez

____

____

6. tú y Gerardo (ustedes)

____

____

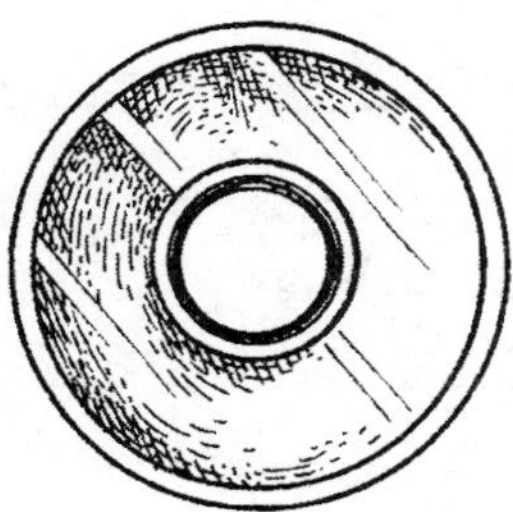

7. Alicia

____

____

8. Tú

____

____

Nombre ______________________ Fecha ____________

P2-4 **¿De quién es?** Use the sentences from the preceding exercise (**P2-3**) to answer the following questions.

1. ¿De quién es el televisor? ______________________
2. ¿De quién es la bicicleta? ______________________
3. ¿De quién es el disco compacto? ______________________
4. ¿De quién es la computadora portátil? ______________________

P2-5 **Personas ocupadas.** Describe what these people do during the week.

Modelo: yo / hablar por teléfono
Yo hablo por teléfono.

1. yo / descansar por una hora
____
2. Ernesto / trabajar en la oficina
____
3. nosotros / tomar muchos exámenes
____
4. tú / escuchar a la profesora
____
5. Teresa y sus amigas / bailar en las fiestas
____

P2-6 **En mi opinión.** Write original sentences expressing your opinion about the following people and things. Use one word from each of the lists below and add or change the words when necessary.

Modelo: *Nuestras bicicletas son buenas.*

mi	televisores	es (no es)	bueno(a)
su	radio	son (no son)	moderno(a)
nuestro(a)	profesor(a) de español		fácil
tu	computadora		difícil
	bicicleta		simpático(a)
			pequeño(a)
			grande

1. ______________________
2. ______________________
3. ______________________
4. ______________________

Nombre ______________________________ Fecha ______________

P2-7 Me gusta / No me gusta. Adriana and Trinidad need a roommate to help out with the rent. They discuss the ideal roommate. Fill in the blanks with the correct form of the words from the list below. Think carefully about the words you choose to fill in the blanks in this exercise. Some words will be used more than once.

mi	me gusta	necesitar
su	querer	tener
	le gusta	

Adriana: En ______________ opinión, nosotras ______________ una compañera de cuarto inteligente y estudiosa.

Trinidad: Nuestra amiga Raquel es inteligente, ______________ una computadora y ______________ estudiar mucho.

Adriana: Y la computadora que Raquel ______________ es de buena calidad.

Trinidad: A mí ______________ ______________ trabajar con la computadora de Raquel.

Adriana: ¿______________ usar ______________ computadora?

Trinidad: ¡Sí! En mi opinión, la compañera de cuarto perfecta para nosotras es Raquel... ¡porque ______________ una computadora muy buena!

Cultura

P2-8 Cultura. Answer the following questions in English.

Consider the information you read in **Lección 2** about the differences and similarities between studies in U.S. universities and those in Latin American and Spanish universities.

1. What are two similarities?

____

____

2. What are two differences?

____

____

¡A leer!: ¡Estudia tu vocación!

Antes de leer

P2-9 Answer these questions before reading.

1. Do you know what type of profession you would like to enter? Have you discovered your vocation?

____

2. Do you know what values, abilities and skills, and personality traits you need to have in order to enter the profession you have chosen?

Values: ____

Abilities and skills: ____

Personality traits: ____

Nombre ______________________ Fecha ____________

Vamos a leer

Remember, before reading it is sometimes helpful to go over the questions you will have to answer later. That way, you can focus your attention on the information you need to find.

In Spain, *informática* = *computación*

Profesiones	Asignaturas que domina	Valores	Habilidades	Personalidad
Ciencias de la salud	Matemáticas Ciencias Química	Altruismo Prestigio Buen sueldo	Científica Manual	Científica Social
Comercial Económicas	Administr. Matemáticas Informática Idiomas	Prestigio Relación Buen sueldo Responsabilidad	Liderazgo Persuasión Administrativa	Negocios
Ciencias	Matemáticas Ciencias Informática	Independencia Prestigio Variedad Creatividad	Científica Matemática Espacial	Científica
Servicios Sociales	C.Sociales Administr.	Altruismo Relación Variedad Seguridad	Persuasión Administr. Didáctica	Social
Cultura Educación	Lenguaje C.Sociales Arte Ciencias	Altruismo Creatividad Seguridad Responsabilidad	Didáctica Lingüística Social	Social
Artística	Arte Música Plástica Imagen	Creatividad Independencia Variedad Prestigio	Artística Manual Musical Lingüística	Artística
Deporte	Ed.Física Ciencias Tecnología Tiempo libre	Relación Altruismo Variedad Didáctica	Física Manual Espacial	Realista
Oficina	Contabilidad Informática Lenguaje Idiomas	Trabajo guiado Rutinas Seguridad Relación	Administr. Lingüística Concentración	Oficina

P2-10 Answer the questions according to the information in the chart.

1. ¿En qué profesión necesitas estudiar informática o computación?

   ____

2. ¿Qué habilidades necesitas para las profesiones comerciales y económicas?

   ____

3. ¿En qué profesiones necesitas tener una personalidad realista?

   ____

4. ¿Qué valores necesitas tener para las profesiones científicas?

   ____

Nombre ______________________ Fecha ____________

Después de leer

P2-11 Now, create lists of your favorite classes, your values, your abilities, and your personality traits. These lists should be helpful in guiding you toward a career choice; or, if you have already made a choice, they should help you to confirm that choice.

1. Mis cursos favoritos:
____
2. Mis valores:
____
3. Mis habilidades:
____
4. Mi personalidad:
____

¡A escribir!

Antes de escribir

P2-12 Ask a classmate the questions below and write his/her answers in Spanish.

1. ¿Cómo te llamas?
____
2. ¿De dónde eres?
____
3. ¿Cuántos años tienes?
____
4. ¿Cómo eres?
____
5. ¿Qué te gusta estudiar?
____
6. ¿Cuál es tu clase favorita?
____
7. ¿Cómo se llama tu compañero(a) de cuarto?
____
8. ¿Tienes perros o gatos?
____
9. ¿Cómo se llaman?
____

Nombre ______________________ Fecha ______________

Vamos a escribir

Phrases: Describing people
Vocabulary: Family members; Nationality; People; Studies
Grammar: Adjective agreement; Adjective position; Possesion with ***de;*** Possesive adjectives; Verbs: ***ser, tener,*** present tense

P2-13 Write a paragraph about your classmate using the information that you just gathered.

Modelo: *Mi compañero de clase se llama Miguel. Miguel es de Ecuador. Tiene 22 años. Es trabajador y sincero. Le gusta estudiar español, pero su clase preferida es la clase de historia. Su profesora preferida se llama Michelle Evers. No tiene compañero de cuarto. Tiene dos gatos. Sus gatos se llaman el Gordo y el Flaco.*

Después de escribir

P2-14 Trade your paragraph with that of a different classmate from the one you just wrote about.

Look over each other's paragraphs for the following:

1. Agreement of adjectives: Do all of the adjectives match the nouns they describe in gender and number?
2. Subject/verb agreement: Do all verb endings correspond to the subject(s) of each sentence?

   (Note: The present tense endings for **-ar** verbs are listed on page 55 in the ***Intercambios*** textbook.)

Nombre ______________________ Fecha ______________

Práctica auditiva

Pronunciación esencial

Spanish *e, i, y*

Remember that Spanish vowels are always short, crisp, and tense.

CD 1-17 **P2-15** Spanish **e** has two pronunciations. When stressed, it is pronounced approximately like the *e* in *eight.* When unstressed, it is pronounced approximately like the *e* in *bet.* Listen to the following sentences and repeat after the speaker.

—¿Cómo s**e** llama tu compañ**e**ra?
—L**e**onor. **E**s **e**studiant**e** aquí.
—¿D**e** dónd**e** **e**s?
—**E**s d**e** M**é**rida, M**é**xico.
—¿Qu**é** **e**studias **e**n la univ**e**rsidad?
—**E**studio **e**spañol, d**e**r**e**cho **e** ingl**é**s.

CD 1-18 **P2-16** Spanish **i** and the word **y** are pronounced approximately like the *i* in *machine.* Listen to the following sentences and repeat after the speaker.

—¿Qué estud**i**as aqu**í,** Mar**í**a?
—Estud**i**o **i**nglés **y** f**i**losof**í**a.
—**Y** yo estud**i**o med**i**c**i**na.
—¡Uy! Qué **i**nteresante, am**i**ga!
—Hay muchos estud**i**antes, ¿eh?
—S**í.** ¡En med**i**c**i**na hay muchos!

CD 1-19 **P2-17** Spanish has open and closed vowels; these terms refer to how much the mouth is opened or closed when pronouncing them. When an open vowel **(a, e, o)** and a closed vowel **(i, y, u)** come together, they are pronounced as one syllable, called a diphthong (e.g., **buenos**). When an open vowel comes between two closed vowels, they are pronounced as one syllable, called a triphthong (e.g., **Uruguay**). Listen to the following sentences and repeat after the speaker.

—¡B**ue**nas noches! ¿Eres estud**ia**nte aquí en la esc**ue**la?
—Sí. Estud**io** histor**ia** y c**ie**nc**ia**s políticas. ¿Y tú?
—S**oy** estud**ia**nte tamb**ién**. Estud**io** b**io**logía y leng**ua**s.
—¡Qué b**ue**no! S**oy** de Asunc**ió**n, Parag**uay.** ¿De dónde eres?
—S**oy** de Montevideo, Urug**uay.** Es una c**iu**dad enorme. Y tú, ¿de dónde eres?
—S**oy** de B**ue**nos **Ai**res. Es una c**iu**dad enorme tamb**ién**.
—Sí, ¡y m**uy** bonita!

Nombre ______________________ Fecha ____________

En contexto

CD 1-20 **P2-18 ¿Le gusta estudiar y trabajar en México?** Listen to the following conversation. Based only on the information you hear, decide whether the statements below are true **(V: verdadero)** or false **(F: falso)**, or whether there is not sufficient information to decide **(N: No hay información suficiente).** Write the corresponding letter next to each statement.

____ 1. A Alicia le gusta la clase de contabilidad.

____ 2. A Enrique le gusta la clase de contabilidad.

____ 3. El profesor de contabilidad habla rápido.

____ 4. Enrique tiene dos clases.

____ 5. Alicia enseña una clase.

Vocabulario esencial

CD 1-21 **P2-19 Los compañeros de Alicia.** Listen to the following descriptions of three of Alicia's classmates. Fill in the blanks below with the appropriate information for each one.

¿Cuál es su nombre?	¿Cuántos años tiene?	¿De dónde es?
1. ____________	____________	____________
2. ____________	____________	____________
3. ____________	____________	____________

CD 1-22 **P2-20 Recados telefónicos.** Alicia and the González family are out of town for the weekend. Listen to the messages that their friends leave on their answering machine and write the messages in the spaces below.

1. Recado para: ____________________
   De parte de: ____________________
   Recado: ____________________
   ____

2. Recado para: ____________________
   De parte de: ____________________
   Recado: ____________________
   ____

3. Recado para: ____________________
   De parte de: ____________________
   Recado: ____________________
   ____

LECCIÓN 3 ¡NECESITO UNA PASANTÍA DE TRABAJO PARA JUNIO!

Práctica esencial

VOCBULARIO ESENCIAL

P3-1 **¿Qué hora es?** Look at the clocks below. Write out what time Alicia has each activity.

Modelo: A *las nueve,* Alicia tiene clase de matemáticas.

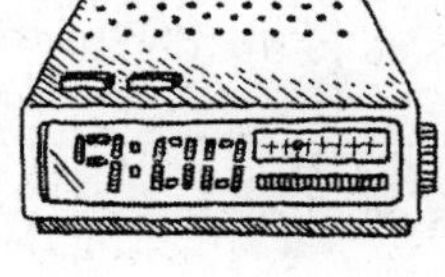

1. A ______________, Alicia habla con su amiga Trinidad.

2. A ______________,Alicia estudia con Enrique.

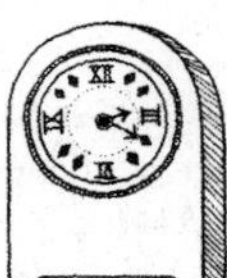

3. A ______________, Alicia toma un café con Blanca.

4. A ______________,Alicia tiene clase de contabilidad.

5. A ______________, Alicia camina a casa.

6. A ______________, Alicia regresa a la universidad para enseñar.

Nombre ______________________ Fecha ____________

P3-2 Los días y los meses. Answer the following questions in Spanish about what days and months the following events take place.

Modelo: ¿Qué día de la semana es hoy *(today)*?
Hoy es martes.

1. ¿Qué días de la semana tienes clase de español?
2. ¿Qué días de la semana trabajas?
3. ¿En qué mes es tu cumpleaños *(birthday)*?
4. ¿En qué mes es el día de San Patricio *(St. Patrick's)*?
5. ¿En qué mes es el día de San Valentín?
6. ¿Cuál es la fecha de hoy?

Gramática esencial

P3-3 ¡Horarios llenos! Describe the activities of the following people.

Modelo: tú / escribir una carta
Tú escribes una carta a las nueve y quince.

1. Adriana y Arturo / comer en casa
2. yo / comer el almuerzo *(lunch)*

3. nosotros / leer el periódico
4. Gerardo / deber estudiar

Nombre ______________________ Fecha ____________

P3-4 **¿Qué quieren hacer?** Alicia and her friends want to do a lot today. Write original sentences about what they want to do, following the model.

Modelo: Teresa / mirar la televisión
Teresa quiere mirar la televisión.

1. Alicia / correr por el parque
____
2. Blanca y Ernesto / decidir los planes para el fin de semana
____
3. Arturo / bailar salsa con su profesora
____
4. Adriana / ir al cine
____
5. Trinidad / leer el periódico
____
6. yo / estudiar para la clase de español
____

P3-5 **¿Qué van a hacer?** Look at Arturo, Adriana, and Alicia's schedule below. Fill in the column for **yo** to indicate what you are going to do on the days listed. Then, on page 32 write five original sentences stating what you, Arturo, Adriana, and Alicia plan on doing using **ir** + **a** + infinitive.

	Arturo y Adriana	**Alicia**	**Yo**
lunes	mirar televisión	enseñar inglés	
martes		ir a la biblioteca	
miércoles	comer en un restaurante		
jueves			
viernes		bailar en una discoteca	
sábado	ir al cine		
domingo		leer el periódico	

Nombre ______________________________ Fecha ______________

Modelo: *El lunes Alicia va a enseñar inglés.*

1. ______________________________
2. ______________________________
3. ______________________________
4. ______________________________
5. ______________________________

P3-6 ¡Hacemos una fiesta! Complete the following paragraph with the correct form of the verbs below. You can use these words more than once.

beber deber querer comer ir ser

La fiesta de Arturo y Adriana

Este sábado nosotros __________ a hacer una fiesta de cumpleaños para Arturo. Su cumpleaños __________ el 20 de septiembre. Nosotros __________ invitar a Alicia, a Trinidad y a Enrique. __________ a invitar a la familia González también. La fiesta __________ a ser a las nueve y nosotros vamos a __________ mucha comida mexicana. También vamos a __________ margaritas y refrescos. ¿__________ venir, Enrique?

Cultura

P3-7 Pareado. Write the letter of the correct response in the space for each of the following.

____ 1. A train that is scheduled to depart at 8:30 P.M.

____ 2. The time to arrive at a party that starts at 10:00.

____ 3. 3.12.07

____ 4. You want to know if something is starting at the exact hour given.

____ 5. A TV program listed to begin at 11:30 P.M.

a. ¿En punto?

b. el 3 de diciembre del año 2007

c. 23:30

d. 20:30

e. 22:30

Nombre ______________________________ Fecha ______________

P3-8 Los gestos. Write the correct phrase below each of the following gestures.

tacaño	¡No!
Un momento.	¡Fantástico!
Vamos a tomar.	¡Estás loco!
¡Cuidado!	dinero

1. ______________________________

2. ______________________________

3. ______________________________

4. ______________________________

5. ______________________________

6. ______________________________

7. ______________________________

8. ______________________________

¡A leer!: Programas de televisión

P3-9 Look at the following TV schedule from the Spanish magazine *Hola* and use the information to answer the questions below. Remember your skimming and scanning skills from earlier chapters. First, take a look at the questions so that you know what information you are seeking.

08.00 TELETRASTO.
09.00 LA ISLA DE FLORA.
09.25 NOTICIAS.
09.30 LAS MAÑANAS DE CANAL SUR.
10.30 FIESTAS DE ANDALUCIA.
11.00 NOCTURNO.
12.05 ARRIBA Y ABAJO.
13.00 LAS COSAS DEL COMER.
13.10 CANCIONERO.
13.35 VECINOS
14.30 EL DIARIO-1.
15.00 EL TIEMPO.
15.05 BOLA DE DRAGON.
15.30 CINE DE TARDE: «Si fulano fuese mengano».
17.20 EL HOMBRE Y LA TIERRA.
17.40 BAHIA PELIGROSA.
18.10 BOLA DE DRAGON Z.
18.35 MIS DOS PADRES.
19.05 TAL COMO SOMOS.
20.30 EL DIARIO-2.
21.00 GRANDES EXITOS DEL CINE HISTORICO: «Alfredo El Grande».
23.35 TEMAS 7.
00.45 INDICIOS.
02.10 DESPEDIDA Y CIERRE.

07.30 TRAFICO DE MADRID.
08.50 A SABER.
10.00 TELENOTICIAS.
10.40 LA NOCHE SE MUEVE.
11.40 BELLEZA Y PODER.
12.45 LA BANDA DE LA FAMILIA BIONICA.
14.00 TELENOTICIAS MADRID.
14.30 TELENOTICIAS.
15.00 MIRA QUIEN HABLA..
15.30 CINE: «Sudie y Simpson» y «Sol negro».
19.00 AVANCE INFORMATIVO.
19.10 A TRAVES DEL ESPEJO.
20.30 TELENOTICIAS.
21.00 EN ACCION.
21.30 RAVEN, GUERRERO AMERICANO.
22.30 CINE. LA NOCHE DE PELICULA: «El gran enredo».
00.10 LA NOCHE SE MUEVE.
01.30 CINE. SALA DE MADRUGADA: «Un chico con gancho».
03.00 INFORMACION CULTURAL DE LA C. A. M.

1. ¿A qué hora es el programa *La isla de flora*? ______________

   ¿En qué canal? ______________
2. ¿A qué hora hay programas de noticias? ______________

   ¿En qué canal? ______________

   ¿Cómo se llaman los programas? ______________
3. ¿Qué canal tiene información cultural? ______________

   ¿Cómo se llama el programa? ______________

   ¿A qué hora es? ______________
4. A las 6:35 de la tarde, ¿qué hay en el Canal Sur? ______________
5. ¿Qué película hay a la 1:30 de la mañana o madrugada? ______________

Nombre ______________________ Fecha ____________

¡A escribir!

Antes de escribir

P3-10 Read the news item titled "Los españoles trabajamos más horas" and answer the questions that follow.

Los españoles trabajamos más horas

Según la Oficina Estadística de las Comunidades Europeas, Eurostat, los españoles trabajamos una media de 39,2 horas a la semana. Esto significa siete horas más de trabajo que un holandés, seis horas más que un alemán y cuatro horas más que un belga. Sólo los portugueses, con 40,5 horas semanales, y los griegos con 40,1, nos superan en trabajo. Pero, curiosamente, en proporción somos los que más fiestas hacemos al año, en concreto, catorce, sólo superados por los quince días al año de los italianos.

1. ¿Qué quiere decir el título de la noticia "Los españoles trabajamos más horas"?
____
2. ¿Cuántas horas trabajan los españoles a la semana?
____
3. ¿Cuántas horas trabajan los alemanes y los holandeses?
____
4. ¿Cuántas horas trabajan los portugueses?
____
5. ¿Cuántas fiestas hacen los españoles al año? ¿Y los italianos?
____

Vamos a escribir

Phrases: Describing people
Vocabulary: Nationality; Personality; Studies
Grammar: Adjective agreement; Verbs: present tense, **ser**

P3-11 Imagine that you are asked to write a short article for your university newspaper describing the number of hours that students study per week at your institution. You will also want to mention that many students, apart from the work that they do for their classes, also hold jobs outside of the university. Compare the hours that you and your fellow students work with the number of hours worked by students you know at other universities. Write your article on a separate sheet of paper.

Modelo: Los estudiantes de la Universidad X trabajamos mucho.

Después de escribir

P3-12 Exchange your article with that of a classmate, and correct each other's mistakes.

Nombre ______________________________ Fecha ______________

Práctica auditiva

Pronunciación esencial

Word stress

A syllable is a word or part of a word pronounced with a single, uninterrupted sounding of the voice; for example, the word **el** has one syllable and the word **padre** has two syllables: **pa - dre.**

Word stress refers to the syllable that is most strongly stressed by the voice in a word; for example, in the word **padre,** the syllable **pa** is stressed. Spanish has three simple rules for word stress.

CD 1-23 **P3-13** Words of more than one syllable ending in a vowel, **n,** or **s** are stressed on the next-to-the-last syllable. Listen to the following sentences and repeat after the speaker.

—¿**Bue**no?
—**Ho**la, En**ri**que. **Ha**bla Ar**tu**ro. ¿**Có**mo estás?
—**Ho**la, Ar**tu**ro. ¿Qué hay de **nue**vo?
—El sábado voy a hacer **u**na **fies**ta **pa**ra celebrar mi cumple**a**ños. ¿**Quie**res venir?
—Sí, **mu**chas **gra**cias. ¿A qué **ho**ra **de**bo llegar?
—Pues, **es**te... a las **nue**ve.
—Muy bien. ¡**Has**ta el sábado!
—¡**Has**ta el sábado! Chao.

CD 1-24 **P3-14** Words ending in a consonant other than **n** or **s** are stressed on the last syllable. Listen to the following sentences and repeat after the speaker.

—Arturo, ¿qué vamos a ha**cer** en la fiesta?
—Este... ¡Vamos a co**mer** mucho! ¡Voy a reci**bir** muchos regalos!
—Ay, Arturo. ¿No vamos a escu**char** música? ¿No vamos a bai**lar**?
—Sí, Trini**dad,** sí. Es una fiesta, ¿no?

CD 1-25 **P3-15** When a word has a stress pattern that does not follow the rules in Exercises P3-13 and P3-14, it carries a written accent mark over the stressed vowel. Question words always carry a written accent. Some one-syllable words, such as **tú** and **él,** carry an accent mark to distinguish their grammatical category and their meaning. Listen to the following sentences and repeat after the speaker.

—**Dí**game. ¿**Quién** habla?
—Hola, Adriana. Habla Alicia. ¿**Cómo** es**tás**?
—Bien, gracias. ¿Vas a ir el **sá**bado a la fiesta?
—Sí. Yo voy a ir con Gerardo. Oye, ¿**qué** necesita Arturo para su fiesta?
—Pues, no necesita más comida... ¡lo **ú**nico que necesita son sus amigos!

En contexto

CD 1-26 **P3-16** **¡Qué padre!** Listen to the following conversation. Based only on the information you hear, decide whether the statements below are true **(V: verdadero)** or false **(F: falso),** or whether there is not sufficient information to decide **(N: No hay información suficiente).** Write the corresponding letter next to each statement.

____ 1. Alicia tiene planes para el sábado.

____ 2. Gerardo no tiene planes para el sábado.

____ 3. El escritor Carlos Fuentes es mexicano.

____ 4. La conferencia es en la universidad.

____ 5. La conferencia es a las 9:00 de la noche.

Nombre ______________________ Fecha ______________

VOCABULARIO ESENCIAL

CD 1-27 **P3-17 La vida activa de doña Carmen.** Doña Carmen is a very active woman. She keeps track of her appointments on the calendar below. Listen to her speak with her family, and write her activities on the calendar.

lunes	martes	miércoles	jueves	viernes	sábado	domingo
1	2	3	4	5	6	7
8	9	10	11	12	13	14
15	16	17	18	19	20	21
22	23	24	25	26	27	28
29	30	31				

CD 1-28 **P3-18 La fiesta de Arturo.** Arturo is going to have a party in his house to celebrate his birthday. Listen to Arturo talking about the party and write the different activities mentioned.

______________	______________	______________
______________	______________	______________
______________	______________	______________
______________	______________	______________
______________	______________	______________
______________	______________	______________

Nombre ______________________________ Fecha ______________

PASO 2 Ecoturismo en Centroamérica

LECCIÓN 4 ¡TENEMOS QUE ESTAR DE ACUERDO!

Práctica esencial

VOCABULARIO ESENCIAL

P4-1 ¡Adivina quién! *(Guess who!)* ¿Quién es la persona de la familia? Escribe el parentesco *(relationship)* de cada una de las personas siguientes.

Modelo: El esposo de mi abuela es mi *abuelo.*

1. El hijo de mi hermano es mi ______________.
2. La esposa de mi hermano es mi ______________.
3. El esposo de mi hermana es mi ______________.
4. El hermano de mi papá es mi ______________.
5. La hermana de mi mamá es mi ______________.
6. Los padres de mis padres son mis ______________.
7. Los hijos de mis tíos son mis ______________.
8. Los hijos de mis abuelos son mis ______________.

P4-2 ¿Cuál no concuerda *(does not match)*? Mira las listas y subraya el objeto que no corresponda al grupo.

Modelo: la estufa, el fregadero, *la cama*

1. el horno, la bañera, la estufa
2. la bañera, la ducha, la mesa de noche
3. el inodoro, la cama, la mesa de noche
4. el sillón, el lavamanos, el sofá
5. la lámpara, el refrigerador, el armario

Nombre ______________________________ Fecha ______________

GRAMÁTICA ESENCIAL

P4-3 ¿Cómo y dónde están? Completa las siguientes oraciones sobre Ileana, Tomás y Luis con la forma apropiada de *estar*.

1. Mi amigo Tomás no ______________ casado ahora, pero quiere casarse en el futuro. Ahora, él y su novia ______________ muy contentos con su relación.
2. Ahora, Ileana, Tomás y yo ______________ en Guatemala. Mañana vamos a ir a Tikal por el fin de semana, donde ______________ las ruinas mayas.
3. Cristina, mi hermana, ______________ en casa hoy porque ella ______________ enferma. ¡Pobrecita! Nosotros ______________ tristes porque ella no come con nosotros hoy.

P4-4 Verbos irregulares en la primera persona: *yo*. Completa este párrafo con la forma correcta del verbo entre paréntesis.

Los sábados por la noche, yo siempre _________ (salir) con mis amigos. Yo _________ (estar) muy contenta cuando estoy con ellos. Yo _________ (conocer) a muchas personas en Antigua, y también _________ (saber) que mis amigos son muy simpáticos y buenos. A veces yo _________ (dar) fiestas en casa. Otras veces yo _________ (hacer) mi tarea en casa con una amiga. Si voy a la casa de mi amiga Josefina, yo siempre _________ (traer) algo para comer. Si estudiamos en mi casa, yo siempre _________ (poner) un poco de música.

P4-5 *¿Saber* o *conocer?* Lee las siguientes oraciones y subraya *(underline)* la forma correcta de **saber** o **conocer** según el contexto. Después, escribe la forma correcta del verbo en el espacio en blanco.

Modelo: Yo *sé* hablar un poco de inglés. (saber / conocer)

1. Ahora, Rodrigo y Teresa ______________ a Ileana. (saber / conocer)
2. Tú ______________ bien Guatemala. (saber / conocer)
3. Cristina ______________ los restaurantes de comida típica guatemalteca. (saber / conocer)
4. Nosotros ______________ mucho sobre las ruinas del Tikal. (saber / conocer)

P4-6 *¿Saber* o *conocer?* Llena los espacios en blanco con la forma correcta de **saber** o **conocer.**

¿Ileana, _________ a mi hermana mayor, Cristina? Ella es de aquí, de Guatemala, pero _________ muchos países latinoamericanos y _________ hablar inglés y un poco de francés. Cristina es una persona muy activa. Trabaja, estudia, _________ muchos restaurantes en la ciudad y además _________ preparar comida guatemalteca muy bien.

También es una buena hermana.

Nombre ______________________ Fecha ____________

P4-7 Adverbios: Mis actividades. Contesta las siguientes preguntas sobre tus actividades. Usa las palabras de la lista a continuación.

a veces	frecuentemente	normalmente	todos los días
todas las semanas	muchas veces	nunca	un poco
casi siempre	muy poco	siempre	

1. ¿Con qué frecuencia estudia usted español?

____

2. ¿Con qué frecuencia sale usted con sus amigos?

____

3. ¿Con qué frecuencia escribe usted en una computadora?

____

4. ¿Con qué frecuencia come usted comida hispana?

____

5. ¿Con qué frecuencia habla usted con su familia?

____

Cultura

P4-8 ¿Verdadero o falso? Decide si las siguientes oraciones son verdaderas **(V)** o falsas **(F)**, o si no hay suficiente información para contestar **(N)**.

____ 1. No es común tener varias generaciones en la misma casa.

____ 2. Los abuelos viven con sus hijos y nietos muchas veces.

____ 3. Muchos niños reciben nombres de santos.

____ 4. No es común tener más de una persona en la familia con el mismo nombre.

____ 5. Memo es un sobrenombre para Guillermo.

____ 6. Los hispanos tienen dos apellidos.

Nombre ______________________ Fecha ______________

¡A leer!: La leyenda del quetzal

Antes de leer

The **quetzal** is a beautiful and colorful bird that is the national symbol of Guatemala. It is also the name of its monetary currency, and it represents the spirit of freedom for the indigenous people.

Cognates **(Cognados)** *are words that are identical or very similar in spelling and meaning in English and in Spanish. Scan the legend below and see if you can find some.*

P4-9 Escribe los cognados de la lectura.

____

____

____

Vamos a leer

P4-10 Lee el artículo sobre el quetzal.

La leyenda del quetzal

El quetzal es uno de los pájaros *(birds)* más hermosos *(beautiful)* y raros del mundo. El quetzal es el emblema nacional de Guatemala. Tiene plumas *(feathers)* de colores brillantes. Sus plumas son rojas, verdes y azules, y tiene una cola *(tail)* muy bonita de tres pies de largo *(three feet long)*. Este pájaro es un símbolo religioso para los indígenas mayas y representa el espíritu de la libertad. El quetzal no puede vivir en cautiverio *(captivity)*. La imagen del quetzal aparece en las estampillas y en la moneda de Guatemala.

Después de leer

P4-11 Contesta las preguntas sobre la leyenda.

1. ¿Cuál es la idea principal *(main idea)* de "La leyenda del quetzal"?

   ____

2. ¿Qué es un quetzal?

   ____

3. ¿Qué representa el quetzal para los indígenas mayas?

   ____

Nombre ______________________________ Fecha ______________

¡A escribir!

Antes de escribir

P4-12 Entrevista a un(a) compañero(a) de clase e incluye la siguiente información. *Remember to formulate questions in Spanish to ask for this information! Write your notes in the space below.*

1. Estado civil ______________________________

____

2. Número de hijos que tiene ______________________________

____

3. Nombres de tres de las personas de su familia y las actividades preferidas de estas personas

Persona #1: Nombre: ______________ Actividades: ______________ ______________

Persona #2: Nombre: ______________ Actividades: ______________ ______________

Persona #3: Nombre: ______________ Actividades: ______________ ______________

4. ¿Con qué frecuencia practican estas actividades? ¿Qué días de la semana?

____

____

____

Vamos a escribir

Phrases: Describing people
Vocabulary: Days of the week; Family members; Leisure; Time expressions; Time of day
Grammar: Adverbs; Adverbs ending in ***-mente***

P4-13 Escribe un párrafo sobre un compañero(a) de clase, su familia y sus actividades favoritas. Sigue el ejemplo.

Modelo: *Hay tres personas en la familia de Nicolás: Nicolás, su esposa Mary y su hija, Kelly. Nicolás tiene cuarenta y un años y es una persona activa. Le gusta hacer ejercicios. Todos los días por la mañana corre en el parque con su perro, Ralph. Su esposa, Mary, es una persona más tranquila. A ella le gusta leer el periódico y tomar café por la mañana. Su hija, Kelly, es una persona activa como su papá. Por la tarde ella ayuda a su mamá a preparar la comida. Después, va al centro con sus amigas. Luego Kelly hace su tarea en la computadora, mira televisión un poco y habla por teléfono con su novio.*

Después de escribir

P4-14 Haz un círculo alrededor de todos los verbos que tú usaste en el párrafo. Subraya los sujetos.

¿Concuerdan *(Do . . . agree)* los verbos con los sujetos? Si no, haz las correcciones necesarias.

Nombre ______________________ Fecha ______________

Práctica auditiva

Pronunciación esencial

Linking words

Spanish speakers do not pronounce words as isolated elements. Instead, they link words together without interrupting the flow of sound.

CD 1-29 **P4-15** A final consonant is linked with the initial vowel of the next word. Two identical consonants coming together are pronounced as a lengthened one. Listen to each sentence and repeat after the speaker.

In this conversation, Luis and Ileana speak to each other by using linking words.

—Luis, ¿Qué vamos + a + hacer hoy?

—Bueno, Ileana, tenemos muchas cosas que hacer. Tenemos que ir + a la Ciudad de Guatemala, a la ciudad de Antigua, al lago de Atitlán...

—Sí, pero necesitamos descansar... Estoy cansada. ¿No estás cansado, Luis?

—No, no estoy cansado. ¿Dónde quieres descansar... aquí en mi casa o en + el hotel?

—Quiero descansar + aquí en tu casa.

—¡Estás + en tu casa!

CD 1-30 **P4-16** A final vowel is linked with the initial vowel of the next word. Two or more identical vowels coming together are pronounced as one. Listen to each sentence and repeat after the speaker.

—Tomás, voy + a + ir a la reunión sobre + ecoturismo a las siete. ¿Quieres ir?

—Sí, Luis, quiero + ir. ¿Sobre qué va + a hablar el director del hotel esta noche?

—Sobre la + hotelería *(hotel business)* en la zona del Tikal. Va + a ser interesante.

—¡Creo que sí! ¡Ya sabemos qué + importante son los hoteles para + el turismo *(tourism)*.

En contexto

CD 1-31 **P4-17 ¡Tenemos muchas cosas que hacer!** Escucha la siguiente conversación. Decide si las oraciones son verdaderas **(V)** o falsas **(F)**, o si no hay suficiente información para contestar **(N)**.

____ 1. Ileana viaja a Guatemala por primera vez.

____ 2. Tomás no conoce la Ciudad de Guatemala.

____ 3. Tomás no quiere visitar el Lago Atitlán.

____ 4. En Tikal están las ruinas de origen maya.

____ 5. Ileana va a ver las ruinas mañana.

Nombre ______________________ Fecha ______________

Vocabulario esencial

CD 1-32 **P4-18** **La familia de Luis Chávez.** Escucha la descripción de la familia de Luis y escribe el nombre de la persona que él describe debajo de cada dibujo.

1. ______________________

3. ______________________

2. ______________________

4. ______________________

5. ______________________

Nombre ______________________ Fecha ______________

CD 1-33 **P4-19 Las actividades de la familia Chávez.** Vas a escuchar a doña Cristina Arzú de Chávez hablar de las actividades de su familia. Mientras escuchas, escribe las actividades que hace cada persona.

Cristina

____

Luis

____

Rodrigo

____

Nietos

____

LECCIÓN 5 ¿QUÉ CARRERA QUIERES SEGUIR?

Práctica esencial

VOCABULARIO ESENCIAL

P5-1 Las vidas profesionales. Escribe el nombre de cada profesión en el espacio debajo del dibujo indicado. Escoje de la lista a continuación. No vas a usar todas las palabras.

trabajadora social	guías de turismo	programador	escritora
hombre/mujer de negocios	médica	músico	agentes de viajes

1. ______________________

2. ______________________

3. ______________________

4. ______________________

5. ______________________

6. ______________________

Nombre ______________________________ Fecha ______________

P5-2 ¿Qué carrera sigue? Escoje la respuesta más lógica.

1. Una persona que estudia ciencias quiere ser...
   a. abogado(a).
   b. periodista.
   c. programador(a).
   d. científico(a).
2. Una persona que trabaja en un hospital es...
   a. policía.
   b. médico(a).
   c. gerente.
   d. comerciante.
3. Una persona que estudia periodismo quiere ser...
   a. investigador(a).
   b. abogado(a).
   c. oficinista.
   d. periodista.

P5-3 ¿Adónde voy? Ileana no sabe adónde ir para las siguientes actividades. ¿Puedes recomendarle a ella adónde puede ir? No necesitas usar todas las palabras de la lista.

tienda por departamentos	hospital	agencia de viajes
restaurante	estación de policía	banco
librería de la universidad	laboratorio	biblioteca

1. Para comprar libros, puedes ir a la ______________.
2. Si necesitas dinero, puedes ir al ______________.
3. Si estás enferma, necesitas ir al ______________.
4. ¿Vas de viaje? ¿Quieres el número de mi ______________?
5. En caso de un robo *(theft)*, hay que ir a la ______________.
6. Si necesitas comprar ropa y zapatos *(clothing and shoes)*, puedes ir a la ______________.

GRAMÁTICA ESENCIAL

P5-4 Las obligaciones y los deseos de Ileana y sus amigos. Llena los espacios en blanco con la forma correcta del verbo apropiado de la lista siguiente.

almorzar	pensar	pedir	tener
decir	preferir	poder	volver

Esta tarde, Ileana _________ que hablar con sus tíos sobre el ecoturismo en el Pacífico. Ahora, ellos _________ en el restaurante de los padres de Ileana. Su mamá _________ que los frijoles negros son muy buenos aquí. Ileana _________ el arroz con leche *(rice pudding)* que es el mejor del mundo y Tomás _________ que el café es el mejor también. Después de almorzar, ellos _________ a casa y aquí _________ mirar el juego de fútbol. Luis y Tomás _________ descansar mirando el juego.

Nombre ______________________________ Fecha ____________

P5-5 Diálogo. Ileana está hablando con María Elena, una amiga de San José. Llena los espacios en blanco con la forma correcta del verbo apropiado de la lista siguiente.

comenzar poder seguir volver pensar preferir recenter

Ileana: ¿Cuándo ____________ ustedes a clases en la Universidad de San José?

María Elena: El lunes ____________ la universidad.

Ileana: ¿Qué carrera ____________ tú?

María Elena: Yo ____________ ser médica.

Ileana: Ah, por eso estudias medicina. ¿____________ tú trabajar como voluntaria en el hospital este semestre?

María Elena: Sí. Pero ____________ trabajar en la sala de emergencias porque es muy interesante.

P5-6 Preguntas personales. Contesta las siguientes preguntas con oraciones completas.

1. ¿Trabajas? ¿Dónde?

____

2. ¿A qué hora comienzas a trabajar? Si no trabajas, ¿a qué hora comienzas a estudiar?

____

3. ¿Dónde prefieres almorzar?

____

4. ¿Qué tienes que hacer hoy?

____

5. ¿Qué piensas hacer mañana?

____

6. ¿A qué hora vuelves a tu casa hoy?

____

P5-7 ¿Qué están haciendo estas personas? Describe con oraciones completas lo que están haciendo las personas indicadas en este instante. Cambia las palabras o agrega *(add)* más palabras cuando sea necesario.

1. Tomás / viajar a / San José

____

2. la señora Gamboa / enseñar / a cocinar *(to cook)* / el restaurante

____

3. Alejandro / volver / casa

____

4. el señor Gamboa / servir / comida / el restaurante

____

Nombre ______________________________ Fecha ______________

P5-8 Una familia ocupada. ¿Qué están haciendo Ileana, su familia y sus amigos a la hora indicada?

Modelo: Ileana habla con sus amigos. (12:00 P.M.)
Ileana está hablando con sus amigos a las doce del día.

1. La señora Gamboa trabaja en el restaurante. (8:00 A.M.)

   ____

2. El señor Gamboa estudia la contabilidad del restaurante. (9:00 A.M.)

   ____

3. Ileana y sus amigos almuerzan en el Café Tico. (12:00 P.M.)

   ____

4. Sara prepara la información turística para Ileana. (2:00 P.M.)

   ____

5. Alejandro mira las noticias sobre el Parque Nacional de Santa Rosa. (4:00 P.M.)

   ____

Cultura

P5-9 En la universidad. Lee las siguientes oraciones y escribe la letra de la respuesta correcta en el espacio en blanco.

____ 1. Before students in Latin America and Spain can enroll in a university, they must complete...
   a. college.
   b. primary school.
   c. secondary school.

____ 2. Competition for acceptance in government-run universities is intense because...
   a. everyone can enroll.
   b. students must pass rigorous entrance exams.
   c. many students enter the labor force instead of going to the university.

____ 3. Most students live...
   a. in residence halls.
   b. in boardinghouses or in their parents' homes.
   c. in their own apartments.

____ 4. The administrations of most universities in Spanish-speaking countries...
   a. can determine their own policies.
   b. receive direction from the government.
   c. answer to policies set by the voting public.

Nombre ______________________________ Fecha ______________

¡A leer!: Los anuncios clasificados

Antes de leer

Vocabulario

los beneficios	*benefits*
la dirección	*address*
los requisitos	*requirements*
el puesto	*job, position*

P5-10 Muchas compañías buscan personal y ponen anuncios en la sección de anuncios clasificados de un periódico. Indica el orden en que aparece normalmente la siguiente información.

1. _____ a. los beneficios del puesto
2. _____ b. los requisitos para el puesto
3. _____ c. el nombre de la compañía o empresa
4. _____ d. la dirección de la compañía
5. _____ e. el número de teléfono de la compañía
6. _____ f. el nombre del puesto

Vamos a leer

P5-11 Mira los seis anuncios del periódico en la página siguiente y completa el cuadro a continuación con la información indicada.

Puesto Anunciado	Compañía/Empresa	Requisitos	Sueldo
1. ________	________	________	________
2. ________	________	________	________
3. ________	________	________	________
4. ________	________	________	________
5. ________	________	________	________
6. ________	________	________	________

Nombre ______________________ Fecha ______________

EMPRESA TURISTICA

requiere

ADMINISTRADOR

en nuevo desarrollo en el Pacífico

Requisitos:

- Mayor de 25 años, con experiencia en hotelería y turismo, dispuesto a residir la mayor parte del tiempo en la zona. Requisito mínimo idioma inglés, preferiblemente con otro idioma adicional.
- Conocimientos básicos de pesca y lanchas.

Interesados enviar currículum y foto reciente al apartado 1373–1000, San José.

COSTA RICA DENTAL & MEDICAL SUPPLY CO.

2. Dr. M. Fischel Co. S.A

REQUIERE:

SECRETARIA EJECUTIVA BILINGÜE

Requisitos:

- Grado académico que la capacite para el desempeño del puesto.
- Inglés fluido, tanto oral como escrito
- Carácter y disposición para trabajar bajo presión
- Excelente presentación
- Buen trato personal
- Destrezas en el uso de télex, fax y microcomputadoras

Se ofrece:

- Salarios a convenir
- Magnífico ambiente de trabajo
- Estabilidad laboral
- Asociación solidarista
- Otros beneficios.

Interesados favor enviar currículum vitae, con fotografía reciente y pretensiones salariales al Apdo. 434–1000, San José Depto. Recursos Humanos.

EMPRESA NACIONAL

requiere los servicios de

QUÍMICO

Requisitos:

- Licenciado en Química
- Incorporado al colegio respectivo
- Dispuesto a residir en Guápiles
- Deseable experiencia mínima de un año en análisis químicos de suelos y plantas

Se ofrece:

- Estabilidad laboral
- Excelente ambiente de trabajo
- Asociación solidarista
- Médico de empresa

Los interesados deberán presentar su currículum vitae a más tardar el día 10-01-05, incluyendo fotocopias de los títulos, fotografía reciente y pretensiones de salario al apartado 1859–1000, San José.

Nota: No se considerarán solicitudes incompletas.

4.

COMPAÑÍA EXPORTADORA EN EXPANSION

requiere los servicios de un

CONTADOR

Requisitos:

1. Amplia experiencia en contabilidad
2. Incorporado al colegio respectivo
3. Experiencia en trámites bancarios de exportación
4. Conocimiento del sistema computadorizado de contabilidad
5. Amplia disposición para el trabajo

Ofrecemos agradable ambiente de trabajo, incentivos y salario acorde con el puesto.

Interesados favor concertar cita al teléfono 55–29–92 en horas de oficina.

PARKE-DAVIS

solicita los servicios profesionales de

DOS VISITADORES MÉDICOS

que reúnan los siguientes requisitos:

Profesión:	Farmacéutico–a (graduado) (a)
Vehículo:	Modelo reciente – buen estado
Edad:	25–35 años
Experiencia:	Preferencia con experiencia en visita médica
Otros:	Buena presentación, relaciones humanas, deseo de trabajar y progresar
Se ofrece:	Salario base Bonos sobre ventas Depreciación vehículo Gasolina – viáticos y 55% seguro vehículo.

Interesados enviar currículum a Dismercasa de Costa Rica, S.A. Barrio La Pitahaya, de Pollos Kentucky en el Paseo Colón 500 metros al norte y 125 al este, o apartado postal: 6–2100, Guadalupe.

S.A.

REQUIERE LOS SERVICIOS DE

UN INGENIERO INDUSTRIAL

REQUISITOS:

Preferiblemente con experiencia en programación de la producción y operación de equipo de cómputo sencillo.

SE OFRECE:

Salario según capacidad
Magníficas condiciones de trabajo
Oportunidad de desarrollo

Interesados enviar currículum vitae al apartado 2000–1000 San José a: **INGENIERO INDUSTRIAL.**

Nombre ______________________________ Fecha ______________

Después de leer

P5-12 Buscas un(a) programador(a) de computadoras para tu compañía. Escribe un anuncio para el periódico. Incluye:

el nombre, la dirección y el número de teléfono de su compañía

el nombre del puesto

los requisitos para el puesto

el sueldo que se ofrece

los beneficios que se ofrecen

otra información necesaria

____

____

____

____

____

____

____

____

____

____

¡A escribir!

Antes de escribir

P5-13 Contesta las siguientes preguntas con oraciones completas.

1. ¿Qué carrera sigues?

   ____

2. ¿Qué clases tomas para esta carrera?

   ____

3. ¿Qué otras clases necesitas tomar en el futuro?

   ____

4. ¿Qué sueldo quieres?

   ____

5. ¿Dónde quieres trabajar?

   ____

Nombre ______________________ Fecha ______________

Vamos a escribir

Vocabulary: Professions; Studies; Trades
Grammar: Accents; General rules; Verbs; Gerunds; **Poder;** Progressive tenses

P5-14 Escribe un párrafo sobre tus planes para tu carrera futura. Incluye la información de las preguntas anteriores *(previous)* y agrega otra información necesaria.

____

____

____

____

____

____

____

____

____

____

Después de escribir

P5-15 Intercambia el párrafo de arriba con el de un(a) compañero(a) de clase. Examina el párrafo de tu compañero(a) para ver si todos los acentos están bien puestos. Si una palabra lleva acento y no lo tiene, agrégaselo. Si una palabra no debe llevar acento pero lo tiene, bórraselo *(erase it).*

Nombre ______________________ Fecha ______________

Práctica auditiva

Pronunciación esencial

Spanish *j* and *g*

CD 1-34 **P5-16** Spanish **j** has a sound somewhat like the *h* in *hill,* but harder. It is never pronounced like the English *j* of *jet*. Listen to the following sentences and repeat after the speaker.

—¿Traba**j**a Tomás el **j**ueves por la tarde?

—Sí, Ileana. Ese *(That)* **j**oven es muy traba**j**ador.

—¿Cuándo va a **j**ugar al fútbol con sus amigos?

—Siempre **j**uega los domingos.

CD 1-35 **P5-17** Spanish **g** before an **e** or **i** is pronounced like the Spanish **j.** Listen to each sentence and repeat after the speaker.

—¿Cómo se llama tu hijo, José?

—Se llama Jor**g**e.

—Jor**g**e vive en Guatemala, ¿no?

—Sí, estudia in**g**eniería allí.

—¿Es inteli**g**ente tu Jorge?

—Sí. Va a ser un in**g**eniero in**g**enioso *(ingenious)*.

CD 1-36 **P5-18** In all other cases, **g** is pronounced approximately like the *g* in *go*. Listen to each sentence and repeat after the speaker.

—Yolanda, éste es mi ami**g**o **G**ustavo **G**onzález.

—Mucho **g**usto, **G**ustavo.

—El **g**usto es mío, Yolanda.

Spanish *h*

CD 1-37 **P5-19** Spanish **h** is never pronounced. Listen to the following sentences and repeat after the speaker.

—**H**ija, ¿qué estás **h**aciendo?

—Estoy **h**ablando con mi **h**ermano por teléfono, mamá.

Nombre ______________________ Fecha ______________

En contexto

CD 1-38 **P5-20** **¡Pura vida!** Escucha la siguiente conversación. Decide si las siguientes oraciones son verdaderas **(V)** o falsas **(F)**, o si no hay suficiente información para contestar **(N)**.

____ 1. Son las dos de la tarde; es hora de beber algo.

____ 2. Ileana quiere café con leche.

____ 3. Tomás quiere café con leche.

____ 4. Después, ellos van a una agencia de viajes.

____ 5. A Luis le gusta la idea de ir a una agencia de viajes.

Vocabulario esencial

CD 1-39 **P5-21** **Los amigos de Ileana.** Ileana va a hablar de sus amigos Luis y Tomás. Escucha a Ileana y escribe la información apropiada en los espacios indicados.

1. ¿Cómo son Luis y Tomás?

   ____

2. ¿Son casados o solteros?

   ____

3. ¿Qué estudian Luis, Ileana y Tomás?

   ____

4. ¿Dónde estudian?

   ____

5. ¿Qué quieren hacer ellos en San José?

   ____

Nombre ______________________ Fecha ______________

LECCIÓN 6 ¡HACE MUCHO CALOR EN PANAMÁ!

Práctica esencial

VOCABULARIO ESENCIAL

P6-1 **¿Qué tiempo hace?** Describe el tiempo que hace en los siguientes dibujos e indica la estación.

1. Estación: ______________________

   Tiempo: ______________________

   ¿Tienes sed? ______________________

2. Estación: ______________________

   Tiempo: ______________________

   ¿Tienes calor? ______________________

3. Estación: ______________________

   Tiempo: ______________________

   ¿Tienes calor? ______________________

4. Estación: ______________________

   Tiempo: ______________________

   ¿Tienes frío? ______________________

Nombre ______________________ Fecha __________

5. Estación: ______________________

   Mes: enero

   Tiempo: ______________________

   ¿Tienes calor? ______________________

6. Estación: ______________________

   Mes: abril

   Tiempo: ______________________

   ¿Tienes frío? ______________________

7. Estación: ______________________

   Tiempo: ______________________

   ¿Tienes frío? ______________________

P6-2 **¿Cuánto es?** El señor Gamboa tiene que escribir cheques para pagar las cuentas *(bills)* del restaurante. Ayúdale a escribir el número de cada cheque.

Modelo: $300 *trescientos*

1. $198 ______________________
2. $420 ______________________
3. $541 ______________________
4. $399 ______________________
5. $1.524 ______________________
6. $2.006 ______________________

Nombre ______________________________ Fecha ______________

Gramática esencial

P6-3 La rutina de todos los días. Completa las siguientes oraciones con la forma correcta de los verbos entre paréntesis.

Modelo: Tomás *se despierta* a las 6:00. (despertarse)
¿A qué hora *te despiertas* tú?
Yo *me despierto a las 7:00.*

1. Ileana ______________ a las once de la noche. (acostarse)

   ¿A qué hora ______________ tú?

   Yo ______________________________.

2. A veces Luis ______________ con dificultad. (dormirse)

   ¿ ______________ tú fácilmente o con dificultad?

   Yo ______________________________.

3. Alejandro ______________ a las siete. (levantarse)

   ¿A qué hora ______________ tú?

   Yo ______________________________.

4. La señora Gamboa ______________ y el señor Gamboa ______________ (bañarse / ducharse).

   ¿Qué prefieres, ______________ o ______________ por la mañana?

   Yo ______________________________.

5. Tía Sara ______________ elegantemente para ir a trabajar los lunes. (vestirse)

   ¿Cómo ______________ tú los lunes?

   Yo ______________________________.

P6-4 ¿Qué pasó ayer? Lee los siguientes párrafos y luego cambia los verbos al pretérito para expresar lo que pasó ayer con los amigos.

Hoy Tomás se levanta a las 5:00, se lava los dientes, se afeita y se ducha. Luego se viste y toma café con leche. A las 6:00 llama a Luis e Ileana al hotel para despertarlos. Luis e Ileana se levantan también. Se bañan, se visten y esperan a Tomás en el hotel. A la 1:00 ellos vuelven al hotel, descansan un poco y luego almuerzan. A las 2:00 vuelven a la oficina de ecoturismo y trabajan hasta las 6:00 de la tarde.

Tomás invita a Ileana y a Luis a cenar en el restaurante El Pacífico. Luis e Ileana comen muy bien. Ellos beben café panameño.

Ayer,

____

____

____

____

Nombre ______________________________ Fecha ______________

P6-5 **¿Qué hicieron ayer?** Describe con oraciones en el pasado lo que hicieron varias personas. Cambia las palabras.

Modelo: Ileana / cenar con sus amigos anoche
Ileana cenó con sus amigos anoche.

1. Luis / salir a tomar una cerveza
____
2. Tomás / comprar regalos para sus parientes
____
3. el señor Gamboa / servir comida en el restaurante
____
4. Ileana / hablar con su mamá
____
5. la señora Gamboa / volver al restaurante por la tarde
____

Cultura

P6-6 **¿Dónde estoy?** Escoge la mejor respuesta para las siguientes preguntas.

____ 1. Las estaciones del año en el hemisferio norte son... al hemisferio sur.
a. iguales
b. un poco más frías
c. opuestas

____ 2. Los latinoamericanos usan... para medir *(to measure)* la temperatura.
a. grados Farenheit
b. grados Centígrados
c. grados bajo cero

____ 3. Tu comida tiene muchísimo chile. Tú dices:...
a. ¡Ay! ¡Qué caliente!
b. ¡Ay! ¡Qué calor!
c. ¡Ay! ¡Qué picante!

¡A leer!: El pronóstico del tiempo

Antes de leer

P6-7 Haz una lista de las expresiones que conoces en español para expresar qué tiempo hace.

____
____
____

Nombre ______________________ Fecha ______________

Vamos a leer

P6-8 Usa la información sobre el clima en la Ciudad de Panamá, Panamá, y describe el pronóstico del tiempo *(weather report)* para los siguientes días.

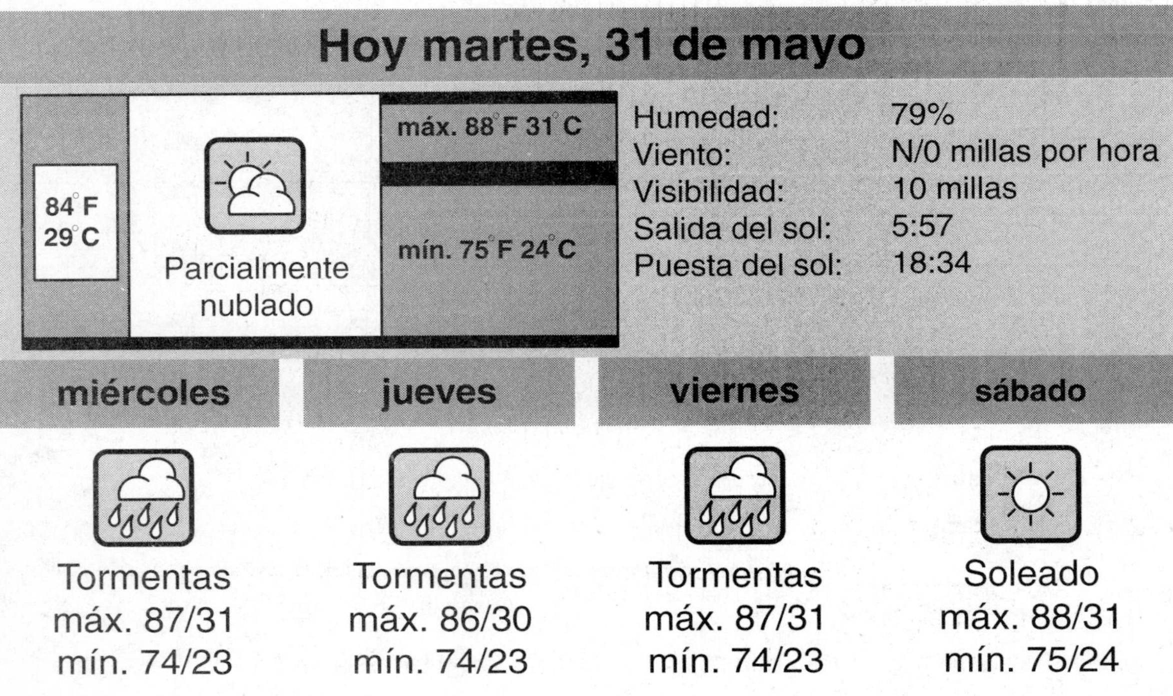

1. ¿Cuál es la temperatura en la Ciudad de Panamá el día martes, 31 de mayo?
____
2. ¿Qué tiempo hace? ______________________
3. ¿A qué hora sale el sol (*sunrise*)? ______________________
4. ¿A qué hora se pone el sol (*sunset*)? ______________________
5. ¿Qué tiempo hace el miércoles, el jueves y el viernes? ______________________
6. ¿Cuál es la temperatura máxima y mínima el sábado? ______________________
7. ¿Qué tiempo hace el sábado? ______________________

Nombre ______________________ Fecha ______________

Después de leer

P6-9 Escribe el pronóstico del tiempo para la región donde vives. Puedes dibujar un cuadro con las temperaturas y usar los símbolos del tiempo para reportar el clima.

EL TIEMPO

Nombre ______________________________ Fecha ______________

¡A escribir!

Antes de escribir

P6-10 Eres periodista de la revista **"Gente en Español"** y tu compañero(a) de clase es una persona muy famosa así que quieres escribir un artículo sobre él/ella. Haz las siguientes preguntas para saber más sobre la vida de esta persona famosa. ¡Sé muy creativo(a) *(Be creative)*!

1. ¿Qué trabajo tienes para ser famoso(a)?
   ____
2. ¿A qué hora te levantas?
   ____
3. ¿Te bañas por la mañana?
   ____
4. ¿Quién te peina?
   ____
5. ¿Quién te maquilla/te afeita? o ¿Te maquillas/Te afeitas tú mismo(a)?
   ____
6. ¿A qué hora llegas a tu trabajo?
   ____
7. ¿Dónde almuerzas? ¿Con quién almuerzas?
   ____
8. ¿Qué comes en el almuerzo?
   ____
9. ¿Cómo te mantienes en forma *(to be in good shape)*?
   ____
10. ¿Qué bebes cuando tienes sed?
    ____

Nombre ______________________ Fecha ______________

Vamos a escribir

Phrases: Sequencing events; Talking about daily routines
Vocabulary: Leisure; Studies; Time of day
Grammar: Adverb types; Adverbs ending in **-mente;** Verbs: present, preterite, reflexives

P6-11 Usando la información anterior, escribe un ensayo sobre la rutina diaria de la persona famosa. Incluye todos los detalles necesarios.

Modelo: *Es famoso(a) porque juega voleibol en la playa por 8 horas todos los días. Todos los días se despierta a las cinco y media de la mañana, pero no se levanta hasta las cinco y cuarenta y cinco. Se baña rápidamente pero nadie le peina o le maquilla. Como juega voleibol no necesita maquillarse o peinarse. Almuerza con su compañero(a) de juego y comen una ensalada. Él/Ella siempre come un helado porque hace mucho sol y mucho calor en la playa en California.*

Hace 8 horas de ejercicios y toma 8 vasos de agua diariamente así que esta es su manera de mantenerse en forma...

Ahora, imaginando que tú eres el/la famoso(a) explica por qué eres famoso(a) y escribe sobre tu propia vida diaria en otra hoja de papel.

Después de escribir

P6-12 Cambia el ensayo que escribiste sobre tu vida diaria al pasado. ¿Por qué fuiste famoso(a) la semana pasada y qué hiciste esa semana? Agrega o cambia la información cuando sea necesario.

Modelo: *Fui famoso(a) porque... El lunes de la semana pasada **me desperté** a las cinco y media de la mañana, pero no **me levanté** hasta las cinco y cuarenta y cinco. **Me bañé** rápidamente pero nadie **me peinó** o **me maquilló.** Como **jugué** voleibol no **necesité** maquillarme o peinarme. **Almorcé** con mi compañero(a) de juego y **comimos** una ensalada. Yo **comí** 4 helados porque hice mucho ejercicio....*

____
____
____
____
____
____
____
____
____
____

Nombre ______________________ Fecha ______________

Práctica auditiva

Pronunciación esencial

Spanish *d*

Spanish **d** has two sounds, depending on its position within a word or a phrase.

CD 1-40 **P6-13** At the beginning of a phrase or a sentence, or after **l** or **n**, Spanish **d** is pronounced like English *d* in *dance,* but somewhat softer. Listen to the following sentences and repeat after the speaker.

—**D**iego, ¿qué estás hacien**d**o?
—¡Ah, Raquel! Estoy leyen**d**o una carta.
—¿**D**e quién?
—Es de **D**aniel **D**urán.
—¿**D**ónde vive **D**aniel ahora?
—En **D**urango, México. Tiene trabajo allí.
—¡Qué bien!

CD 1-41 **P6-14** In all other positions, especially between vowels, Spanish **d** is pronounced like the *th* in *then.* Listen to the following sentences and repeat after the speaker.

—¡Hola, Tomás! ¿Qué tal?
—Estoy cansa**d**o, Ileana. El trabajo **d**e la oficina es muy **d**uro.
—Luis está preocupa**d**o por ti. Piensa que **d**ebes pasear con nosotros.
—Debo trabajar, pero **d**ebo pasear también. ¡Tienen razón!

Spanish *r* and *rr*

CD 1-42 **P6-15** Spanish **r** is pronounced like the *tt* sound in the sentence *Betty had a little bitty kitty.* Listen to the following sentences and repeat after the speaker.

—Luis e Ileana, ¿quie**r**en cena**r** aho**r**a?
—Sí, Tomás, g**r**acias. Pe**r**o, ¿tenemos que camina**r**?
—Sí, pe**r**o el luga**r** está ce**r**ca, a veinte minutos.
—¡Perfecto! Vamos a camina**r** y a hace**r** eje**r**cicio.

CD 1-43 **P6-16** In Spanish, **rr** is pronounced like the single **r,** but the tongue bounces several times against the ridge behind the upper teeth. The **rr** is trilled somewhat like a child imitating the sound of a motor. The single **r** is also trilled when it begins a word, and within a word after **l, n,** or **s.** Listen to the following sentences and repeat after the speaker.

—Estoy abu**rr**ido, Luis. Quiero caminar **r**ápido.
—Vamos al **r**estaurante.
—Sí, vamos. Allí viene un pe**rr**o que co**rr**e **r**ápido.
—A mí no me gustan los pe**rr**os.

Nombre ______________________________ Fecha ______________

EN CONTEXTO

CD 1-44 **P6-17** **¡Hace mucho sol en Panamá!** Escucha la siguiente conversación. Decide si las siguientes oraciones son verdaderas **(V)** o falsas **(F)**, o si no hay suficiente información para contestar **(N)**.

____ 1. Ileana y Luis comenzaron el viaje a las seis de la mañana.

____ 2. Ellos almorzaron en el fuerte San Lorenzo.

____ 3. Ellos almorzaron muy bien.

____ 4. El almuerzo es bueno y económico.

____ 5. Ellos van a cenar en el restaurante Balboa Club esta noche.

VOCABULARIO ESENCIAL

CD 1-45 **P6-18** **¿A cuánto está la temperatura?** Vas a escuchar una descripción del tiempo en diferentes ciudades del mundo. Escribe la temperatura para cada ciudad.

Ciudad	Tiempo	Temperatura
Guatemala	*Hace buen tiempo*	*28° C, 84° F*
Acapulco	____________	____________
Barcelona	____________	____________
Moscú	____________	____________
Sydney	____________	____________

CD 1-46 **P6-19** **La rutina diaria.** Luis y Tomás están hablando de su rutina diaria. Lee las actividades que aparecen a continuación y ponlas en orden según la información que escuches.

La rutina de Tomás	La rutina de Luis
_____ Se levanta.	_____ Se levanta.
_____ Se baña.	_____ Se baña.
_____ Se desayuna.	_____ Se desayuna.
_____ Se viste.	_____ Se viste.
_____ Se lava los dientes.	_____ Se lava los dientes.
_____ Se va a la oficina.	_____ Se va a la oficina.

Nombre ______________________________ Fecha ______________

PASO 3 ¡Buena Onda!

LECCIÓN 7 ¡TENGO GANAS DE IR A LA PLAYA!

Práctica esencial

VOCABULARIO ESENCIAL

P7-1 Deportes y pasatiempos. Pon la letra de la actividad que se describe a continuación.

____ 1.	para escuchar música en vivo *(live)*	a. acampar en las montañas
____ 2.	para investigar usando la computadora	b. ir a un concierto
____ 3.	para ser como Ronaldo o Beckham	c. ir a la playa
____ 4.	para estar en las montañas	d. ir al teatro
____ 5.	para ser como Sammy Sosa	e. navegar por la red
____ 6.	para ver el arte de Picasso, Dalí y Miró	f. visitar museos
____ 7.	para ser como Michael Jordan	g. montar en bicicleta
____ 8.	para nadar en el mar	h. jugar al baloncesto
____ 9.	para ver las obras de Shakespeare y Lope de Vega	i. jugar al béisbol
____ 10.	para ser como Lance Armstrong	j. jugar al fútbol

GRAMÁTICA ESENCIAL

P7-2 Una fiesta. ¿Qué pasó en la fiesta que hicieron los padres de Alicia para despedirse *(to say good-bye)* de ella? Escribe oraciones completas, según el modelo.

Modelo: muchos amigos y parientes / ir a la fiesta
Muchos amigos y parientes fueron a la fiesta.

1. Alicia les / dar un abrazo a todos

____

2. la señora Benson / estar muy contenta / en la fiesta

____

3. algunos de los invitados / poder bailar toda la noche

____

Nombre ______________________________ Fecha ______________

4. el señor Benson / ir al supermercado donde / tener que comprar más refrescos

____

5. los amigos de Alicia / querer regresar a sus casas

____

6. la tía Matilde / servir su famosa tortilla

____

7. muchos amigos de la universidad / venir a la fiesta y / traer bebidas frías

____

8. cuando los invitados irse / Alicia / ponerse el pijama / acostarse y / dormirse

____

9. todos / decir que la fiesta / ser realmente maravillosa

____

P7-3 ¿Qué hicieron los Benson durante las vacaciones? Lee la siguiente narración de Alicia sobre las vacaciones y llena los espacios en blanco con la forma correcta del pretérito del verbo indicado.

El año pasado, nosotros __________ (ir) al norte de Wisconsin para esquiar. __________ (Ser) muy divertido visitar esa zona. La noche antes de salir para el norte, todos nosotros __________ (acostarse) temprano. Por la mañana mi mamá y yo __________ (levantarse) a las cinco, y __________ (ducharse) antes de despertar a los otros. Mi papá no __________ (levantarse) hasta las seis y __________ (ser) muy difícil levantarlo. Por fin, nosotros __________ (salir) a las siete y __________ (llegar) al norte al mediodía.

Al día siguiente, Miguel y yo __________ (ir) a esquiar. Mi mamá y Shawn __________ (llegar) un poco más tarde porque ellos __________ (tener) que desayunar primero. Shawn __________ (sacar) fotos con su cámara digital nueva y __________ (comprar) chocolates. A ver... ¿qué más __________ (hacer) nosotros?

Otro día __________ (ver) una película estupenda en el cine. __________ (Ir) a un concierto y __________ (esquiar) mucho por todas las montañas. En fin __________ (divertirse) mucho y lo __________ (pasar) muy bien.

Nombre ______________________________ Fecha ______________

P7-4 Los pasatiempos y los deportes. Completa las siguientes oraciones lógicamente, indicando los pasatiempos y deportes apropiados para cada situación.

1. Cuando voy a la piscina, me gusta

   ____

2. En diciembre voy a Colorado. Cuando estoy allí, me gusta

   ____

3. Me gustan los animales, por eso, voy a

   ____

4. Me gusta mucho hacer ejercicio; por eso, cuando hace buen tiempo, voy a

   ____

P7-5 Todos tenemos diferentes gustos. Mira las listas de personas, lugares y cosas que aparecen a continuación. Escribe lo que les gusta o no les gusta a las siguientes personas que conoces.

Lugares	**Cosas**
las islas tropicales	las frutas
las montañas	los regalos
los océanos	las grabadoras (iPods)
el desierto	los trajes de baño
los países europeos (sudamericanos, asiáticos)	los juegos electrónicos
los restaurantes étnicos (románticos)	la música de rock/jazz/clásica
las universidades grandes (pequeñas)	los deportes acuáticos / en equipo
las ciudades modernas	las bebidas frías/calientes

Modelos: *A mi papá le gustan los deportes en equipo como el fútbol.*
A mi papá no le gustan los restaurantes románticos.

1. A mi papá

   ____.

2. A mi mamá

   ____.

3. A mis compañeros de clase

   ____.

4. A mi profesor(a)

   ____.

5. A mi mejor amigo(a) y a mí

   ____.

6. A mí

   ____.

Nombre ______________________ Fecha ____________

P7-6 Busca compañero(a). Mira la encuesta *(poll)* de abajo y decide si a tí te gustan las actividades de la lista. Si te gusta cierta actividad, escriba **sí** en el espacio indicado. Si no te gusta, escriba **no.** Luego entrevista a un(a) compañero(a) y escribe la respuesta en el espacio indicado.

	Actividad	**¿Me gusta?**	**¿Te gusta?**
1.	sacar fotos	______	______
2.	jugar cartas	______	______
3.	comer palomitas de maíz	______	______
4.	ver un partido de fútbol	______	______
5.	ir a la playa	______	______
6.	esquiar	______	______
7.	el submarinismo	______	______
8.	los museos de arte moderno	______	______
9.	comer helado de chocolate	______	______
10.	montar en bicicleta	______	______

P7-7 A mí me gusta... Ahora escribe cinco oraciones siguiendo el modelo a continuación.

Modelo: sacar fotos (nombre)
A mí me gusta sacar fotos, pero a Miguel no le gusta.

1. ______________________.
2. ______________________.
3. ______________________.
4. ______________________.
5. ______________________.

P7-8 *¿Por* o *para?* Ileana habla con Alicia sobre un examen en la clase de economía. Para completar la conversación, decide si es necesario poner **por** o **para** en el espacio.

Ileana: Alicia, ________ favor, ¿puedo usar tu libro de economía?

Alicia: ¿Lo necesitas ________ tu examen mañana, ¿no?

Ileana: Sí. Sólo quiero tu libro ________ dos horas hoy ________ la noche.

Alicia: Claro que sí. Yo te lo traigo ________ la tarde. ¿Vale?

Ileana: Ay, gracias ________ todo, amiga.

Nombre ______________________________ Fecha ______________

Cultura

P7-9 Deportes y pasatiempos en el mundo hispano. Completa las siguientes frases según las lecturas de la **Lección 7.**

____ 1. Es muy común participar en actividades ________ en el mundo hispano durante el tiempo libre.
a. individuales
b. peligrosas e ilegales
c. sociales y familiares

____ 2. Todos los países hispanos tienen un equipo nacional de ________
a. jugadores de universidades.
b. fútbol.
c. golf.

____ 3. El béisbol es el deporte más popular en ________
a. el Brasil.
b. España.
c. el Caribe.

____ 4. Hoy en el mundo hispano hay equipos deportivos ________
a. solamente para los hombres.
b. solamente para los profesionales.
c. para mujeres, hombres, profesionales y semiprofesionales.

____ 5. Algunos entrenadores norteamericanos emplean a los mejores jugadores latinoamericanos de béisbol y algunos entrenadores latinoamericanos emplean a los mejores jugadores americanos de ________
a. básquetbol.
b. béisbol.
c. fútbol.

¡A leer!: Submarinismo

Antes de leer

P7-10 Contesta las preguntas antes de leer el artículo.

Remember your scanning skills from earlier chapters. It may be helpful to look over the questions following the reading before beginning. That way, you can scan the article for the information you need and use that to guide you.

1. ¿Sabes algo de submarinismo *(scuba)*?

____.

2. ¿Te gustaría hacer submarinismo?

____.

Vamos a leer

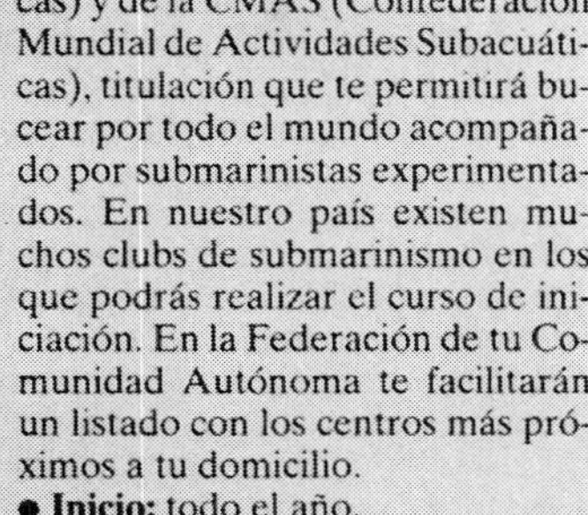

◆ SUBMARINISMO ◆

Si te atrae la idea de practicar un deporte de aventura y te gusta el mar, el submarinismo puede ser la mejor opción. Ahora es posible seguir un curso de iniciación que en sólo 2–3 semanas te permitirá hacer las primeras inmersiones. Este curso combina la formación teórica con las prácticas en piscina y mar. Al finalizar el curso obtendrás la titulación B1E (Buceador una estrella) de la FEDAS (Federación Española de Actividades Subacuáticas) y de la CMAS (Confederación Mundial de Actividades Subacuáticas), titulación que te permitirá bucear por todo el mundo acompañado por submarinistas experimentados. En nuestro país existen muchos clubs de submarinismo en los que podrás realizar el curso de iniciación. En la Federación de tu Comunidad Autónoma te facilitarán un listado con los centros más próximos a tu domicilio.

- **Inicio:** todo el año.
- **Duración:** 2–3 semanas.
- **Horario:** de lunes a viernes tardes-noche, fines de semana.
- **Grupos:** 5 y 10 personas.
- **Precio:** entre 40.000 y 45.000 ptas.
- **Teléfonos:**
  - Federació Catalana d'Activitats Subaquàtiques. Tel. (93) 330 44 72.
  - Federación Andaluza de Actividades Subacuáticas. Tel. (950) 27 06 12.
  - Federación Madrileña de Actividades Subacuáticas. Tel. (91) 442 21 69.
  - Federación Balear de Actividades Subacuáticas. Tel. (971) 46 33 15.
  - Federación Española de Actividades Subacuáticas. Tel. (93) 200 67 69.

A.G.E.

La Federación de Actividades Subacuáticas de tu Comunidad te informará de dónde puedes aprender.

te atrae... *you are attracted by . . .*
iniciación *introduction*
buceador *diver*
titulación *qualification, license*
te permitirá bucear *it will allow you to dive*

P7-11 Contesta las preguntas con información del artículo.

1. ¿Qué características son necesarias para hacer submarinismo?
   ____.
2. ¿Cuánto tiempo dura el curso de iniciación?
   ____.
3. Al final del curso, ¿qué titulación vas a tener?
   ____.
4. ¿Qué te va a permitir esa licencia?
   ____.
5. ¿Dónde puedes aprender a hacer submarinismo en tu comunidad/universidad/escuela?
   ____.

Nombre ______________________________ Fecha ______________

Después de leer

P7-12 Diseña un anuncio de un pasatiempo. Si en tu universidad o en tu comunidad enseñan a nadar, a patinar, a navegar o a esquiar, escribe un anuncio sobre esta actividad para tu universidad o tu comunidad, en español para la comunidad hispana.

Modelo: *¿Quiere aprender a navegar para el verano? El centro de la comunidad de Mystic tiene clases de navegación los meses de junio y julio. Las clases son todos los sábados de las ocho de la mañana hasta las doce del día.*

P7-13 Hablen sobre los anuncios de los pasatiempos en la clase y expliquen lo que pueden aprender en las diferentes comunidades.

¡A escribir!

Antes de escribir

P7-14 Haz una lista de tus pasatiempos favoritos durante las siguientes estaciones del año.

Primavera	Verano	Otoño	Invierno
____________	____________	____________	____________
____________	____________	____________	____________
____________	____________	____________	____________

Vamos a escribir

Phrases: Greeting; Inviting, accepting, and declining; Saying good-bye; Stating a preference; Writing a letter (informal)
Vocabulary: Leisure; Sports; Time expressions
Grammar: Verbs: present, irregular preterite, preterite

P7-15 Vas a mandarle un mensaje electrónico *(e-mail)* a un(a) compañero(a) de clase a quien quieres conocer mejor. También quieres saber más sobre sus pasatiempos y deportes favoritos.

1. Begin by asking how he or she is.
2. Next, ask if he or she has something to do this coming weekend, if he or she likes sports, and if so, which sport he or she practices and when.
3. End by asking him or her if he or she would like to do something with you next weekend.

Nombre ______________________ Fecha ______________

De:	
Para:	
Tema:	

Después de escribir

P7-16 Ahora discute con un(a) compañero(a) de clase los pasatiempos y los deportes que a ti te gusta hacer y que le gusta hacer a tu amigo(a) ideal.

Práctica auditiva

Pronunciación esencial

Spanish *c* and *z*

CD 2-2 **P7-17** In Latin America and some areas in Spain, **z** and the letter **c** before **e** or **i** are pronounced like the *s* in *swim*. Listen to the following sentences and repeat after the speaker.

—¡Martín! ¡Pancho! Es hora de almor**z**ar.
—No podemos, mamá. Vamos a ha**c**er ejer**c**i**c**io.
—¿Y qué van a ha**c**er que es tan importante?
—Vamos al parque a montar en bi**c**icleta. ¿Podemos llevarnos el almuer**z**o?
—¡Ay, cómo no!... ¿Qué voy a ha**c**er con ellos?

CD 2-3 **P7-18** In most of Spain, **z** and **c** before **e** or **i** are pronounced like the *th* in *think*. Listen to the following sentences and repeat after the speaker.

—Vi**c**ente, ¿quieres ir al con**c**ierto de "Alejandro Saenz" en Bar**c**elona?
—Sí, **C**e**c**ilia. Me gustaría ir. Me gusta su música.
—El con**c**ierto es el quin**c**e de mar**z**o. Comien**z**a a las **c**inco de la tarde.
—¿Quieres **c**enar después del con**c**ierto? Cono**z**co unos restaurantes fabulosos.
—Vale.

CD 2-4 **P7-19** In all other positions, Spanish **c** has a hard sound like the *c* in *car*. Listen to the following sentences and repeat after the speaker.

—Voy a ir al parque a **c**aminar, Silvia. ¿Me a**c**ompañas?
—Sí, **c**ómo no, Jaime. Pero hace mucho **c**alor.
—Después de la **c**aminata, te invito a tomar una **C**o**c**a-**C**ola.
—¡Qué simpáti**c**o eres, Jaime!

Spanish *q*

CD 2-5 **P7-20** Spanish **q** also has a hard *k* sound as in *Katy*. In written form, **q** is always followed by **u**. Listen to the following sentences and repeat after the speaker.

—Silvia, ¿**q**uieres ir a **Q**uito a visitar a mis padres este fin de semana?
—Es una buena idea, **q**uerido. ¿No es el cumpleaños de tu papá?
—Sí, es el **q**uince de este mes.
—¿**Q**ué le llevamos de regalo?
—Bueno... a él le gusta el e**q**uipo nacional de fútbol. ¿**Q**ué tal dos billetes para un partido?
—¡Perfecto!

Nombre ______________________________ Fecha ______________

En contexto

CD 2-6 **P7-21 ¡Vamos a la playa!** Escucha la siguiente conversación. Decide si las siguientes oraciones son verdaderas **(V)** o falsas **(F)**, o si no hay suficiente información para contestar **(N)**.

____ 1. David visita a Alicia en México.

____ 2. El trabajo de Alicia fue muy interesante.

____ 3. Alicia fue a un partido de fútbol entre México y Chile.

____ 4. Ellos van a nadar en el mar.

____ 5. David está contento de ver a Alicia.

Vocabulario esencial

CD 2-7 **P7-22 Pasatiempos en Santiago de Chile.** Escucha la descripción de los pasatiempos de David y Alicia en Santiago. Escribe los números del 1 al 5 en el orden en que las actividades se describen.

_____ a. Compraron boletos para ir a ver un partido de fútbol.

_____ b. Caminaron por el Parque de la República.

_____ c. Tomaron fotografías del Palacio de Bellas Artes.

_____ d. Fueron al viñedo.

_____ e. Fueron a las tiendas de compras.

CD 2-8 **P7-23 Mi experiencia en Monterrey.** Alicia le está contando sus experiencias a David en México. Escucha las siguientes actividades de Alicia y completa las oraciones a continuación.

1. Mi familia fue
____

2. Con los amigos fuimos a
____

3. Una noche oímos cantar
____

4. Los Mariachis cantaron
____

Nombre ______________________________ Fecha ______________

CD 2-9 **P7-24 Una familia activa.** Todos los meses Alicia llama por teléfono a su mamá. Escucha su conversación y anota qué actividades hizo cada persona el mes pasado. Escribe los nombres de la familia y de los amigos de Alicia donde correspondan.

Persona(s)	**Actividad**
1. ______________	Jugó al fútbol.
2. ______________	Fue a Florida.
3. ______________	Compró un libro sobre vinos chilenos.
4. ______________	Tomó clases de golf.
5. ______________	Corrió y ganó un maratón.
6. ______________	Llamó para saber de ti.
7. ______________	Comenzó a hacer ejercicio.

Nombre ______________________ Fecha ____________

LECCIÓN 8 ¡SALUD Y BUEN PROVECHO!

Práctica esencial

VOCABULARIO ESENCIAL

P8-1 **¿Qué comen estas personas?** Mira los siguientes dibujos y completa las oraciones con las comidas y bebidas apropiadas.

1. David come ______________________
____
____
____
y toma/bebe ______________________
____

2. Alicia come ______________________
____
____
____
y toma/bebe ______________________
____

3. La señora Torreón come ______________________
____
____
____
y toma/bebe ______________________
____

4. El señor Torreón come ______________________
____
____
____
y toma/bebe ______________________
____

Nombre ______________________________ Fecha ______________

P8-2 ¡Planifique el menú! Vas a ayudar a la señora Torreón a planificar un menú para esta noche. Piensa en una entrada, un plato principal, un vegetal, un postre y bebidas. Escribe las comidas que quieres incluir en el menú a continuación.

de entrada:

____

____

de plato principal:

____

____

los vegetales:

____

____

de postre:

____

____

de bebidas:

____

____

GRAMÁTICA ESENCIAL

P8-3 En el restaurante. Estás en un restaurante con unos amigos. Tus amigos te hacen preguntas. Sigue el modelo y haz las siguientes cosas:

1. Contesta las preguntas de tus amigos con una oración completa.
2. Subraya el objeto directo.
3. Escribe la oración otra vez, esta vez con el pronombre correcto **(lo, los, la, las).** Si hay dos posibilidades para la nueva oración, escriba dos oraciones en el espacio indicado.

Modelo: ¿Quieres pedir aperitivos?
—Sí, quiero pedir aperitivos.
—Sí, quiero pedirlos. No, no los quiero pedir.

1. ¿Estás leyendo la lista de postres?

____

____

2. ¿Tomas el café con azúcar o sin azúcar?

____

____

Nombre ______________________ Fecha ______________

3. ¿Pediste las papas fritas?

____

____

4. ¿Conoces los restaurantes de la ciudad de Santiago de Chile?

____

____

5. ¿Vas a pedir los mariscos esta noche?

____

____

6. ¿Bebes vino tinto?

____

____

7. ¿Vas a dejar propina *(tip)*?

____

____

8. ¿Vas a pagar la cuenta?

____

____

P8-4 En la cocina. Los señores Torreón están conversando en su cocina. Lee su conversación y llena los espacios indicados con la forma correcta de los pronombres de objeto directo **(lo, la, los, las).**

Rodolfo: ¿Ya preparaste el desayuno, Rosario?

Rosario: Sí, Rodolfo, ya ______________ preparé. Aquí tienes tu café con leche y tu pan tostado.

Rodolfo: ¿Y la mermelada? ¿ ______________ tienes allí?

Rosario: Ya no hay mermelada, solamente hay mantequilla. ¿ ______________ quieres?

Rodolfo: Sí, gracias. Y por ser domingo, ¿puedo comer huevos fritos, verdad? Los huevos fritos, ¿ya ______________ preparaste?

Rosario: Sí, y las papas fritas también. ¿ ______________ quieres probar?

Rodolfo: ¡Cómo no! Ay, Rosario, ¡David tiene razón! Cocinas excelentemente. Gracias, mi amor.

Nombre ____________________ Fecha ____________

P8-5 Los gustos de los señores Torreón. Los señores Torreón van a un restaurante a almorzar. Hablan sobre la comida que se sirve allí. Lee la conversación y llena los espacios en blanco con las siguientes formas: **lo, la, los** o **las.**

Remember that the direct object pronouns ***(me, te, lo, la, nos, los, las)*** *always answer the question "who(m)?" or "what?"*

Señora Torreón: ¿Con qué quieres almorzar, Rodolfo?

Señor Torreón: Quiero comer carne.

Señora Torreón: ¿ __________ quieres comer con papas o con arroz?

Señor Torreón: Quiero comer__________ con papas. Y tú, Rosario, ¿qué quieres almorzar?

Señora Torreón: Quiero comer pescado al horno.

Señor Torreón: ¿ __________ quieres con papas también?

Señora Torreón: Sí, exactamente. __________ quiero con papas también. ¿Llamamos al camarero?

Señor Torreón: Señor, por favor, estamos listos para pedir.

Camarero: ¿Qué desean almorzar los señores?

Señora Torreón: Yo quiero el pescado con papas.

Camarero: Se __________ traigo enseguida. Y usted, señor, ¿qué quiere comer?

Señor Torreón: Yo quiero la carne con papas también.

Camarero: Se __________ traigo enseguida. Y para beber, ¿qué desean?

Señora Torreón: Yo quiero una botella de agua mineral.

Camarero: __________ ordeno rápidamente.

Señor Torreón: Yo quiero una copa de vino blanco.

Camarero: Se __________ traigo inmediatamente.

Señora Torreón: Yo quiero un flan de caramelo.

Señor Torreón: Yo también.

Camarero: Se __________ traigo después de la comida. ¿Dos cafés?

Señora Torreón: Sí, nos __________ trae al final con la cuenta. Gracias.

P8-6 Alicia recuerda Monterrey. A continuación Alicia describe cómo era su vida cuando vivía en Monterrey. Ayúdala a completar la historia, poniendo los verbos entre paréntesis en el imperfecto del indicativo.

Cuando yo __________ (vivir) en Monterrey, __________ (estar) muy contenta. Yo __________ (tener) muchas responsabilidades y __________ (estudiar) constantemente, pero mis amigos y yo __________ (salir) de vez en cuando, y mis compañeros de clase me __________ (ayudar) mucho. En un día típico, yo __________ (levantarse) a las siete. Mi familia y yo __________ (desayunar) con pan y café, y después yo __________ (caminar) a la universidad. Por la tarde, siempre __________ (tomar) un café con algún amigo. Por la noche, nosotros __________ (comer) en casa, y nosotros __________ (acostarse) para las once. ¡Qué vida tan tranquila!

Nombre ______________________________ Fecha ______________

Cultura

P8-7 Por el mundo hispano. Lee las siguientes oraciones y decide si son verdaderas **(V)** o falsas **(F)**. Si una oración es falsa, corrígela para que sea verdadera.

____ 1. La comida corriente es la comida a precio fijo.

____

____ 2. En muchos restaurantes españoles y latinoamericanos hay una sección de no fumar.

____

____ 3. El camarero no trae la cuenta hasta que usted se la pida.

____

____ 4. La cuenta siempre incluye la propina.

____

____ 5. En general, el desayuno consiste en una taza de café, pan con mermelada o mantequilla y, a veces, fruta.

____

____ 6. La sobremesa es la costumbre de dormir la siesta después del almuerzo.

____

____ 7. Se sirve la cena más tarde que en los Estados Unidos. Generalmente es después de las siete de la noche.

____

____ 8. Algunos hispanos comen una merienda entre las cinco y las seis de la tarde.

____

____ 9. La tortilla de maíz es una tapa muy común que se sirve con jamón y queso.

____

____ 10. En los bares de tapas se sirven solamente bebidas alcohólicas como vino y cerveza.

____

¡A leer!: El restaurante Versailles

Antes de leer

P8-8 Contesta las preguntas antes de leer el artículo.

1. Típicamente, ¿qué información se incluye en el menú de un restaurante?

____

2. ¿Cómo se organiza la información en un menú normalmente?

____

3. ¿Qué parte del menú miras primero cuando va a un restaurante?

____

Nombre ______________________ Fecha ______________

Vamos a leer

P8-9 Mira el menú a continuación y busca esa información.

Versailles

VERSAILLES SURTIDO CUBANO

Pequeñas Porciones de los mas Típicos Platos Cubanos

EL CLASICO
Arroz Blanco y Frijoles Negros, Picadillo, Lechón Asado, Plátanos Maduros, Croqueta de Jamón, Yuca y Tamal
$7.85

EL CRIOLLO
Arroz Amarillo y Frijoles Negros, Ropa Vieja, Masas de Puerco, Croqueta de Jamón, Plátanos Maduros y Yuca.
$7.85

Pollo

POLLO FRITO ESTILO CUBANO (½)
Con Papas Fritas o Plátanos (146) 5.75
Con Arroz, Frijoles y Plátanos (46) 5.95
POLLO FRITO ESTILO CUBANO (¼) (147) 4.25
Con Papas Fritas o Plátanos.
POLLO "VERSAILLES" DESHUESADO (73) 6.95
POLLO BAR-B-CUE (½) (111) Moros y Plátanos 5.95
POLLO POLINESIO (37) 7.65
Pechuga Empanizada, Cubierta con Jamón, Salsa de Tomate, Queso Gratinado y Piña. Arroz y Plátanos.

Pescados

PESCADO DEL DIA "GRILLE" (34) 6.95
Filete Cocinado con Mantequilla y Limón.
Servido con Puré de Papas y Vegetales.
CHURRASCO DE DORADO (112) 7.95
Filete a la Plancha Encebollado o al Ajillo, con Arroz Amarillo y Plátanos.
PARGUITO ENTERO FRITO (1½ lb) (165) 10.85
Papas Fritas y Ensalada.
FILETE DE MERO A LA CATALANA (68) 6.95
Puré de Papas y Vegetales.

Especiales Diarios

SOPA DE POLLO 1.55 1.85
FRIJOLES NEGROS 1.30 1.65
SOPA CEBOLLA GRATINADA 2.75
CALDO GALLEGO 1.65 2.35
27 ARROZ CON POLLO 1.75
Con maduros

Sopas

FRIJOLES NEGROS 1.30 1.65
SOPA DE POLLO 1.55 1.85
SOPA DE CEBOLLA AL GRATEN 2.75
CALDO GALLEGO 1.65 2.35

Ensaladas

ENSALADA CESAR 2.75
CHEF SALAD 4.95
ENSALADA MIXTA 2.25
LECHUGA Y TOMATE 1.30

En Temporada

ENSALADA DE AGUACATE 2.45
AGUACATE RELLENO
Con Ensalada de Pollo 3.95
Con Cangrejo y Camarones 4.95
ENSALADA DE FRUTAS NATURALES 4.35
Con Cottage Cheese.

DRESSINGS
French - Low Cal Italian
Blue Cheese - Creamy Italian
Ranch - Thousand Island

Fuente de Soda

CAFE EXPRESSO o COFFEE .... .60
TE FRIO o CALIENTE .... .65
SANKA .... .65
REFRESCOS DE LA FUENTE .... .75
REFRESCOS EN LATAS .... .95
LECHE .... .95
CAFE CON LECHE .... .95
CHOCOLATE CALIENTE .... .95
CHOCOLATE FRIO .... .95
CORTADITO .... .70
MALTA .... .95

SUNDAES O SODAS

CHOCOLATE 2.25
VAINILLA 2.25
FRESA 2.25

BATIDOS

CHOCOLATE, VAINILLA O FRESA 1.75
MAMEY 1.75
FRUTA BOMBA 1.75
MALTEADA 1.75
TRIGO 1.75

ABIERTO DESDE las 8 a.m. a 2 a.m. (Domingo a Jueves)
Viernes hasta las 3:30 a.m. Sábados hasta las 4:30 a.m.

PROPINA NO ESTA INCLUIDA

3555 S. W. 8th Street
Miami, Florida
Teléfono: 444-0240 o 444-7614

1. nombre del restaurante ______________________
2. dirección ______________________
3. ciudad ______________________
4. ¿A qué hora abre el restaurante? ______________________

Nombre ______________________ Fecha ______________

P8-10 Haz un círculo alrededor de todas las palabras que reconoces en el menú.

P8-11 Escribe algunas categorías que encuentras en el menú y una comida o bebida en cada categoría que a ti te gustaría comer o beber.

Categoría

1. ______________________
2. ______________________
3. ______________________

Comida o bebida

1. ______________________
2. ______________________
3. ______________________

P8-12 ¿Qué tipo de restaurante es el Versailles? Escribe el nombre de un plato típico que se sirve allí.

____

Después de leer

P8-13 Imagínate que fuiste a cenar al Restaurante Versailles. Escribe una crítica del restaurante para el periódico de tu universidad o para el periódico de tu ciudad. Describe alguno de los platos y explica si fue bueno o no y por qué...

VERSAILLES

Lugar: ______________________

Tipo de Cocina: ______________________

Precio: ______________________

de estrellas: ______________________

Información: (305) 444-0240

____

____

____

____

____

____

Nombre ______________________________ Fecha ______________

¡A escribir!

Antes de escribir

P8-14 Lee cada descripción e identifica si es carne, postre, bebida, fruta o verdura. Luego adivina qué es exactamente.

Modelo: Cuando hace calor, se toma frío en un vaso grande, pero contiene cafeína. Se le puede poner limón.
bebida, té

1. Se pone en el cereal y se bebe también. Se le puede poner chocolate.
____
2. Es uno de los ingredientes principales de una ensalada básica y es de color rojo.
____
3. Es frío y viene en sabores de fruta, chocolate o vainilla y contiene muchas calorías.
____
4. Viene de un animal que pone huevos *(lays eggs)* y es la parte principal de una comida.
____
5. Se come con un bistec de varias maneras: frita, asada con mantequilla, etcétera.
____

P8-15 ¿Cuáles son tus comidas y bebidas preferidas en casa y en los restaurantes? Escribe tus respuestas con oraciones completas.

En casa

1. ¿Con qué desayunas normalmente? ______________________________
____
2. ¿Qué tomas para el desayuno? ______________________________
____
3. ¿Con qué almuerzas generalmente? ______________________________
____
4. ¿Comes merienda entre *(between)* comidas? ¿Qué comes? ______________________________
____
5. ¿Con qué te gusta cenar? ______________________________
____
6. ¿Qué comidas étnicas sabes preparar? ______________________________
____
7. ¿Cuál es tu postre preferido? ______________________________
____

Nombre ______________________________ Fecha ______________

8. ¿Qué comidas fritas comes? ______________________________

9. ¿Qué carne prefieres? ______________________________

10. ¿Qué tomas cuando tienes mucha sed? ______________________________

En el restaurante

1. ¿Qué comida te gusta pedir cuando vas a un restaurante? ______________________________
2. ¿Qué comidas de otros países te gusta pedir en un restaurante? ¿De qué países son? ______________________________
3. ¿Qué restaurantes étnicos hay en tu ciudad? ______________________________
4. ¿Cuál es tu restaurante preferido? ______________________________
5. ¿Qué bebidas pides con más frecuencia en un restaurante? ______________________________
6. ¿Cuándo te gusta ir a los restaurantes? ______________________________

Vamos a escribir

P8-16 Eres dueño(a) *(owner)* de un restaurante. ¿Qué tipo de restaurante es? ¿Cómo se llama? ¿Qué comida se sirve en el restaurante? ¿Qué bebidas hay? Diseña *(Design)* un menú a continuación. Incluye el nombre del restaurante, las comidas y bebidas que vas a ofrecer y los precios.

Phrases: Appreciating food; Asking the price
Vocabulary: Food: bread, cereals, drinks, fish & seafood, fruits, legumes & vegetables, meals, meat; Restaurant
Grammar: Verbs: present, past

Nombre ______________________ Fecha ______________

Restaurante ______________________

Aperitivos **Precio**

- ______________________ ________
- ______________________ ________
- ______________________ ________

Platos Principales

- ______________________ ________
- ______________________ ________
- ______________________ ________
- ______________________ ________

Postres

- ______________________ ________
- ______________________ ________
- ______________________ ________

Bebidas

- ______________________ ________
- ______________________ ________
- ______________________ ________
- ______________________ ________

Nombre ______________________________ Fecha ______________

Después de escribir

P8-17 Los señores Torreón almorzaron en tu restaurante esta tarde. Prepara su cuenta abajo. En la cuenta no te olvides de incluir el nombre del restaurante, la dirección y el número de teléfono.

RESTAURANTE ______________________

Dirección: ______________________

Número de teléfono: ______________________

	Pesos chilenos
____________	________
____________	________
____________	________
____________	________
____________	________
____________	________
____________	________
Propina 10%–15%	________
Total	________

1 dólar $ = 536 pesos chilenos (noviembre 2005)

Nombre ______________________ Fecha ____________

Cultura

P8-18 Lectura. Lee las siguientes preguntas primero. Luego lee la historia sobre el origen del helado en la página siguiente y conteste las preguntas.

1. Lee el título del artículo. ¿De qué se trata?

____

2. Según el primer párrafo de la lectura, ¿dónde y cuándo nació el helado?

____

3. ¿Quiénes dieron a conocer *(made known)* el uso del helado en el siglo XVII?

____

4. ¿En qué partes geográficas lo dieron a conocer?

____

5. ¿Cuándo se introdujo el helado en los Estados Unidos?

____

6. ¿Cuándo se introdujo en México?

____

7. La "nieve" se preparaba con

____

8. ¿Cómo se llama y dónde está la primera heladería que ofreció el helado? ¿En qué ciudad está?

____

9. ¿Cómo se llama la persona que introdujo el helado a Francia a través de sus cocineros *(chefs, cooks)*?

____

10. ¿Qué grupo de emigrantes se dedicó a la producción de leche? ¿Dónde?

____

11. ¿Qué es la "Flor de Leche" europea?

____

12. ¿Por qué se considera el helado de Danesa uno de los diez mejores helados del continente?

____

Nombre ______________________ Fecha ______________

La aparición de los helados data de hace 600 años aproximadamente. Se cree que fue en Italia donde nació el tipo de helado que actualmente conocemos, aunque en ese entonces su elaboración era solamente doméstica.

Fueron también los italianos —genoveses y venecianos— del siglo XVII, quienes lo dieron a conocer, dado los nexos comerciales que tenían con las distintas regiones de Asia y norte de Europa, posteriormente, éstos últimos, propagaron las recetas en sus países antes del descubrimiento de América.

En el continente Americano, el helado se introdujo durante la colonización de los ingleses, hace más de 200 años en Estados Unidos de Norteamérica y en México, apenas unos 40 años.

Cabe señalar que en nuestro país durante la época porfiriana ya existía una forma de helado, mejor conocida como "nieve", la cual era preparada con agua, fruta y azúcar. Era algo derivado del raspado, que conocieron aquí los españoles en el Imperio de Moctezuma II. El raspado era un tipo de golosina helada que consistía en hielo picado al que se le agregaba una miel de frutas como el capulín, garambuyo, tuna o tejocote, posteriormente, naranja y limón.

Fue en Francia donde por primera vez el helado se elaboró con fines comerciales, siendo el Café Precope, la primera heladería ofrecida al público consumidor y la cual aún existe en París. Se cuenta que Catalina de Medici introdujo esta golosina a través de sus cocineros.

En nuestro continente, debido a la escasa relación —casi nula— entre los sajones americanos y los latinoamericanos, el conocimiento del helado de crema fue muy tardío. Este ocurrió después de la independencia de las colonias americanas, pues antes los intereses religiosos y costumbristas de los europeos, impedían todo tipo de comunicación o intercambio ideológico entre los pobladores.

Por otra parte, tocó a México el privilegio de ser el primer país latinoamericano en conocer el helado de crema, gracias a la afluencia de emigrantes de origen europeo que se dedicaron a la producción de leche, desarrollando una infraestructura adecuada para su impulso comercial.

Este gran empuje se dio principalmente en la región del Bajío, donde el terreno era propio para la producción lechera, a diferencia de las cuencas poblana, queretana y mexiquense. Así, se vio nacer por primera vez un helado con todas las características cualitativas y naturales, superiores a la "Flor de Leche" europea, nombre original del helado de crema.

En México, aunque ya se tenía conocimiento de este tipo de helado, fue Industrias *Danesa*, quien en golpe de iniciativa se arriesgo a presentar ante el público consumidor un auténtico helado, el cual, primero por curiosidad o por novedad, empezó a tener aceptación hasta hacerse un hábito alimenticio en la dieta mexicana.

Actualmente, el helado de Danesa está ubicado entres los diez mejores helados del continente, dada la calidad de sus ingredientes y el tipo de leche que se produce en la cuenca del Bajío.

Nombre ______________________ Fecha ______________

Práctica auditiva

Pronunciación esencial

Spanish *ll* and *y*

CD 2-10 **P8-19** Pronunciation of **ll** and **y** varies widely in the Spanish-speaking world. In general, **ll** and initial **y** are pronounced like the *y* in *yo-yo*. As you know, the word **y** *(and)* is pronounced like the *i* in *machine*. Listen to the following sentences and repeat after the speaker.

—Alicia, te presento a mi amiga **Y**olanda **Y**añez de Cari**ll**o. E**ll**a es de Sevi**ll**a.
—Mucho gusto, **Y**olanda. ¿Cuándo **ll**egaste a Chile?
—**Ll**egué a las dos de la tarde a**y**er y **ll**amé a Rosario inmediatamente.
—¿Quieres desa**y**unar con nosotros mañana? Vamos a desa**y**unar en la terraza del hotel si no **ll**ueve.
—Sí, gracias.

Spanish *ñ*

CD 2-11 **P8-20** Spanish **ñ** is pronounced approximately like the *ny* sound in *canyon*. Listen to the following sentences and repeat after the speaker.

—¿Dónde están los ni**ñ**os, Alicia?
—Creo que Miguel está ba**ñ**ándose y Shawn está jugando al fútbol con su compa**ñ**ero de escuela. Oye, ma**ñ**ana es el cumplea**ñ**os de Shawn, ¿verdad?
—No, Alicia. Ma**ñ**ana es mi cumplea**ñ**os.
—Ay, ¿sí? ¡Feliz cumplea**ñ**os, I**ñ**aki!
—Gracias.

En contexto

CD 2-12 **P8-21** **¡Salud!** Escucha la siguiente conversación. Decide si las siguientes oraciones son verdaderas **(V)** o falsas **(F)**, o si no hay suficiente información para contestar **(N)**.

____ 1. Los señores Torreón invitaron a Alicia a cenar en su casa.

____ 2. Los señores Torreón son buenos cocineros.

____ 3. David es también un buen cocinero.

____ 4. El guisado es de pollo y papas.

____ 5. La comida huele muy bien.

Nombre ______________________________ Fecha ______________

VOCABULARIO ESENCIAL

CD 2-13 **P8-22 ¡Tengo ganas de comer!** David siempre tiene hambre. Ahora está en Viña del Mar con Alicia, después de nadar y de hacer submarinismo. David tiene hambre y le pregunta a Alicia si tiene hambre también. Escucha muy bien la conversación entre David y Alicia y escoge la mejor respuesta para completar cada oración.

____ 1. David tiene...
a. sed.
b. hambre.
c. sueño.

____ 2. Alicia tiene...
a. hambre.
b. razón.
c. sed.

____ 3. David quiere almorzar...
a. carne con papas fritas.
b. sopa y ensalada.
c. pescado con arroz.

____ 4. Alicia quiere almorzar...
a. sopa.
b. ensalada.
c. carne con arroz.

____ 5. De postre, David quiere...
a. arroz con leche.
b. flan.
c. helado de vainilla.

Nombre ______________________ Fecha ____________

CD 2-14 **P8-23** **Las comidas.** Escucha la siguiente narración de David. Mientras escucha la conversación, haz un círculo alrededor de las comidas que David va a comer hoy. No vamos a usar todos los dibujos.

Nombre ______________________ Fecha ______________

LECCIÓN 9 ¿VACACIONES DE VERANO EN DICIEMBRE?

Práctica esencial

VOCABULARIO ESENCIAL

P9-1 Asociaciones. Empareja las siguientes palabras con la oración más lógica. No vas a tener que usar todas las palabras de la lista.

los aretes	los juegos de video	el reproductor de DVD
el anillo	la máquina de afeitar	la cámara de fotografía digital
la pulsera	la radio grabadora	el escáner plano
el collar	el secador de cabello	el juego de pesas
la computadora	la cámara de video	la caminadora
el reproductor de CD portátil		

1. Se usa para navegar el Internet
____
2. Joya que se lleva en la muñeca
____
3. Joyas que se llevan en los dedos
____
4. Se usa para sacar fotos para ver en la computadora
____
5. Se usa para ver películas en disco
____
6. Game Cube, Play Station, X-Box
____
7. Se usa para tener músculos *(muscles)* muy fuertes
____
8. Se usa para secar el cabello
____
9. Es para escuchar música mientras se corre por el parque
____
10. Joyas que se llevan en las orejas
____

Nombre ________________________________ Fecha ________________

Gramática esencial

P9-2 Hermanos opuestos *(opposites)*. Shawn y su hermano Miguel son muy diferentes. Son opuestos. Lo que hace Shawn no lo hace Miguel. Cambia las siguientes oraciones para reflejar las diferencias entre los dos hermanos.

Modelo: Shawn siempre le trae flores a su mamá. (nunca / nada)
Miguel nunca le trae nada a su mamá.

1. Shawn siempre estudia. (nunca)

   Miguel

   ____

2. A Shawn le gustan todos los deportes. (ningún)

   A Miguel

   ____

3. Miguel conoce a todos los estudiantes de la escuela. (nadie)

   Shawn

   ____

4. Shawn siempre juega al básquetbol y al fútbol con sus amigos. (ni... ni / con nadie)

   Miguel

   ____

P9-3 De mal humor *(In a bad mood)*. David está de mal humor hoy con sus amigos. A todos les contesta negativamente. Escribe lo que responde David a las preguntas usando las palabras entre paréntesis.

Modelo: —¿Quieres nadar conmigo *(with me)* hoy? (con nadie / nunca)
—No, no quiero nadar con nadie nunca.

1. ¿Practicas algún deporte? (ningún)

   ____

2. ¿Te gusta nadar? (tampoco)

   ____

3. ¿Prefieres jugar al tenis? (nunca / con nadie)

   ____

4. ¿Te gusta correr o jugar al básquetbol? (ni... ni)

   ____

Nombre ______________________ Fecha ____________

P9-4 Sí y no. Escribe las siguientes oraciones dos veces: primero, positivamente y después, negativamente.

Modelo: David / siempre / levantarse / a tiempo / para / ir / a / trabajar
David siempre se levanta a tiempo para ir a trabajar.
David nunca se levanta a tiempo para ir a trabajar.

1. el señor Torreón / siempre / regalarle / o / flores / o / dulces / a / la señora Torreón

____

____

2. yo / pensar / visitar / Viña / también

____

____

3. Alicia, ¿hay / algunos / brazaletes / bonitos / aquí?

____

____

4. David, ¿tú / ver / algo / barato / en / almacén?

____

____

P9-5 Así era yo. Alicia les describe a los señores Torreón las cosas que ella hacía con su familia en Wisconsin.

Modelo: mi familia y yo / ir a esquiar los fines de semana
Mi familia y yo íbamos a esquiar los fines de semana.

1. yo / comer muchos chocolates cuando mi mamá no / estar en casa

____

2. mis hermanos / jugar al fútbol todos los días

____

3. mis hermanos y yo / montar en bicicleta todo el tiempo

____

4. mi papá / trabajar mucho en casa los fines de semana

____

5. mi mamá / hacer comida típica para el día de Navidad

____

6. mi familia y yo / ir a Chicago y a los museos en el verano

____

7. nosotros / divertirse mucho juntos

____

Nombre ______________________________ Fecha ______________

P9-6 Hace muchos años... La señora Torreón les describe su vida cuando era joven a Alicia y a David. Completa el siguiente relato usando la forma correcta del imperfecto.

Cuando (tener) doce años, __________ (vivir) en una casa en Viña. Cuando __________ (tener) dieciocho años, regresamos a Santiago y por eso asistí a la Universidad de Santiago. Cuando __________ (estar) en la universidad, me __________ (gustar) ver los juegos de fútbol y __________ (practicar) tenis todos los fines de semana durante el verano. En el invierno __________ (ir) con mi familia a esquiar. Mis amigos y yo __________ (ir) a patinar los viernes por la noche. Después de patinar, __________ (cenar) en casa de alguna de las muchachas y después __________ (cantar) y __________ (bailar) toda la noche. Nosotros lo __________ (pasar) muy bien en la universidad. Ahora administro este viñedo y recuerdo mi vida de joven con ustedes.

Cultura

P9-7 La religión en Hispanoamérica. Lee cada oración y decide si es verdadera **(V)** o falsa **(F)**, o si no hay información suficiente para contestar **(N)**.

_____ 1. Los españoles trajeron a América la religión católica.

_____ 2. Los indígenas no tenían religión cuando llegaron los españoles.

_____ 3. Hoy en día, los santos tienen mucha importancia en Latinoamérica.

_____ 4. La religión que llegó de África influyó en un 80% de la religión de Latinoamérica.

P9-8 Celebraciones. Completa las siguientes oraciones sobre las celebraciones en el mundo hispano.

1. En España, comienza la celebración de la Navidad el ______________________________.
2. En España y en Puerto Rico, los niños reciben sus regalos el día de ______________________.
3. En México, las posadas se celebran ______________________________________.
4. En Venezuela, la gente patina después de __________________________________.

¡A leer!: La historia de la tarjeta de Navidad

Antes de leer

P9-9 La siguiente lectura es sobre la historia de la tarjeta de Navidad. Haz una lista con la información que esperas encontrar en esta lectura.

____

____

____

____

Nombre ______________________ Fecha ______________

Vamos a leer

HISTORIA

La costumbre de mandar tarjetas de Navidad, tal como las conocemos, comenzó en Londres en 1848.

La idea fue de un próspero comerciante, quien le pidió al artista John Calcott Horsley, de la Real Academia, que le diseñara algo para mandar a sus amigos y relacionados saludándolos por Navidad.

La tarjeta estaba dividida en tres paneles, con la ilustración principal mostrando a una familia brindando en una fiesta. Los paneles de ambos lados ilustraban dos antiguas tradiciones de Navidad — dando de comer a los pobres y vistiendo a los necesitados. Un breve mensaje, deseando una alegre Navidad y un feliz año nuevo, acompañaba la ilustración.

En Inglaterra, las tarjetas se comenzaron a imprimir y popularizar en los años que siguieron. Como salieron tres años después que se había pasado en Inglaterra una ley que permitía el envío de cartas por un centavo, las tarjetas fueron recibidas con entusiasmo.

Durante las primeras décadas, las tarjetas más populares eran las de paisajes, niños, flores, pájaros y animales. También se vendían escenas religiosas.

Para 1870, en Boston, se había perfeccionado el proceso de impresión en colores y las reproducciones eran tan bien hechas que sólo los expertos podían distinguir entre una impresión y un original.

Para 1881 la editorial de Boston imprimía 5 millones de tarjetas al año, la mayoría de Navidad.

A comienzos de siglo, las postales alemanas de a centavo invadieron el mercado. La compañía de Boston no podía competir sin bajar la calidad y cerró. Alemania monopolizó el mercado hasta la I Guerra Mundial.

La mayoría de los impresores de tarjetas de saludo surgieron en 1910 y para 1920 ya ofrecían una variedad de diseños y mensajes.

Fue en 1929, cuando la Depresión golpeó al país, que las tarjetas expresando fe y esperanza para mejores tiempos se popularizaron.

La industria sobrevivió la Depresión y para la II Guerra los mensajes reflejaban los sentimientos de la época, apareciendo saludos a través de las millas o expresando añoranza.

Durante unos años se vendían mucho las tarjetas con versos cómicos. Amoldándose a los tiempos, aparecieron los mensajes de paz y los diseños celebrando la llegada del hombre a la Luna. Luego siguieron las tarjetas que reflejaban el afán de mantenerse en buena salud. Hasta a Santa le pusieron patines.

Ahora las valijas del correo se llenan diariamente con millones de artísticos mensajes impresos —sentimentales, picarescos y tradicionales— cada uno es portador de deseos para un cumpleaños, una fiesta u otra ocasión especial. Los modernos diseños y las nuevas técnicas de imprenta hacen que haya tarjetas de todo tipo, tamaño y precio para todas las ocasiones y parentescos.

NACIMIENTO DE UN GIGANTE

Uno de los arquitectos de esta costumbre es el fundador de la compañía de tarjetas Hallmark, Joyce C. Hall, quien se abrigó en una ola de moda de mandar postales y la transformó en una costumbre social que no da indicios de estar por desaparecer.

El negocio comenzó en 1910 y desde entonces se ha convertido en una corporación millonaria y en líder de su industria.

Hallmark es ahora una organización internacional con sede en Kansas City, estado de Missouri, publica más de 11 millones de tarjetas cada día, las imprime en 20 idiomas y las distribuye en más de 100 países.

P9-10 Completa la historia de la tarjeta de Navidad.

Según *(According to)* la historia de mandar tarjetas de Navidad, la costumbre comenzó en el año __________ en __________. Fue idea de un próspero *(prosperous)* __________ quien le pidió al __________ John Calcott Horsley que le diseñara *(he asked . . . to design)* algo especial para mandarles a sus __________ y __________ saludándolos *(greeting them)* por __________.

Nombre ______________________________ Fecha ______________

P9-11 Describe la primera tarjeta. Marca **sí** en todas las descripciones que se aplican *(apply)* a esta tarjeta.

1. _____ Estaba dividida en tres paneles.
2. _____ Estaba dividida en dos ilustraciones principales.
3. _____ La ilustración principal era una familia en una fiesta.
4. _____ Una ilustración era de Santa Claus.
5. _____ Un panel ilustraba tradiciones antiguas *(old)* de Navidad.
6. _____ Un panel ilustraba alguien que daba de comer a *(was giving food to)* personas necesitadas *(needy)*.
7. _____ Tenía un breve mensaje *(message)* para una alegre Navidad y un Feliz Año Nuevo.

P9-12 Qué pasó en los años siguientes? Escribe la letra de la respuesta correcta en el espacio indicado.

a. en 1870
b. en 1881
c. en 1910
d. en 1920
e. en 1929

1. _____ Las tarjetas de la Depresión expresaban la esperanza *(hope)* de mejores tiempos *(better times)*.
2. _____ Se perfeccionó el proceso de impresión en colores *(color printing)* y las reproducciones en las tarjetas.
3. _____ Surgieron la mayoría de impresores *(printers)* de tarjetas de saludo *(greeting cards)*.
4. _____ La editorial de Boston imprimía *(printed)* 5 millones de tarjetas al año.
5. _____ Se ofrecía una variedad de diseños *(designs)* y mensajes.

P9-13 Completa la siguiente oración con los números necesarios.

El negocio de Hallmark, que comenzó en _________, publica más de _________ de tarjetas por día y las imprime en _________ idiomas para distribuirlas en más de _________ países.

Nombre ______________________ Fecha ____________

Después de leer

P9-14 Diseña y dibuja una tarjeta de Navidad, de cumpleaños, de día del santo o de alguna otra ocasión especial para dársela a un(a) compañero(a) de clase. El diseño puede ser como el de las primeras tarjetas de 1848 o un diseño moderno.

Nombre ______________________ Fecha ______________

¡A escribir!

Antes de escribir

P9-15 Completa las siguientes oraciones de una manera breve para describir tu juventud.

Cuando yo tenía diez años...

1. Mi deporte favorito era ______________________.
2. Mi día festivo preferido era ______________________.
3. Mi comida preferida era ______________________ y mi bebida preferida era ______________________.
4. Yo vivía en ______________________.
5. Mi libro preferido era ______________________.
6. Mi canción preferida era ______________________.
7. Mi mejor amigo(a) era ______________________.
8. Mi programa de televisión preferido era ______________________.
9. Mi escuela preferida era ______________________.
10. Mi pasatiempo favorito era ______________________.

Vamos a escribir

P9-16 Escribe un ensayo breve sobre tu juventud. Incluye la siguiente información y toda la información anterior que sea apropiada para tu ensayo. Puedes agregar más información si quieres.

- ¿Cómo eras tú cuando tenías quince años?
- ¿Dónde vivías?
- ¿Cómo eran tus padres y hermanos?
- ¿Cómo se divertían ustedes? ¿Adónde iban? ¿Con quién?

Phrases: Describing the past; Expressing time relationships
Vocabulary: Family members; Leisure; Sports; Studies
Grammar: Verbs: imperfect

Nombre ______________________ Fecha ______________

Cuando yo tenía quince años…

Después de escribir

P9-17 Haz una lista de todos los verbos y sujetos que usaste en tu ensayo. Luego escribe el infinitivo y la forma correcta del presente, del imperfecto y del pretérito en el espacio indicado. El primer verbo ya está escrito en la forma correcta.

As you learn more verb tenses in Spanish, it becomes increasingly important to be able to choose among them in your writing. Charts of this type will help you to select the correct verb form. Remember, you will need plenty of time to acquire the different verb forms in your speech. Be patient with yourself. It is well worth the time and effort!

Infinitivo	Sujeto	Presente	Imperfecto	Pretérito
tener	*yo*	*tengo*	*tenía*	*tuve*

Nombre ______________________________ Fecha ______________

Práctica auditiva

Pronunciación esencial

Spanish *b* and *v*

In Spanish, **b** and **v** are pronounced the same. Their pronunciation depends on their position in a word or in a group of words.

CD 2-15 **P9-18** At the beginning of a single word or a group of words (after a pause) and after **m** or **n,** Spanish **b** and **v** are pronounced very much like the *b* in *boy.* Listen to the following sentences and repeat after the speaker.

—**B**uenos días, señorita. **B**usco un regalo para la **b**oda de mis amigos este **v**iernes.
—**B**ueno... un reloj es un **b**uen regalo. Este reloj es muy **b**onito.
—Sí, lo es *(Yes, it is)*..., pero creo que **v**oy a regalarles un álbum para fotos.
—**B**uena idea... así **v**an a recordar su **b**oda para siempre.

CD 2-16 **P9-19** In all other positions, particularly between vowels, Spanish **b** and **v** are pronounced softly.

To pronounce them correctly, start to say **b,** but at the last moment, do not quite close your lips.

Listen to the following sentences and repeat after the speakers.

—¿En qué puedo ser**v**irles, jó**v**enes?
—Buscamos un regalo para nuestra mamá. Su cumpleaños es el sá**b**ado. ¿Nos ayuda, por fa**v**or?
—¡Cómo no! Este brazalete es bonito, ¿no?
—Claro. Pero si hu**b**iera uno menos caro...

En contexto

CD 2-17 **P9-20** **¡Felices vacaciones de verano!** Escucha la siguiente conversación. Decide si las siguientes oraciones son verdaderas **(V)** o falsas **(F),** o si no hay suficiente información para contestar **(N)**.

____ 1. Los señores Torreón, Alicia y David celebran las Navidades en Chile.

____ 2. La Navidad en Chile se celebra en el verano.

____ 3. En Wisconsin no hace mucho frío en el invierno.

____ 4. A Alicia le gusta nadar en el mar.

____ 5. Alicia y David van a la playa en Viña del Mar.

Nombre ______________________ Fecha ______________

VOCABULARIO ESENCIAL

CD 2-18 **P9-21 Regalos de Navidad.** Alicia llama a su familia para desearles una Feliz Navidad. Alicia y su madre están conversando sobre los regalos de Navidad que se dieron en Santiago y en Madison. Escribe el nombre del regalo que recibió cada uno y quién se lo regaló.

	Regalo(s)	**¿De quién?**
Señora Torreón	______________	______________
Señora Benson	______________	______________
Señor Torreón	______________	______________
Shawn	______________	______________
Miguel	______________	______________
Alicia	______________	______________
David	______________	______________
Señor Benson	______________	______________

CD 2-19 **P9-22 Cuando éramos niños.** David y Alicia están hablando sobre su niñez *(childhood)* en Wisconsin. Lee las oraciones de abajo y escucha su conversación. Indica si cada oración es verdadera **(V)** o falsa **(F).**

____ 1. Cuando Alicia era niña, jugaba con la nieve.

____ 2. A David no le gustaba esquiar.

____ 3. Alicia y David jugaban en la calle.

____ 4. Nunca practicaban juegos de video.

____ 5. Alicia nadaba todas las mañanas.

____ 6. David veía la televisión.

____ 7. Alicia no tenía bicicleta.

____ 8. Alicia y David se divertían mucho cuando eran niños.

Nombre ______________________________ Fecha ______________

PASO 4 De Compras

LECCIÓN 10 ¿DESEA ALGO MÁS?

Práctica esencial

VOCABULARIO ESENCIAL

P10-1 ¡Adivina qué es! Aquí hay descripciones de varias frutas, vegetales y carnes. Adivina qué es y escribe el nombre en el espacio en blanco.

Modelo: Es rojo, no es dulce *(sweet)*, pero es una fruta. Se come en muchas ensaladas.
el tomate

1. Es una fruta amarilla. Es la fruta favorita de los monos *(monkeys)*.

   ____

2. Es como una naranja, pero es más grande y es amarga *(bitter)*. Se come mucho en el desayuno.

   ____

3. Es un vegetal blanco que se parece mucho al bróculi.

   ____

4. Es un vegetal que da sabor *(flavor)* a muchos platos. Las ensaladas muchas veces tienen tomate y este vegetal.

   ____

5. Es una fruta roja y se usa para hacer pasteles *(pies)*.

   ____

6. Es un vegetal verde de hojas *(leaves)* que se come en las ensaladas.

   ____

7. Es un vegetal de color anaranjado y es largo de tamaño. Es el vegetal favorito de Bugs Bunny.

   ____

8. Es una fruta pequeña, redonda y roja. Se sirve muchas veces encima de la tarta de queso *(cheesecake)*.

   ____

Nombre ______________________________ Fecha ______________

P10-2 **¿Dónde se compra?** A continuación hay cinco tiendas diferentes. Haz una lista de tres o cuatro cosas que se pueden comprar en cada una.

Productos: ______________________________

____

Productos: ______________________________

____

Productos: ______________________________

____

Productos: ______________________________

____

Productos: ______________________________

____

Nombre ______________________ Fecha ____________

GRAMÁTICA ESENCIAL

P10-3 Consejos para una entrevista. Susana va a tener una entrevista de trabajo mañana con el señor Navarro en su mercado. Un amigo le da consejos sobre lo que debe y no debe hacer. Usa los mandatos informales para hacer oraciones completas.

1. no estar nerviosa

   ____

2. responder honestamente

   ____

3. contestar cada pregunta

   ____

4. llegar a tiempo a la entrevista

   ____

5. no fumar ni cigarrillos ni cigarros

   ____

6. no comer nada mientras hablas

   ____

7. mirar directamente al señor Navarro

   ____

8. escribirle una tarjeta para darle las gracias al señor Navarro

   ____

P10-4 En el mercado. Dos amigos están en un mercado de comestibles. Comparan las verduras y las frutas que venden allí. ¿Qué dicen?

Modelo: lechuga / estar / caro / bróculi
La lechuga está más cara que el bróculi.

1. plátanos / estar / barato / uvas

   ____

   ____

2. cebolla / estar / fresco / apio *(celery)*

   ____

   ____

Nombre ______________________________ Fecha ______________

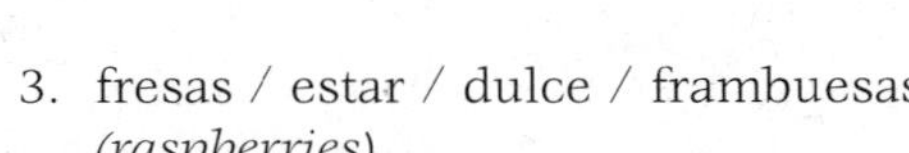

3. fresas / estar / dulce / frambuesas *(raspberries)*

____

____

4. naranjas / tener / fibra / manzanas

____

____

5. pimientos / ser / grande / rábanos *(radishes)*

____

____

6. espinacas *(spinach)* / ser / nutritivo / zanahorias

____

____

P10-5 Les presento a mi familia. María Alexandra, la hija del Sr. Navarro, nos va a describir a su familia y va a exagerar un poco. Completa la descripción con las palabras apropiadas de la lista siguiente. Puedes usar una palabra más de una vez. Asegúrate de hacer todos los cambios necesarios.

el	tan	trabajador
la	más	guapo
los	menos	simpático
las	mejor	amable
	peor	inteligente
	tanto	ocupado
	mayor	bonito
	menor	bajo
		delicioso
		organizado
		responsable
		eficiente

Nombre ____ Fecha ___________________

Mi familia vive en Buenos Aires, Argentina. Mi papá es ________ ________ hombre del mundo. Él es el dueño del mercado ________ pequeño de Buenos Aires. Nuestro mercado es ________ ________ ________ de la calle Independencia. Nuestros precios son ________ ________ ________ de toda la ciudad y nuestras frutas y verduras son ________ ________ ________. Mi mamá nos ayuda con la contabilidad. Ella es contadora y es ________ ________ contadora de Buenos Aires. Mi mamá es ________ ________ como mi papá. También es ________ ________ como él.

Yo trabajo con mi papá en el mercado y hago los pedidos; soy ________ persona ________ ________ del mundo. También estudio negocios por la noche en la universidad y soy muy estudiosa. Trato de ser ________ persona ________ ________ de mi clase. Por ahora, tengo muy buenas notas y el mercado está dando ganancias *(profits)*.

P10-6 Consejos. Elena Aguilar está dándoles consejos a sus empleados. ¿Qué les dice? Usa mandatos formales.

Modelo: La señorita Gómez come sólo postres para el desayuno y no come nada para el almuerzo. De las 3:00 a las 5:00 no puede trabajar porque está cansada.
Señorita Gómez, coma usted fruta para el almuerzo. o *Desayune bien, señorita Gómez.*

1. Un empleado llega cinco minutos tarde todos los días porque tiene problemas mecánicos con su auto.

   ____

2. Una estudiante que trabaja en la tienda veinte horas a la semana pasa el tiempo comprando refrescos y hablando con otros empleados todos los días.

   ____

3. Otra empleada descansa cada treinta minutos pero trabaja muy rápido cuando está trabajando.

   ____

4. Una empleada joven siempre está cansada porque sale a bailar y se acuesta tarde tres o cuatro veces a la semana.

   ____

5. Un empleado sólo hace las cosas cuando Elena Aguilar se lo pide dos o tres veces.

   ____

Nombre ______________________________ Fecha ______________

P10-7 Qué hacer y qué no hacer durante las horas de trabajo. En el mercado central, la gerenta, Elena Aguilar, hizo una lista de mandatos para todos los empleados. Lee la lista siguiente y escribe la lista con mandatos formales en vez de infinitivos. Usa las líneas proveídas en la página 110.

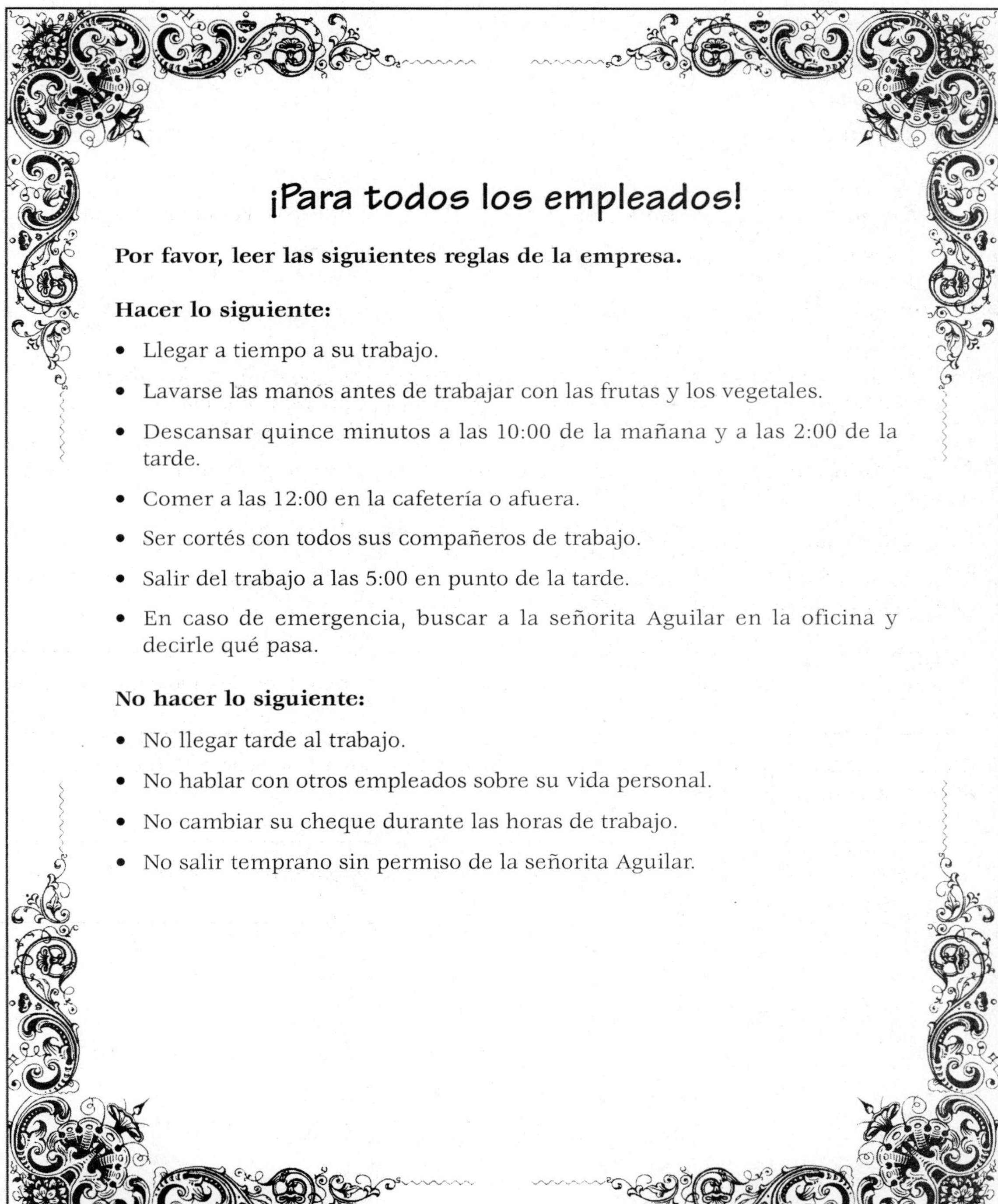

¡Para todos los empleados!

Por favor, leer las siguientes reglas de la empresa.

Hacer lo siguiente:

- Llegar a tiempo a su trabajo.
- Lavarse las manos antes de trabajar con las frutas y los vegetales.
- Descansar quince minutos a las 10:00 de la mañana y a las 2:00 de la tarde.
- Comer a las 12:00 en la cafetería o afuera.
- Ser cortés con todos sus compañeros de trabajo.
- Salir del trabajo a las 5:00 en punto de la tarde.
- En caso de emergencia, buscar a la señorita Aguilar en la oficina y decirle qué pasa.

No hacer lo siguiente:

- No llegar tarde al trabajo.
- No hablar con otros empleados sobre su vida personal.
- No cambiar su cheque durante las horas de trabajo.
- No salir temprano sin permiso de la señorita Aguilar.

Nombre ______________________________ Fecha ______________

Hagan lo siguiente:

____

____

____

____

____

____

____

No hagan lo siguiente:

____

____

____

____

CULTURA

P10-8 Por el mundo hispano. Completa las siguientes oraciones con la información cultural apropiada.

1. En Latinoamérica y en España, muchas personas prefieren comprar comida en
   ____.
2. En una carnicería se compran
   ____.
3. Se compra el pan en
   ____.
4. Hay mejores precios en
   ____.
5. Los productos son más frescos en
   ____.
6. Algunas de las secciones que se encuentran en un mercado son las de
   ____.
7. Si un artículo no tiene precio fijo, se puede
   ____.
8. ¿Dónde es recomendable quedarse si uno está en Buenos Aires?
   ____.
9. ¿Qué cosas especiales se puede comprar en Argentina?
   ____.
10. ¿Qué se come en un asado?
    ____.

P10-9 Lectura. Mira el siguiente anuncio y contesta las preguntas.

CARNICERIA
LA VILLA

"La que no tiene sucursales"

ESPECIALES DE SEMANA SANTA

CARNE PARA ASAR.............. $1.59 LIBRA
PIERNAS DE POLLO............. 49¢ LIBRA
PALOMILLA.......................... $1.99 LIBRA

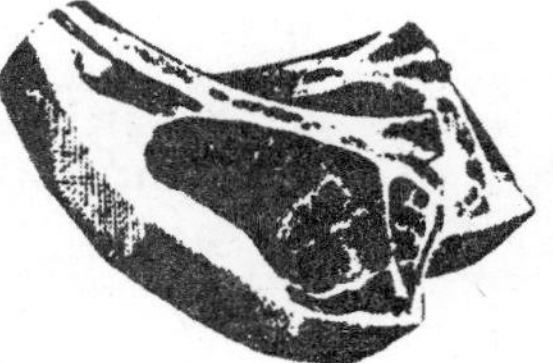

CARNE TIERNA RANCHERA. $2.25 LIBRA
MENUDO.............................. 39¢ LIBRA
PATITAS DE PUERCO.......... 39¢ LIBRA

TAPATIO, 5 oz.......................... 2 x 89¢
ACEITE DE MAIZ GALÓN.................. $4.79
FARAON JALAPEÑO 28 OZ. $1.19
GAMESA PASTAS 7 OZ. .... 5 x $1.00
PAPEL BOSIC.............................. 2 x 89¢
SARDINAS ROYAL CROWN 15 OZ...... 99¢
PAN BLANCO.............................2 x 89¢
HUEVOS BLANCOS (PAQ. DE 20).......... $1.99
RABANITOS.......................4 lbs. x $1.00
CEBOLLAS VERDES..........5 lbs. x $1.00
CILANTRO............................... 5 x $1.00

2214 SO. SAN PEDRO ST., LOS ANGELES, CA 90011

(213) 748-6014

*Con la compra de un mínimo de $5 dólares, reciba una docena de tortillas "La Tapatía"

1. ¿Qué se vende en esta tienda? ¿Dónde se encuentra la tienda?

____.

2. ¿Cuánto cuesta una libra de piernas de pollo?

____.

3. ¿Cuál es la carne más cara? ¿Cuál es la carne más barata?

____.

4. Necesitas dos litros de refrescos, una libra de cebollas verdes, un galón de aceite de maíz y tres libras de carne para asar. ¿Cuánto dinero necesitas llevar a la carnicería?

____.

5. Si gastas más de 5 dólares en esta tienda, ¿qué recibes gratis?

____.

Nombre ______________________________ Fecha ______________

¡A leer!: Los avisos clasificados

Antes de leer

P10-10 Muchas tiendas que se especializan en la venta de ciertos productos ponen un anuncio *(ad)* en la sección de anuncios clasificados de un periódico. ¿Qué tipo de información sobre los productos se incluye en estos anuncios?

____

____

Vamos a leer

P10-11 Examina los anuncios clasificados de la página 113 y escoge dos anuncios y escribe la siguiente información en los espacios indicados.

Nombre de la tienda	Productos que se venden	Dirección (calle y número)
1. ______________	______________	______________
2. ______________	______________	______________

SECCIÓN ESPECIAL DE AVISO OPORTUNO CLASIFICADO POR TEMAS

TELEFONOS

18•59•28
18•12•45
18•47•51

COMO REDACTAR SU ANUNCIO: 1. SEA CONCRETO. Anuncie sin perderse en detalles, con un texto comprensible, y datos que den una idea clara. 2. SEA VERAZ. Si busca comprar o vender, especifique las condiciones, y realizará su operación con mayor rapidez. La verdad vende. 3. NO OMITA DATOS. Números telefónicos y dirección son muy indispensables. Incluya horarios en los que se le localice.

AVISOS DISPONIBLES: El regular, en mayúsculas y minúsculas, $370 pesos palabra; El DESTACADO, TODAS EN MAYUSCULAS, $390 pesos palabra; EL ESPECIAL, EN MAYUSCULAS o minúsculas, en tipo negro. $480 pesos palabra. TODOS ESTOS PRECIOS YA INCLUYEN EL I.V.A.

LLAME a cualquiera de estos 3 números, de 8 AM a 5 PM, lunes a sábado, y ordene su anuncio. Nuestras operadoras tomarán su orden, se confirmará telefónicamente su inserción, y en su domicilio u negocio recibirá Ud. la factura correspondiente. EN NUESTRAS OFICINAS se reciben avisos de ocasión en el mismo horario.

- A/ ANUNCIOS
- B/ TRANSPORTE
- C/ EMPLEOS
- D/ MERCANCÍA
- E/ RANCHOS
- F/ EDICTOS Y OFICIALES
- G/ RENTA DE BIENES RAÍCES
- H/ VENTA DE BIENES RAÍCES
- I/ SALONES, FIESTAS, ETC.
- J/ SERVICIOS VARIOS

Nombre ______________________ Fecha ____________

FLORERIA Y REGALOS

"ALI" | "JAZMIN"

MAR DEL NORTE #5117 FOVISSTE TERESIANO | MONTES APENINOS Y SIERRA LEONA # 5479

TEL. 16-53-70 | LA CUESTA

Arreglos florales naturales y artificiales para toda ocasión arreglos con globos gigantes, plantas naturales y coronas, especial del mes, decoraciones para bodas o quinceañeras, 78 arreglos naturales, salón, iglesia y carro todo por $495,000.- M.N. aparte el suyo con tiempo ENTREGA GRATIS A DOMICILIO. Atendidos personalmente por su propietaria ALI LUCERO.

E18J-F30J

CARNICERÍA

HERMANOS CÁRDENAS

Le ofrece las mejores carnes, frutas y legumbres. Lo esperamos en Guadiana #5375 entre Suiza y Luxemburgo Col. San Antonio.

E15J-F10A

P10-12 Los símbolos y las letras de las diferentes secciones de los anuncios clasificados (página 112) indican la clasificación por tema de los anuncios. Contesta las siguientes preguntas sobre estas secciones.

1. Si buscas trabajo, ¿cuál es la letra y el nombre de la sección que necesitas?

   ____

2. ¿En qué sección se encuentran los apartamentos que puedes alquilar *(to rent)*?

   ____

3. Imagínate que vas a vender un televisor que ya no necesitas. ¿En qué sección se encuentra tu anuncio?

   ____

4. Si quieres llamar para poner un anuncio clasificado en el periódico, ¿a qué números puedes llamar?

   ____

5. ¿Cuál es el horario para llamar para poner un anuncio? (las horas) de ________ a ________ (los días) de ________ a ________.

Nombre ______________________ Fecha ____________

Después de leer

P10-13 Vas a tener una fiesta especial con mucha comida, un pastel para la ocasión y decoraciones para la mesa y la casa. Con un(a) compañero(a) de clase, escriban un conversación con los dueños de las varias tiendas que están en los anuncios clasificados (página 113) para preguntar lo siguiente:

- si la tienda tiene ciertas cosas para su fiesta especial
- el precio de cada cosa
- si la tienda acepta tarjetas de crédito
- dónde está cada tienda

____

____

____

____

____

____

¡A escribir!

Antes de escribir

P10-14 Piensa en los anuncios que ves con frecuencia en las revistas y en los periódicos. Llena la tabla a continuación con información sobre los productos y las publicidades.

Productos	¿En qué tipo de tiendas se vende(n)?	¿Quiénes van a comprar estos productos?	¿Qué mandatos formales se usan en los anuncios?
Cereal azucarado (*sweetened*)	*en el mercado*	*adultos y niños*	*descruba, pruebe*
Café descafeinado			
Suplementos de calcio			
Verduras congeladas (*frozen*)			
Helados naturales			
Salsas y especies (*spices*) orientales			
Pan y pan dulce frescos			

Nombre ______________________ Fecha ______________

Vamos a escribir

Phrases: Appreciating food
Vocabulary: Food: Bread, Cereals, Drinks, Fish and seafood, Fruits, Legumes and vegetables, Meat; Quantity
Grammar: Comparisons: adjectives, equality, inequality; Verbs: imperative usted(es)

P10-15 Eres dueño(a) de una tienda pequeña y quieres vender más productos. Diseña y escribe un anuncio para tu tienda. Incluye lo siguiente:

- el nombre de tu tienda, la dirección y el teléfono
- el tipo de tienda
- qué se vende
- los precios y las ofertas especiales
- dibujos o fotos de los productos (puedes recortarlos de una revista)
- otra información importante

Don't forget to use formal commands in your ad!

Nombre ______________________ Fecha ______________

Después de escribir

P10-16 Examina el anuncio de un(a) compañero(a) de clase y contesta las siguientes preguntas sobre su anuncio.

1. ¿Cómo se llama la tienda?

____

2. ¿Dónde está situada?

____

3. ¿Qué productos se venden en la tienda?

____

4. ¿Qué vas a comprar allí?

____

5. ¿Qué productos tienen precios especiales?

____

6. ¿Cómo puedes ahorrar dinero en esa tienda?

____

7. ¿Piensas volver a esa tienda frecuentemente? ¿Por qué sí o por qué no?

____

Nombre ______________________________ Fecha ______________

Práctica auditiva

En contexto

CD 2-20 **P10-17** **¿Desea algo más?** Escucha la siguiente conversación. Decide si las siguientes oraciones son verdaderas **(V)** o falsas **(F)**, o si no hay suficiente información para contestarlas **(N)**.

____ 1. El señor Navarro quiere hacer un pedido de vinos para el mercado.

____ 2. Los vinos argentinos son tan buenos como los vinos franceses.

____ 3. En el mercado se venden vinos italianos.

____ 4. En este mercado las frutas no son frescas.

____ 5. La idea de vender bebidas y comidas en el mismo lugar es práctica.

Vocabulario esencial

CD 2-21 **P10-18** **En la tienda de comestibles.** Vas a escuchar una conversación entre María Alexandra Navarro y la señora Álvarez, una de sus clientes. Mientras escuchas la conversación, indica los productos que compra la señora Álvarez.

_____ cebollas

_____ pimientos

_____ fresas

_____ lechuga

_____ zanahorias

_____ manzanas

_____ bananas

_____ piñas

_____ tomates

_____ uvas

_____ vino blanco

_____ vino tinto

Nombre ______________________ Fecha ______________

CD 2-22 **P10-19 El señor Peraza y María Alexandra hacen pedidos para el mercado.** El señor Navarro les va a decir al señor Peraza, su socio, y a María Alexandra varios productos que deben pedir para el mercado. Escucha la siguiente conversación entre el señor Navarro, el señor Peraza y María Alexandra y escribe a continuación los mandatos formales que escuchas. Incluye los pronombres directos e indirectos cuando sea necesario.

Before you listen to the conversation, review the command forms if you need to. Think about when a person would use a command form and what tone of voice he or she might use.

1. ______________________________
2. ______________________________
3. ______________________________
4. ______________________________
5. ______________________________
6. ______________________________
7. ______________________________
8. ______________________________
9. ______________________________

Nombre ______________________________ Fecha ______________

LECCIÓN 11 ¡VAMOS DE COMPRAS! ¡QUÉ CHÉVERE!

Práctica esencial

Vocabulario esencial

P11-1 Asociaciones. ¿Qué colores asocias con los siguientes días festivos o con las siguientes cosas? Escribe los colores en los siguientes espacios:

1. Halloween (el día de las brujas) ____________ y ____________
2. la Navidad ____________ y ____________
3. el Día de Acción de Gracias ____________ y ____________
4. el 4 de julio (en los Estados Unidos) ____________, ____________ y ____________
5. la Coca-Cola ____________ y ____________
6. Los Bulls de Chicago ____________ y ____________
7. La organización "Greenpeace" ____________
8. Pepsi ____________, ____________ y ____________
9. las manzanas, los tomates y el vino tinto ____________
10. La bandera de México ____________, ____________ y ____________;

P11-2 ¿Qué me voy a poner? Graciela les pregunta a sus amigas Eli y Beatriz qué ropa debe usar en las siguientes situaciones. Dale sugerencias según la situación.

Modelo: las montañas para esquiar
unos anteojos de sol, una chaqueta grande, unos guantes

1. Ir a la oficina para trabajar ____________, ____________, ____________.
2. Ir a la playa ____________, ____________, ____________.
3. Ir de compras con su mamá ____________, ____________, ____________.
4. Ir a la iglesia ____________, ____________, ____________.

Gramática esencial

P11-3 ¿Qué harán Beatriz, Graciela y Eli? Graciela, Beatriz y Eli están hablando de su amistad. Se prometen *(They promise each other)* hacer cosas para mantener *(to strengthen)* su amistad. Escribe la forma correcta de los verbos en el futuro para completar sus promesas.

Modelo: (Graciela) Yo las *llamaré* (llamar) más a menudo por teléfono.

1. Nosotras nos ____________ (escribir) más mensajes electrónicos.
2. Beatriz y Eli ____________ (visitar) más a su amiga Graciela.
3. Graciela ____________ (comprar) un teléfono celular para estar en contacto con sus amigas.
4. Graciela, Beatriz y Eli ____________ (divertirse) juntas por lo menos una vez al año.
5. Beatriz ____________ (invitar) a su casa a Eli y a Graciela.

Nombre ______________________________ Fecha ______________

P11-4 Amiga mandona *(Bossy friend).* ¿Qué quiere Beatriz que hagan sus amigas Eli y Graciela? Escribe oraciones completas, usando las siguientes frases.

Modelo: (Eli) hacer más ejercicios
Beatriz quiere que Eli haga más ejercicios.

1. (Eli) descansar mucho más en Caracas
______________________________.
2. (Graciela) pasar más tiempo con ella y Eli
______________________________.
3. (Graciela) ir al cine con ellas el viernes
______________________________.
4. (Eli) no comprar tantos recuerdos
______________________________.
5. (Eli) no correr a toda hora
______________________________.

P11-5 Deseos y preocupaciones. Beatriz está hablando con sus amigas Graciela y Eli sobre sus deseos y preocupaciones *(worries).* Escribe oraciones, usando las siguientes palabras y frases. Haz los cambios necesarios y fíjate bien en si se debe usar el infinitivo o el subjuntivo.

Remember to use the subjunctive here only *if there is a change of subject after the verb* ***querer.*** *Check your completed sentences and make sure that all words are in agreement.*

1. yo / querer pasar / más tiempo con ustedes
____
2. mi / padres / querer / que yo / pasar / más tiempo en casa
____
3. mi / mamá / querer / que yo / limpiar / mi / dormitorio / todos los días
____
4. yo / querer / que ella / me / ayudar
____
5. ¡yo / sólo / querer / ser / feliz!
____

Cultura

P11-6 Por el mundo hispano. Lee las siguientes oraciones. Si la oración es verdadera, escribe **V** en el espacio indicado. Si la oración es falsa, escribe **F.**

____ 1. Carolina Herrera es una pintora famosa de Venezuela.

____ 2. La ropa y los accesorios de Carolina Herrera son populares en muchos países, incluso en los Estados Unidos.

____ 3. Carolina Herrera no quiere que su hija trabaje en su compañía.

Nombre ______________________ Fecha ____________

P11-7 Lectura. Lee el siguiente artículo sobre un desfile de modas de ropa deportiva y contesta las preguntas en la página siguiente con oraciones completas.

DANA Y SU ROPA DEPORTIVA

Fotos: Hugo García Tapia

Dana ha diseñado para los hombres y las mujeres que gustan del deporte una línea de prendas y accesorios inspirados en el diseño italiano: playeras, shorts, calcetas, tines, muñequeras y testieri.

Llegan a México las prendas deportivas y los accesorios que están de moda entre los europeos.

El Club Atlético del Hotel Nikko fue la "cancha" donde Dana presentó su colección primavera-verano de ropa y accesorios deportivos. Las prendas de vestir y los accesorios tienen como color fundamental el blanco, con estampado de muñecos para las activas damas y figuras geométricas para los varones. Los modelos se inspiran en el diseño italiano y, a pesar de que han sido pensados para practicar tenis, dada su comodidad y elegancia se pueden emplear para cualquier otro deporte, e incluso para quien gusta vestir a diario sport. Los anfitriones fueron el Sr. Moiz Dana y su hijo, el Ing. Alberto Dana, y entre los invitados estaban representantes de los mejores almacenes.

Nombre ______________________________ Fecha ______________

1. ¿Qué tipo de ropa se presenta en el artículo y en las fotos de la página 121?

______________________________.

2. ¿Dónde hizo Dana la presentación?

______________________________.

3. ¿Para qué deporte es la ropa?

______________________________.

4. ¿En qué país se hizo la presentación?

______________________________.

5. Para una presentación de nuevos diseños se necesitan diseñadores, anfitriones (las personas que hacen las preparaciones y pagan el costo) e invitados. ¿Quiénes fueron los anfitriones?

______________________________.

¿Quiénes fueron los invitados?

______________________________.

¡A leer!: Baron's

Antes de leer

P11-8 Cuando miras los anuncios para las tiendas de ropa en el periódico, ¿qué tipo de información buscas? ¿Qué tipo de información es importante?

____

____

Vamos a leer

P11-9 Mira el anuncio para el almacén *(department store)* Baron's y contesta las siguientes preguntas.

1. ¿El almacén Baron's tiene solamente ropa para hombres, o también para mujeres?

____

2. ¿En qué estación del año ocurrió *(happened)* esta venta?

____

3. Lee las siguientes oraciones sobre el anuncio de Baron's. Escribe **V** en el espacio indicando si la oración es verdadera o **F** si la oración es falsa.

____ a. Baron's tiene una amplia *(wide)* selección de blusas.

____ b. Todos los pantalones están en venta *(are on sale)*.

____ c. Hay una amplia selección de trajes.

____ d. Hay un grupo selecto de camisas de sport de famosos diseñadores *(designers)*.

____ e. Baron's ofrece hacer alteraciones gratis *(free)*.

____ f. Baron's no abre los domingos.

Nombre ______________________ Fecha ______________

AHORRE

15% a 50%

En Una Amplia
Selección de Diseñadores

Trajes &
Chaquetes de Sport

Marcas : Christian Dior
Lanvin • Pierre Cardin
Givenchy • Adolfo • Marco
Finchley • Oleg Cassini
Groshire • Profilo
Charles Jourdan • Diplomat
... y muchos más

TODOS LOS PANTALONES DE LA TIENDA ESTAN EN

VENTA

Diseños en Mangas
Corta y Larga

Camisas de Sport

Y en Selecto Grupo
de Famosos Diseñadores

Camisas de Sport

Marcas de: Givenchy,
Alan Stuart, Dior,
David Michaels, D'Avila,
Cassini, Damon,
Louis Azzaro, Lanvin
... y más

Regular hasta $32.50

AHORA **$19.99**

Naturalmente, Alteraciones
Gratis por Expertos

Todas las Tiendas Abren el Domingo
No todas las mercancías en todas las tiendas

La leyenda es usted en...

Baron's

La Cadena de Tienda Mayor de la Florida desde 1945, en Ropas para Caballeros.
Dadeland • Miami International Mall • Westland • 445 Lincoln Road Mall • Bal Harbour Shops
The Mall at 163rd Street • Broward Mall • The Galleria • Pompano Square • Coral Square
Boynton Beach Mall • Palm Beach Mall • Altamonte Mall • Florida Mall

Nombre ______________________________ Fecha ______________

Después de leer

P11-10 Escribe un anuncio de publicidad para una tienda, anunciando los artículos de ropa en venta, los precios y los diseñadores. ¿En qué fecha es la venta y qué días y a qué horas se abre la tienda?

¡A escribir!

Antes de escribir

P11-11 Completa las siguientes oraciones con información personal sobre tu ropa.

1. Para ir al cine con mis amigos, me gusta ponerme de color

   ______________________________.

2. Cuando tengo una entrevista de trabajo, llevo el color

   ______________________________.

3. El primer día de clase generalmente me pongo

   ______________________________.

4. Cuando practico algún deporte o pasatiempo, prefiero llevar

   ______________________________.

5. Cuando voy a cenar en un restaurante elegante, me gusta llevar

   ______________________________.

Nombre ______________________________ Fecha ______________

P11-12 Contesta las siguientes preguntas con oraciones completas.

1. Generalmente, ¿cuánto pagas por un par de zapatos?

   ____.

2. ¿Te gusta ir a las tiendas por la mañana, por la tarde o por la noche? ¿Por qué?

   ____.

3. ¿Por cuánto tiempo te gusta estar en las tiendas?

   ____.

4. En tu ciudad, ¿en qué calle hay muchos almacenes o tiendas?

   ____.

Vamos a escribir

Phrases: Describing objects; Talking about past events; Writing a letter (informal)
Vocabulary: Clothing; Colors
Grammar: Verbs: irregular preterite, preterite

P11-13 Eli Miller compró varias cosas en la gran apertura *(grand opening)* de la tienda Gisel's. Cuando llegó a casa de Beatriz, puso todas sus cosas en la sala y le escribió un recado *(message)* a la mamá de su amiga.

Escribe el recado que Eli le dejó a la mamá de Beatriz y haz lo siguiente:

- Describe cada prenda de ropa *(article of clothing)* e incluye su precio.
- Menciona por qué Eli compró cada prenda.
- Incluye las cosas que Eli compró para los otros miembros de su familia.

Nombre _______________ Fecha _______________

Querida señora Arreaza:

¡Mire todo lo que compré en la gran apertura de la tienda Gisel's!

Perdone el desorden. *(Sorry about the mess.)*

Nombre ______________________________ Fecha ______________

Después de escribir

P11-14 Comparte tu recado con un(a) compañero(a) de clase. Luego examinen juntos los dos recados y hagan lo siguiente.

1. Subrayen *(Underline)* todos los sustantivos que hay en el recado.
2. Tracen *(Draw)* un círculo alrededor de cada adjetivo.
3. ¿Concuerdan *(Agree)* los adjetivos con los sustantivos? Si no, corríjanlos.
4. Tracen un cuadro alrededor de cada verbo.
5. Si un verbo está en el tiempo presente, escriban **pres.** arriba del verbo. Si un verbo está en el tiempo pretérito, escriban **pret.** arriba del verbo.
6. Examinen todos los verbos usados. ¿Escogieron ustedes el tiempo verbal correcto? Si no, corríjanlos.

Modelo: La blusa [es] *(pres.)*, (muy bonita) ¿no?

Nombre ______________________________ Fecha ______________

Práctica auditiva

En contexto

CD 2-23 **P11-15 ¡Qué chévere!** Escucha la siguiente conversación. Decide si las siguientes oraciones son verdaderas **(V)** o falsas **(F)**, o si no hay suficiente información para contestar **(N)**.

____ 1. Eli y Beatriz van a ir a una tienda de ropa.

____ 2. La tienda está en Caracas.

____ 3. Eli necesita ropa para ir a fiestas.

____ 4. Eli tiene mucho dinero para comprar ropa.

____ 5. La ropa en Caracas es más económica que en los Estados Unidos.

Vocabulario esencial

CD 2-24 **P11-16 Las compras de Eli (Primera parte).** Eli fue de compras a una tienda que tenía una oferta *(sale)*. Cuando salió de la tienda, su amiga Beatriz le hizo varias preguntas sobre sus compras. Completa el cuadro con la información que ella le dio.

	¿Para quién?	**Artículo de ropa**	**Color**	**Uso (¿Para qué es?)**
1.	____________	____________	____________	____________
2.	____________	____________	____________	____________
3.	____________	____________	____________	____________
4.	____________	____________	____________	____________

CD 2-25 **P11-17 Las compras de Eli (Segunda parte).** Ahora vas a oír cinco oraciones basadas en la conversación de Beatriz y Eli. Después de escuchar cada oración dos veces, escribe **V** si es verdadera o **F** si es falsa.

1. ____
2. ____
3. ____
4. ____
5. ____

CD 2-26 **P11-18 De compras.** Vas a escuchar una conversación entre una dependiente y su cliente. Mientras escuchas la conversación, completa la siguiente información con lo que compra la cliente.

Artículo de ropa: ______________________________

Color: ______________________________

Talla: ______________________________

Precio: ______________________________

LECCIÓN 12 ¡QUÉ DELICIOSO EL CAFÉ!

Práctica esencial

VOCABULARIO ESENCIAL

P12-1 ¡Tantas cosas que hacer! Gloria está haciendo varias actividades en su viaje de negocios. Escribe una conversación que corresponda a cada dibujo.

Modelo: En la agencia de carros
Gloria: *¿Puedo alquilar un auto económico en Bogotá?*
Empleado: *Sí, señora, puedo llamar a nuestra compañía y reservar un auto económico.*
Gloria: *Muchas gracias.*

1. En el banco

Empleado: ____________________
____
____

Gloria: ____________________
____
____

Empleado: ____________________
____
____

Nombre ______________________________ Fecha ______________

2. En la oficina de correos

Gloria: ______________________________

____

____

Empleada: ______________________________

____

____

Gloria: ______________________________

____

____

P12-2 Preguntas personales. Contesta las siguientes preguntas personales, usando oraciones completas. Usa el vocabulario de la **Lección 12** para tus respuestas.

El dinero

1. ¿Prefieres pagar al contado o con cheque?

____

2. ¿Dónde tienes una cuenta de ahorros?

____

3. ¿Dónde está la oficina de correos más cerca de ti?

____

4. ¿Por qué es una buena idea invertir dinero?

____

5. ¿Qué gastos tienes?

____

6. En este país, ¿dónde puedes cambiar un cheque?

____

Los sentimientos

1. ¿Qué te preocupa más?

____

2. ¿De qué se quejan más tus profesores?

____

3. ¿De qué te alegras frecuentemente?

____

4. ¿Qué te gusta que hagan tus amigos por ti?

____

Nombre ______________________________ Fecha ______________

Gramática esencial

P12-3 Las preocupaciones de la mamá de Gloria. La mamá de Gloria le habla a su hija sobre sus opiniones con respecto al viaje a Bogotá. Completa las siguientes oraciones con la forma correcta del verbo.

Modelo: Me gusta que ustedes *vayan* (ir) en avión.

1. Ojalá que ______________ (hacer) buen tiempo durante su visita.
2. Me alegro que ustedes ______________ (tomar) unos días de vacaciones.
3. Siento mucho que tú ______________ (tener) que regresar tan pronto a Medellín para trabajar.
4. Espero que tus tíos te ______________ (llamar) por teléfono.
5. Me preocupa que ustedes no ______________ (ver) a tus abuelos desde hace tanto tiempo.

P12-4 Las opiniones de Gloria. Gloria reacciona a los comentarios de su mamá. ¿Cuál es su opinión? Lee los comentarios del ejercicio anterior.

Modelo: Es mejor que...
Es mejor que nosotros vayamos en avión.

1. Es posible que....

   ____.

2. Es importante que...

   ____.

3. Es triste que...

   ____.

4. Es importante que...

   ____.

5. Es una lástima que...

   ____.

P12-5 Preparaciones para el viaje a Bogotá. Enrique y Gloria están haciendo los planes finales para su viaje a Bogotá. Enrique le habla a Gloria sobre sus emociones y opiniones. ¿Qué le dice a ella?

Modelo: es importante / tú y yo / estar de acuerdo con todas las decisiones
Es importante que tú y yo estemos de acuerdo con todas las decisiones.

1. (yo) esperar / (tú) / ir a comprar los regalos para tu familia

 ____

2. (yo) preocuparse de / (tú) / trabajar mucho en la hacienda de café

 ____

3. (yo) esperar / (nosotros) / ir juntos a decirles adiós a mis padres

 ____

4. (yo) / alegrarse de / (tú) / estar contenta porque vamos por una semana a Bogotá

 ____

5. es una lástima / (nosotros) / no poder quedarnos más días en Bogotá

 ____

P12-6 Querida Gloria. Enrique León regresó de Bogotá y se fue para los Estados Unidos. Enrique le escribió una postal a Gloria desde Miami. Indica la forma correcta de los verbos entre paréntesis.

Querida Gloria,
Me alegro de (estoy / esté / estar) aquí en Miami y siento mucho que tú no (puedes / puedas / poder) estar aquí conmigo. La ciudad de Miami (es / está / ser) muy bonita y el tiempo (es / está / ser) fresco. Espero que tú (vienes / vengas / venir) conmigo en el próximo viaje de negocios. Ojalá que (puedes / puedas / poder) pagar todas las cuentas con el dinero que depositamos en la cuenta corriente. Espero que tú no (tienes / tengas / tener) muchos problemas en la compañía ahora que yo no estoy. Bueno, espero (veo / vea / verte) muy pronto.

Con amor,
Enrique

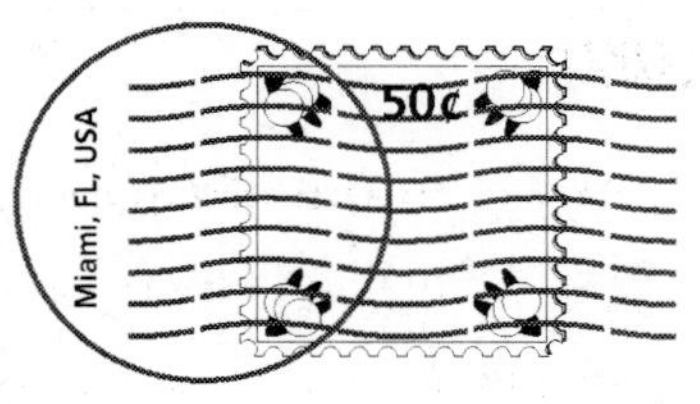

Sra. Gloria León
Calle 12–14, N° 39
Medellín, Colombia
Sur América

P12-7 Las cosas que veo en mi vida diaria. Expresa tus opiniones y actitudes sobre situaciones o cosas que observas en tu vida diaria.

1. Es importante que los estudiantes de esta universidad

   ____

   ____.

2. En la cafetería de la universidad es bueno que

   ____

   ____.

3. Es imposible que todos los profesores

   ____

   ____.

4. Es ridículo que no todos los administradores de la universidad

   ____

   ____.

5. Es lógico que los cursos de los estudiantes

   ____

   ____.

Cultura

P12-8 Por el mundo hispano. Escribe la mejor respuesta posible para las siguientes preguntas. Busca la información en las lecturas sobre cultura que aparecen en el texto.

1. ¿En qué lugares *(places)* puede uno cambiar dinero en Latinoamérica y España?

   ____.

2. ¿Dónde recibe uno el mejor cambio?

   ____.

3. ¿Qué documento de identificación es mejor usar cuando uno quiere cambiar dinero?

   ____.

4. ¿Qué es el Fondo Monetario Internacional?

   ____.

5. ¿Cuál es su propósito?

   ____.

Nombre ______________________ Fecha ____________

¡A leer!: ¡Suscríbase hoy!

Antes de leer

P12-9 Imagínate que quieres suscribirte a una revista. ¿Qué información necesitas incluir en el formulario de inscripción?

____

____

____

Vamos a leer

Nombre ______________________________ Fecha ______________

P12-10 Contesta las siguientes preguntas sobre los anuncios de las revistas.

1. Completa el cuadro siguiente con la información que te pide.

Nombre de la revista	Precio de la suscripción	Número de ejemplares *(copies)*	% de ahorro
a. ______	______	______	______
b. ______	______	______	______
c. ______	______	______	______
d. ______	______	______	______

2. ¿Cuál es la suscripción más barata por ejemplar?

____

3. ¿Qué información personal tienes que completar para recibir tu suscripción?

____

4. Si pagas con tarjeta de crédito, ¿qué otra información necesitas escribir?

____

5. ¿Cuándo vas a recibir el primer ejemplar de *TÚ*?

____

6. ¿Qué frases se encuentran en los formularios que motivan a comprar una suscripción?

____

Después de leer

P12-11 Imagínate que eres editor(a) y estás planeando varios artículos para las revistas indicadas a continuación. Escribe los nombres de los artículos que a ti te gustaría incluir en cada revista en los espacios indicados.

GeoMundo

1. ______________________________
2. ______________________________

Buenhogar

1. ______________________________
2. ______________________________

Mundo21

1. ______________________________
2. ______________________________

TÚ

1. ______________________________
2. ______________________________

Nombre ______________________________ Fecha ______________

¡A escribir!

Antes de escribir

P12-12 Enrique y Gloria van a Bogotá y tienen que hacer un presupuesto porque sus gastos van a ser más altos que en Medellín.

1. Haz una lista de todas las cosas que van a tener que comprar para todos los miembros de la familia de Enrique en Bogotá.

Papá	Mamá	Los hermanos		
		Olga	Mildred	Juan Carlos

2. ¿Cuánto cuestan en Colombia las cosas mencionadas en la lista anterior? Adivina *(Guess)* los precios y escríbelos al lado de cada cosa que ellos quieren comprar para su familia.

Nombre ______________________________ Fecha ______________

Vamos a escribir

Phrases: Agreeing and disagreeing; Apologizing; Asking and giving advice; Asking the price; Persuading
Grammar: Verbs: subjunctive with **ojalá**, subjunctive with **que**

P12-13 Enrique y Gloria tienen que tomar una decisión sobre sus gastos en Bogotá para poder comprar regalos para su familia. A continuación, escribe una conversación entre Enrique y Gloria. Al final del diálogo los dos tienen que ponerse de acuerdo.

Enrique:

____

Gloria:

____

Enrique:

____

Gloria:

____

Enrique:

____

Gloria:

____

Después de escribir

P12-14 Comparte tu conversación con un(a) compañero(a) de clase y entre los dos, practíquenla para presentársela al resto de la clase.

Nombre ______________________________ Fecha ______________

Práctica auditiva

En contexto

CD 2-27 **P12-15 ¡Qué delicioso el café!** Escucha la siguiente conversación. Decide si las siguientes oraciones son verdaderas **(V)** o falsas **(F)**, o si no hay suficiente información para contestar **(N)**.

____ 1. Gloria va a visitar a su familia en Bogotá.

____ 2. Gloria y Enrique van a Bogotá por dos semanas.

____ 3. Ellos trabajan mucho en la hacienda de café.

____ 4. Enrique va a los Estados Unidos a vender café.

____ 5. Enrique va a quedarse cuatro semanas en la Florida.

Vocabulario esencial

CD 2-28 **P12-16 ¡Tenemos muchas cosas que hacer!** Escucha el siguiente diálogo donde Enrique y Gloria León están prepárandose para ir a Bogotá. Hicieron algunas cosas pero todavía tienen que hacer otras. En la lista que ellos prepararon, indica qué cosas hicieron, marcando **sí,** y qué cosas no han hecho todavía, marcando **no.**

	sí	no
1. terminar de preparar el café para las próximas dos semanas		
2. comprar los boletos de avión		
3. comprarle regalos a la familia		
4. visitar a los padres de Enrique para decirles adiós		
5. lavar la ropa		
6. limpiar la casa		
7. llamar al taxi para que venga a buscarlos		

CD 2-29 **P12-17 En el banco.** Escucha la narración e indica la mejor respuesta para completar cada oración.

____ 1. Enrique y Gloria necesitan cambiar pesos por...
a. pesos colombianos.
b. dólares.
c. bolívares.

____ 2. Para Miami, Enrique necesita comprar...
a. cheques personales.
b. cheques de la cuenta de ahorros.
c. cheques de viajero.

____ 3. Enrique y Gloria pagan sus cuentas haciendo cheques de...
a. la cuenta corriente.
b. la cuenta de ahorros.
c. la cuenta de crédito.

____ 4. Cuando vaya a Bogotá, Gloria no quiere usar...
a. sus cheques personales.
b. sus cheques de viajero.
c. su tarjeta de crédito.

CD 2-30 **P12-18 Expresa tu opinión.** El señor Antakly es el gerente general de una empresa de café y sus empleados tienen muchos problemas. Después de escuchar las tres situaciones siguientes de sus empleados, expresa la recomendación del señor Antakly.

Modelo: **Empleado:** Señor Antakly, no me siento bien. Comí demasiada pizza. ¿Qué me recomienda usted?
Señor Antakly: *Le recomiendo que vaya al médico, le recomiendo que descanse en casa.*

1. ______________________________

2. ______________________________

3. ______________________________

Nombre ______________________________ Fecha ______________

PASO 5 ¡Buen Viaje!

LECCIÓN 13 ¡TE ESPERAMOS EN GALICIA!

Práctica esencial

VOCABULARIO ESENCIAL

P13-1 Cuando yo viajo... Completa las siguientes oraciones con la palabra apropiada de la lista siguiente.

1. Cuando yo viajo, normalmente pido una (llave / lámpara / habitación) sencilla.
2. No me gusta subir las escaleras *(stairs),* así que me gustan los hoteles que tienen (ascensor / habitación / reserva).
3. Prefiero un hotel que no sea muy caro, así que si los (recepción / televisor / muebles) son un poco viejos, no me importa.
4. ¡Necesito mi privacidad! Necesito (cocina / cuarto de baño / mesa pequeña) privado(a).
5. Hay mucho ruido en las calles, así que prefiero los cuartos que no dan (a la izquierda / a la calle / recto).
6. Cuando hace mucho calor, me gusta tener (papel higiénico / el espejo / aire acondicionado) en el cuarto.

P13-2 ¿En qué puedo servirle? Tu mejor amigo(a) y tú están en la recepción de un hotel en Madrid. Escribe una conversación entre ustedes y el (la) recepcionista del hotel con los siguientes elementos.

Cliente:

1. dar un saludo apropiado
3. pedir un cuarto para ti y tu amigo(a)
5. responder por cuántos días, qué quieren en el cuarto
7. pedir información sobre precios, restaurantes, dónde cambiar el dinero
9. darle las gracias al (a la) recepcionista

Recepcionista:

2. responder al saludo
4. preguntar cuántos días, qué tipo de cuarto
6. preguntar qué más quieren en el cuarto
8. responder a las preguntas del (de la) cliente
10. darle la bienvenida a su cliente

Nombre ______________________ Fecha ______________

Cliente:

____

Recepcionista:

____

Cliente:

____

Recepcionista:

____

Cliente:

____

Recepcionista:

____

Cliente:

____

Recepcionista:

____

Cliente:

____

Recepcionista:

____

GRAMÁTICA ESENCIAL

P13-3 Optimistas y pesimistas. Normalmente la gente pesimista tiene más dudas que la gente optimista. Escribe oraciones completas que expresen las opiniones de algunos amigos de Ileana.

1. **Tomás:** dudo que Europa / ser más bonita que Panamá, pero creo que el continente europeo / tener muchos lugares interesantes para los turistas

   ____

   ____

2. **Luis:** es dudoso que los hoteles en Europa / estar baratos, pero no dudo que / haber muchos hoteles allá para escoger

   ____

   ____

3. **Alicia:** no creo que los demás europeos *(other Europeans)* / trabajar tanto como los españoles / Creo que los españoles / trabajar más horas

____

____

4. **Luis:** no estoy seguro de que / poderse ver Europa en quince días / ¿Se necesitan más días?

____

____

5. **Teresa:** tal vez / costar mucho dinero viajar por Europa, pero no estoy segura de eso

____

____

P13-4 Hablando de festivales. A Manuel y a Victoria Castro les gustan las fiestas de Santiago de Compostela. Completa la siguiente conversación, usando apropiadamente el indicativo o el subjuntivo de los verbos de la lista de abajo. Se puede usar un verbo más de una vez.

haber	hacer	invitar	ir
ser	vivir	celebrar	

Manuel: No hay ningún festival que _____________ igual a las fiestas de Santiago de Compostela, ¿verdad?

Victoria: Ese festival _____________ el más interesante para mí, pero quizás _____________ otros muy buenos aquí en España y en otros países de Europa.

Manuel: Sí, por ejemplo, algún día quiero ir a celebrar la Semana Santa en Sevilla. Dicen que mucha gente de todas partes del mundo _____________ a Sevilla para celebrarla.

Victoria: Conozco a alguien que _____________ la Semana Santa el próximo año. Se llama María Aquino, y _____________ en Caracas, Venezuela. Tal vez nos _____________ una invitación para visitarla en Sevilla porque es una persona muy generosa.

Manuel: ¡Ojalá que ella nos _____________ a Venezuela algún día también!

P13-5 ¡A comer! Manuel y Victoria están limpiando la casa para la visita de Ileana, pero Victoria tiene mucha hambre. Manuel la invita a comer en un restaurante de la ciudad. Lee la siguiente conversación y decide si se debe usar el indicativo, el subjuntivo o el infinitivo del verbo indicado.

Victoria: Manuel, ¿cuándo (vamos / vayamos / ir) al restaurante? Tengo mucha hambre.

Manuel: Vamos al restaurante inmediatamente después de limpiar para que (puedes / puedas / poder) comer.

Victoria: Pero, Manuel, no podemos ir al restaurante antes de que nosotros (terminamos / terminemos / terminar) de limpiar la casa.

Manuel: Pero Victoria, ya vamos a (terminamos / terminemos / terminar).

Victoria: Ojalá que a Ileana le (gusta / guste / gustar) nuestra casa y Santiago de Compostela.

Manuel: Claro que sí, Victoria. No te preocupes. Tan pronto como ella (llega / llegue / llegar) a nuestra ciudad, todo le va a (gusta / guste / gustar) mucho.

Nombre ______________________ Fecha ______________

Cultura

P13-6 Por el mundo hispano. Escribe la letra de la respuesta apropiada para completar cada frase.

a. tiene pocas habitaciones.

b. dejan su pasaporte con el (la) recepcionista.

c. escriben el número del pasaporte en el registro.

d. ofrece habitaciones y desayuno.

e. la mayoría viaja de una ciudad a otra en tren.

f. muchas veces es un castillo.

g. ofrece una cama, más tres comidas.

h. existe un sistema excelente de autobuses.

i. representa lo mejor y lo más caro.

j. es el modo más barato de alojarse en España.

____ 1. Un hostal residencia...

____ 2. Una pensión completa...

____ 3. En España, los viajeros...

____ 4. Acampar...

____ 5. En Latinoamérica...

____ 6. Un hotel de cinco estrellas...

____ 7. En España...

____ 8. Una pensión...

____ 9. En Latinoamérica, los viajeros...

____ 10. Un parador...

¡A leer!: España en los paradores

Antes de leer

P13-7 Muchas veces las agencias de viajes ofrecen paquetes que incluyen varias excursiones y actividades, así como el costo del vuelo y alojamiento en diferentes hoteles. Imagínate que un turista visita la ciudad donde vives. En el cuadro siguiente, describe un itinerario de un día para este turista. ¿Qué lugares turísticos va a visitar? ¿Dónde va a desayunar, almorzar, cenar? ¿Cómo se llama el hotel que tú le recomiendas? ¿Qué otras excursiones y actividades se incluyen en el paquete?

Nombre ______________________ Fecha ______________

Ciudad:		
Hotel:		
Actividades (mañana)	Actividades (tarde)	Actividades (noche)

Nombre ______________________________ Fecha ______________

Vamos a leer

P13-8 Mira el itinerario de "España en los paradores" y contesta las preguntas que siguen.

España en los Paradores

15 DIAS

INCLUYE:

- Avión Jet de ida y regreso.
- 13 noches alojamiento en hoteles de primera y Paradores Nacionales.
- Desayuno diario y 7 comidas.
- Recorrido en ómnibus de lujo.
- Impuestos y servicio de hoteles.
- Tarjeta de descuento en restaurantes y tiendas.
- Traslado y entrada al Gran Casino de Madrid.

Día 1 – RUMBO A ESPAÑA.
Salida en vuelo intercontinental con destino a Madrid.

Día 2 – MADRID
Llegada a Madrid. Resto del día libre para recorrer la ciudad, sus típicas calles y sus tascas. Alojamiento.

Día 3 – MADRID - TOLEDO - CÓRDOBA
Salida por la mañana hacia Toledo, visita de la ciudad, la Catedral y la Iglesia de Santo Tomé. Continuación hacia Bailén y Córdoba. Llegada. Cena y alojamiento en el Parador Nacional.

Día 4 – CÓRDOBA - GRANADA
Desayuno. Visita de la ciudad, su famosa Mezquita, con el laberinto de columnas; el barrio Judío y la Sinagoga. Por la tarde, salida a Granada. Llegada. Cena y alojamiento en el hotel junto a los jardines de la Alhambra.

Día 5 – GRANADA - COSTA DEL SOL
Desayuno. Por la mañana, visita de esta maravillosa ciudad, situada al pie de Sierra Nevada. La incomparable Alhambra, palacio moro, rodeado de jardines y el Generalife. Por la tarde, salida hacia las playas más conocidas en toda Europa, la Costa del Sol. Alojamiento en el hotel.

Día 6 – COSTA DEL SOL - SEVILLA
Desayuno. Salida hacia Ronda, con su famoso Tajo. Arcos de la Frontera y Jérez. Llegada a Sevilla. Alojamiento en el hotel.

Día 7 – SEVILLA
Desayuno. Visita de la ciudad, con su famosa Catedral, la Torre de la Giralda, el Alcázar, barrio de Santa Cruz, la Torre de Oro. Tarde libre. Alojamiento en el hotel.

Día 8 – SEVILLA - MÉRIDA
Desayuno. Salida hacia Zafra en tierras de Extremadura. Llegada a Mérida. Por la tarde, visita de su famoso Teatro Romano. Cena y alojamiento en el Parador Nacional.

Día 9 – MÉRIDA - SALAMANCA
Desayuno. Salida hacia Cáceres. Recorrido por la ciudad vieja. Continuación a Hervas y Salamanca. Por la tarde, recorrido de la ciudad, su famosa Plaza Mayor y la Universidad. Cena y alojamiento en el Parador Nacional.

Día 10 – SALAMANCA - BAYONA O CAMBADOS.
Desayuno. Salida vía Zamora y Puebla de Sanabria hacia Galicia, donde llegamos a las rías Bajas. Cena y alojamiento en el Parador Nacional de Bayona o Cambados.

Día 11 – BAYONA O CAMBADOS - SANTIAGO DE COMPOSTELA.
Desayuno. Salida hacia la isla de La Toja, con su famoso Balneario. Continuación a Santiago de Compostela. Por la tarde, visita de la ciudad, la Basilica, la Universidad. Cena y alojamiento en el famoso Parador Nacional de los Reyes Católicos.

Día 12 – SANTIAGO DE COMPOSTELA - LEON
Desayuno. Mañana libre en la ciudad, por la tarde, salida a León. Cena y alojamiento en el bello Parador Nacional de San Marcos.

Día 13 – LEON - MADRID
Desayuno. Tiempo libre para recorrer la ciudad y su bella catedral. Salida a Tordesillas y Madrid. Llegada. Alojamiento en el hotel.

Día 14 – MADRID
Desayuno. Por la mañana, visita de la ciudad, recorrido por las calles principales, visitando la famosa pinacoteca de El Prado, así como el Palacio Real. Tarde libre. Alojamiento en el hotel.

Día 15 – MADRID
Desayuno. Tiempo libre- Regreso a América.

SALIDAS: Domingos
Mayo 21; Junio 25; Julio 2, 9, 23; Agosto 6, 20; Sep 3, 17; Octubre 1, 15

PRECIO POR PERSONA	
NEW YORK	$2083
MIAMI	2140
Tierra solo	1461
Sencillo adic.	450
Aumento terrestre 7/1-8/20	85

NUESTROS HOTELES	
MADRID	El Coloso 1*
CÓRDOBA	P. N. de la Arruzafa 1*
GRANADA	Alhambra Palace 1*
COSTA DEL SOL	Meliá Costa del Sol 1*
SEVILLA	Meliá Sevilla 1*
MÉRIDA	P. N. Vía de la Plata 1*
SALAMANCA	P. N. de Salamanca 1*
BAYONA	P. N. Conde de Gondomar 1*
LA TOJA	Gran hotel Lujo
CAMBADOS	P. N. el Albariño TS
SANTIAGO DE COMPOSTELA	P. N. Los Reyes Católicos Lujo/ Hotel Compostela/ Peregrino 1*
LEON	P. N. San Marcos Lujo/ Hotel Conde Luna 1*

NOTA: Las salidas de julio 23 y agosto 6 se alojarán en el gran Hotel de La Toja en lugar del Parador de Bayona. Las salidas de junio 25, julio 9, septiembre 3 y 17 se alojarán en el Hotel Compostela en lugar del Parador de Santiago.
Las salidas julio 9, agosto 20 y septiembre 3 se alojarán en el Parador de Cambados, en lugar de Bayona. La salida de octubre 1 se alojará en Hotel Conde Luna de León en lugar del Parador Nacional.

Nombre ______________________ Fecha ______________

1. ¿Qué ciudades y cuántos días incluye el viaje? ______________________
2. ¿Cuánto cuesta el viaje si usted sale en avión de Nueva York? ______________________

   ¿Y si sale de Miami? ______________________
3. ¿Adónde llega el avión? ______________________

   ¿De dónde sale cuando termina la excursión? ______________________
4. ¿Cuántos días está el viajero en Madrid? ____________ ¿Y en Sevilla? ____________
5. ¿En qué ciudades hay alojamiento en los paradores?

_____ Madrid	_____ Mérida
_____ Toledo	_____ Salamanca
_____ Córdoba	_____ Bayona
_____ Granada	_____ Cambados
_____ Costa del Sol	_____ Santiago de Compostela
_____ Sevilla	_____ León

6. ¿En qué fechas puede usted ir a España con ese itinerario? ______________________

Después de leer

P13-9 Imagínate que fuiste a España con el paquete que ofrece la agencia de viajes en **Vamos a leer.** Selecciona una ciudad y escríbele una tarjeta postal a un(a) amigo(a) desde esa ciudad. Menciona los lugares que visitaste, las actividades que hiciste, qué fue lo que más te gustó, etcétera.

CORREOS
0469
Naturaleza
***21 PTS

Nombre ______________________ Fecha ______________

¡A escribir!

Antes de escribir

P13-10 Lee los anuncios de varios hoteles y balnearios *(resorts)* y contesta las preguntas a continuación.

1. ¿En qué lugar se puede hacer excursiones a caballo?

____

2. ¿Cuál de los hoteles está al lado del mar?

____

3. ¿Qué hotel tiene las habitaciones a mejor precio?

____

4. ¿Dónde se puede cocinar dentro de la habitación?

____

5. ¿En cuál de estos hoteles te gustaría quedarte? ¿Por qué?

____

Hotel Real Miramar

Le invita a descansar al lado del mar y a disfrutar las brisas caribeñas

- 203 habitaciones de lujo
- Conserje las veinticuatro horas
- Servicio de lavandería y tintorería
- Restaurante/Bar
- Minidiscoteca

¡Deje los quehaceres de la vida cotidiana y disfrute de unas vacaciones de primera!

Habitaciones de US$ 87 a US$ 130
Llame para hacer su reservación hoy al 52-94-89 o al 52-94-92.

Albergue de la Plaza

¡Quédese con nosotros y no se pierda de nada!

Ubicado en el centro de la ciudad, nuestro albergue ofrece lo mejor en precio y localidad. A pocos pasos de los más movidos restaurantes, bares, discotecas y centros comerciales de la ciudad, también estamos muy cerca de museos y otras diversiones turísticas.

Servicios

- teléfono y TV en la habitación
- fax y fotocopiadora en el lobby
- piscina y sauna
- guardería infantil
- alquiler de bicicletas y vespas

¡Todo por tan sólo 89 dólares la noche!
LLAME AL 37-93-85

Descanse y disfrute...

Nuestra hacienda cuenta con cinco habitaciones en la casa grande y cuatro cabañas privadas, cada uno con dos dormitorios y cocina propia.

Descanse en los jardines, al lado de la pileta o en la biblioteca.

Si es aventurero, explore la montaña en excursiones a caballo.

Nuestros guías son del lugar y conocen los sitios más bonitos de la región.

...como sólo lo puede hacer en la Hacienda El Monte

Reserve hoy su habitación. Llame al 304-94-68.
¡Precio especial: cabaña $99.00 la noche!

Nombre ______________________ Fecha ______________

P13-11 Lectura. Mira la Guía de Servicios y contesta las siguientes preguntas.

Guía de Servicios

9	INFORMACIÓN
9	DE CUARTO A CUARTO
0	LLAMADAS LOCALES
9	LARGA DISTANCIA
9	DESPERTADOR
6	RECEPCIÓN
5	LOBBY ACUEDUCTO
1	AMA DE LLAVES
2	SERVICIO DE CUARTOS
4	SERVI-BAR
8	RESTAURANTE "LA FONDA"
3	BAR "LA TABERNA"
5	LOBBY BAR "LA ESTANCIA"

Para estos servicios marque Ext. 9

Oficina de Reservaciones
LOCALIZADA JUNTO A RECEPCIÓN HORARIO DE 9:00 a.m. A 16:00 p.m.

Servicio de Botones
ANEXO A RECEPCION

Cajas de Seguridad
SERVICIO LAS 24 HORAS

Servicio de Niñeras
COMUNICARSE CON EL AMA DE LLAVE CON ANTICIPACIÓN DE 5 HORAS

Natación
DOS ALBERCAS DE 9:00 a.m. A 22:00 p.m. NO SE PERMITE QUE NIÑOS MENORES DE 12 AÑOS UTILICEN LAS ALBERCAS SOLOS.

Lavandería y Tintorería
RECIBO 10:00 a.m. ENTREGA 21:30 p.m. SERVICIO DE LUNES A SÁBADO

Sala de Juegos
SERVICIO DE 9:00 a.m. A 24:00 p.m. LOCALIZADA EN LA SECCIÓN ACUEDUCTO BOLICHE. PING-PONG. DOMINO. JUEGOS ELECTRONICOS. CARTAS

Servicio Médico
EL HOTEL PROPORCIONA EL SERVICIO LAS 24 HORAS. CON EL GERENTE DE TURNO

Correo
ENTREGA DE CORRESPONDENCIA EN LA RECEPCIÓN DEL HOTEL.

Agencia de Viajes
VIAJES H.R., S.A. DE 9:00 a.m. A 17 p.m. RENTA DE AUTOMÓVILES TRANSPORTACIÓN AL AEROPUERTO DE MÉXICO RESERVACIONES DE BOLETO DE AVIÓN

Objetos Perdidos
EL HOTEL NO SE HACE RESPONSABLE POR DINERO. JOYAS U OBJETOS DE VALOR EXTRAVIADOS EN EL HOTEL. SIN EMBARGO PUEDE COMUNICARSE A RELACIONES PÚBLICAS

Oficina de Ventas
DE LUNES A SÁBADO HORARIO DE 9:30 a.m. A 18:00 p.m.

Servicio de Convenciones
COPIADORAS Y ENMICADOS. ACETATOS PIZARRONES. ETC.

Nombre ______________________ Fecha ______________

1. Los números que aparecen en la guía son...
   a. los números de las habitaciones.
   b. los números de las extensiones telefónicas del hotel.
   c. los pisos donde se encuentran los servicios.
2. Mira los servicios que aparecen en el directorio. ¿Qué servicios corresponden a las siguientes actividades?
   a. nadar ______________
   b. cuidar niños ______________
   c. lavar la ropa ______________
   d. jugar juegos electrónicos ______________
   e. dejar el dinero y las joyas en el hotel ______________
3. ¿A qué número llama usted para los siguientes servicios?
   a. para pedir toallas extras ______________
   b. si usted está enfermo(a) ______________
   c. si quiere hacer una reservación en el restaurante ______________
4. ¿Qué servicios requieren reservaciones? ______________

Vamos a escribir

Phrases: Planning a vacation
Vocabulary: Traveling
Grammar: Verbs: subjunctive with conjunctions, subjunctive with **ojalá**, subjunctive with **que**

P13-12 Todos deseamos ir a pasar unas vacaciones maravillosas algún día. Escribe en forma detallada cómo quieres que sea tu viaje ideal. Incluye lo siguiente para describir el viaje:

- a qué país o lugar quieres ir
- cuándo y cómo quieres viajar
- quién quieres que vaya contigo y por qué
- cómo quieres que sea el hotel y dónde quieres que esté
- qué facilidades deseas que tenga la habitación del hotel
- qué es posible que haga durante tu viaje ideal

Nombre ______________________ Fecha ______________

Mi viaje ideal

Después de escribir

P13-13 Ahora escribe brevemente sobre una experiencia que tuviste durante un viaje. Puede ser una experiencia positiva o negativa. Comparte esta experiencia con un(a) compañero(a) de clase.

Nombre ______________________ Fecha ______________

Práctica auditiva

En contexto

CD 2-31 **P13-14** **¡Te esperamos en Galicia!** Escucha la siguiente conversación. Decide si las siguientes oraciones son verdaderas **(V)** o falsas **(F)**, o si no hay suficiente información para contestar **(N)**.

____ 1. Ileana va a visitar a sus tíos en Madrid.

____ 2. El tío Manuel mandó información sobre los hostales en Madrid.

____ 3. Ileana quiere quedarse en Madrid más de una semana.

____ 4. Ileana desea visitar a los primos por más de dos semanas.

____ 5. Ileana quiere celebrar las fiestas de Santiago de Compostela con los tíos y los primos.

Vocabulario esencial

CD 2-32 **P13-15** **¡Bienvenidos al Hostal Azul!** Escucha la siguiente conversación por teléfono entre Ileana Gamboa, que está haciendo reservaciones, y el recepcionista del Hostal Azul. Escribe la información que el recepcionista necesita tener en el formulario del hotel.

Reservación

Nombre ______________________

Dirección ______________________

Ciudad ______________________

País ______________________

Día de llegada ______________________

Preferencia:

Sencilla ______________________

Doble ______________________

Nombre ______________________________ Fecha ______________

CD 2-33 **P13-16 Situaciones en el Hostal Azul.** Escucha las cinco conversaciones sobre lo que pasa en el Hostal Azul y escribe el número debajo del dibujo correspondiente.

a. ______________

b. ______________

c. ______________

d. ______________

Nombre ______________________ Fecha ______________

e. ______________

CD 2-34 **P13-17 La vida en España.** Vas a escuchar cinco oraciones sobre la vida en España. Reacciona a cada oración según tu opinión. Comienza tu respuesta con **Dudo que... , No dudo que... , Creo que..., No estoy seguro(a) que..., Estoy seguro(a) que...** o **Es verdad que....**

Modelo: En España todos los hoteles son muy caros.
Dudo que todos los hoteles sean muy caros.

1. ____

2. ____

3. ____

4. ____

5. ____

Nombre ______________________ Fecha ______________

LECCIÓN 14 ¡LO SIENTO, PERO NO ME SIENTO BIEN!

Práctica esencial

Vocabulario esencial

P14-1 Enfermedades y sus remedios. Completa las siguientes oraciones sobre enfermedades con la palabra correcta de la lista.

dolor de cabeza	insomnio	náuseas	catarro
dolor de muela	una receta médica	diarrea	

1. Cuando Alicia tiene ______________________, tiene que ir al dentista.
2. Si Alicia y Mariana tienen ______________________, necesitan tomar pastillas para la tos *(cough drops)*.
3. Alicia tiene ______________________; por eso va a tomar aspirina.
4. El año pasado, Mariana tuvo dolor de oído y fiebre, por eso el médico le dio ______________________ para antibióticos.
5. Cuando Mariana tiene ______________________, ella toma Pepto-Bismol.
6. Cuando una persona no puede dormir tiene ______________________.
7. Cuando Mariana se monta en avión para visitar a su familia en Monterrey, ella sufre de ______________________ algunas veces.

P14-2 Había muchos pacientes en la clínica. Cuando Alicia y Mariana fueron a la clínica, vieron a muchos pacientes allí con todo tipo de problemas médicos. Mira los dibujos y describe los problemas de cada paciente, según el número indicado.

Modelo: ¿Qué tiene esta paciente número uno?
La mujer está embarazada y tiene tos.

Nombre ______________________ Fecha ____________

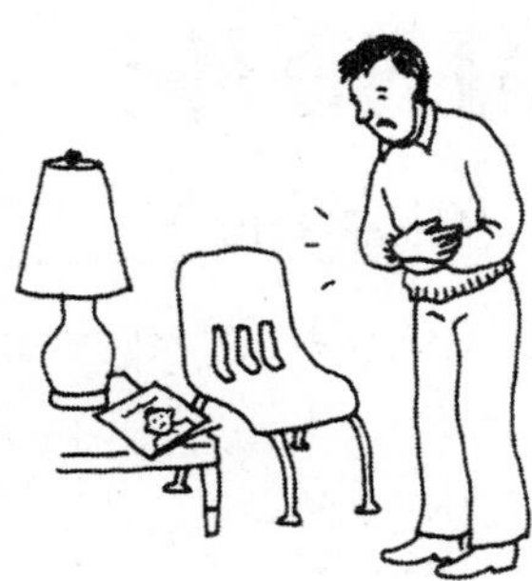

1. ¿Qué tiene esta paciente número dos?

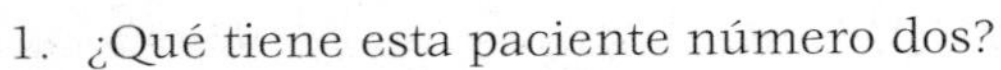

2. ¿Qué tiene esta paciente número tres?

3. ¿Qué tiene esta paciente número cuatro?

4. ¿Qué tiene esta paciente número cinco?

P14-3 ¿Qué haces cuando... ? Escribe una respuesta para cada pregunta sobre problemas médicos.

Modelo: ¿Qué haces cuando te duele la cabeza?
Tomo aspirina y me acuesto.

1. ¿Qué haces cuando tienes gripe y fiebre alta?

2. ¿Qué recomiendas para el dolor de estómago cuando uno come mucho?

3. ¿Qué haces cuando tienes mucha tos y fiebre?

4. ¿Qué haces cuando te duelen las piernas porque hiciste mucho ejercicio?

Nombre ______________________ Fecha ____________

Gramática esencial

P14-4 ¡Qué lástima! Alicia y Mariana están expresando cómo se sintieron durante sus vacaciones. Escribe oraciones utilizando las siguientes palabras y expresiones. Incluye la forma correcta del verbo en el pasado del subjuntivo.

Modelo: fue una lástima que / pasarse / las tres semanas tan pronto
Fue una lástima que se pasaran las tres semanas tan pronto.

1. era imposible que nosotros / visitar / todo Los Ángeles y Arizona en dos semanas

   ____

2. yo preferiría que la próxima vez / nosotros / estar / allí más de un mes

   ____

3. fue una lástima que no / nosotros / poder / viajar a Nevada también

   ____

4. ¡qué malo que me / enfermar / del estómago!

   ____

P14-5 ¿Qué harías en estas situaciones? Primero, pon los verbos entre paréntesis en el condicional para completar las oraciones. Después, decide cuál sería la mejor opción y pon la letra en el espacio en blanco.

____ 1. Si estuvieras estudiando en una universidad española y de repente tuvieras náuseas, ¿qué harías?
   a. ____________ (Beber) leche y ____________ (esperar) hasta que me sintiera mejor.
   b. ____________ (Tomar) dos aspirinas y ____________ (guardar) cama por dos días.
   c. ____________ (Ir) a una clínica para que un médico me examinara.

____ 2. Si acabaras de llegar a un hotel y descubrieras que la recepcionista no tiene tu reservación y ya no hay un cuarto vacante, ¿qué harías?
   a. Le ____________ (pedir) que me permitiera usar el teléfono para llamar a otro hotel.
   b. ____________ (Volver) al aeropuerto para comprar un billete y volver a casa.
   c. ____________ (Hablar) con el gerente del hotel y le ____________ (explicar) el problema.

____ 3. Si fueras doctor(a) y un día un paciente te visitara porque sufre de un dolor de oído horrible, ¿qué harías?
   a. Le ____________ (dar) dos aspirinas y le ____________ (decir) que tú lo (la) llamarías al día siguiente.
   b. Le ____________ (decir) a mi enfermera que le pusiera una inyección.
   c. Le ____________ (examinar) el oído y le ____________ (escribir) una receta médica.

____ 4. Si estuvieras viajando en el extranjero y perdieras tus cheques de viajero, ¿qué harías?
   a. ____________ (Ir) al banco con la lista de los números de mis cheques.
   b. ____________ (Llamar) a mis padres y les ____________ (pedir) más dinero.
   c. ____________ (Ir) a hablar con la policía y ____________ (llenar) un formulario en caso de que los encontraran.

Nombre ______________________________ Fecha ______________

P14-6 Descansaría mucho... Contesta las siguientes preguntas sobre lo que harías si tuvieras gripe.

Modelo: Si tuvieras gripe... ¿irías a una clínica médica o a un hospital?
Si yo tuviera gripe, iría a una clínica médica.

Si tuvieras gripe...

1. ¿tomarías pastillas o preferirías una inyección?

____

2. ¿descansarías un poco o volverías a trabajar inmediatamente?

____

3. ¿le pagarías al médico al contado o usarías su tarjeta de crédito?

____

Cultura

P14-7 Por el mundo hispano. Contesta estas preguntas según la información cultural de la **Lección 14.**

1. En Latinoamérica, los médicos y especialistas cobran (mucho / poco) en comparación con los Estados Unidos y Canadá.
2. En muchas partes del mundo hispano, los farmacéuticos (pueden / no pueden) dar consejos y vender medicinas sin receta médica.
3. Si estás en el extranjero, necesitas beber agua (de botella / del grifo) para evitar "el turista".
4. Antes de comer, es recomendable ______________ las manos. También es mejor ______________ y ______________ las frutas y vegetales.

P14-8 Lectura. Mira el anuncio de la aspirina en la siguiente página y contesta las preguntas.

1. ¿Cuántas aspirinas se consumen en el mundo cada día?

____

2. ¿Cuántos millones de dólares se gastan en los Estados Unidos en aspirinas?

____

3. ¿Cuántas aspirinas toman los españoles como promedio al año?

____

4. ¿Quiénes llevaron aspirinas a la luna?

____

5. ¿Desde hace cuántos años se usa la aspirina?

____

Nombre ______________________ Fecha ______________

La aspirina llegó a la Luna

La aspirina se popularizó rápidamente a principios del siglo XX, debido a las epidemias de gripe, ahora en el siglo XXI se usan masivamente en Europa y en los Estados Unidos. En este país, devastado por una gripe en la década de los cincuenta, la fábrica de aspirina estuvo días fabricando comprimidos *(pills)* in interrumpidamente día y noche debido a la gran demanda.

Después de más de cien años la aspirina incluso ha viajado al espacio: los astronautas Armstrong, Aldrin y Collins, los primeros seres humanos que pisaron la luna, llevaban en el botiquín del Apolo XI, entre otras cosas, varias aspirinas.

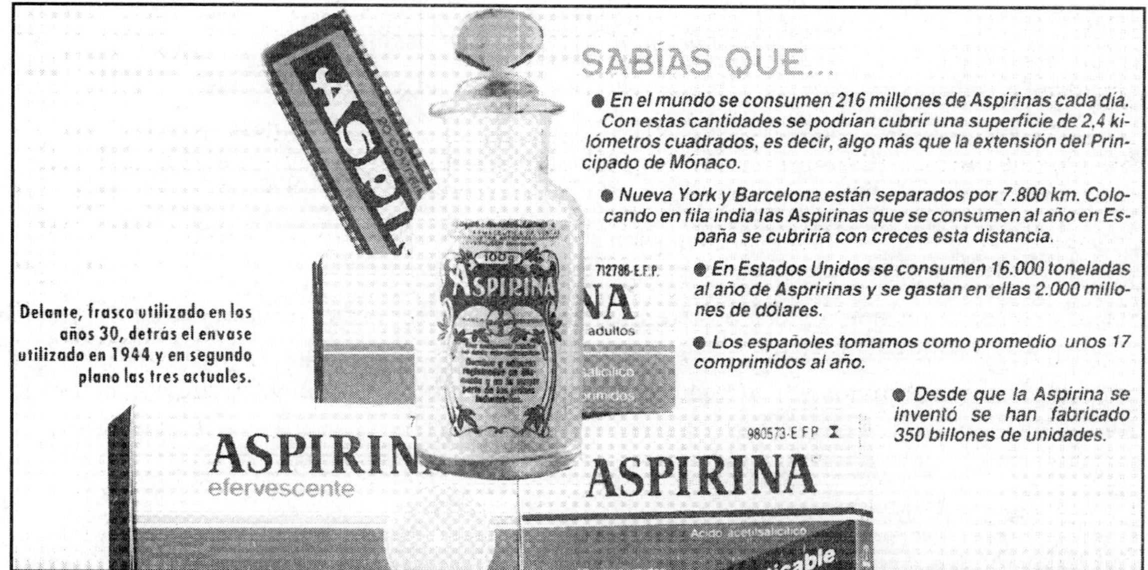

¡A leer!: Médico de familia

Antes de leer

P14-9 En muchas revistas se puede encontrar secciones escritas por médicos o especialistas dedicadas a responder a las preguntas médicas de los lectores *(readers)*. ¿Qué tipo de información piensas que se puede encontrar en una sección médica?

____

____

Nombre ______________________________ Fecha ______________

P14-10 Muchos factores determinan la presión sanguínea *(blood pressure)* de una persona. Algunos son más fáciles de controlar que otros. ¿Qué tipo de factores crees que afectan la presión?

_____ genéticos

_____ climáticos

_____ dietéticos

_____ relacionados con la vida del individuo

_____ hormonales

_____ emocionales

_____ educacionales

P14-11 Hoy en día se puede encontrar a muchas personas que sufren de senilidad. ¿Qué factores crees que puedan ser la causa de la pérdida de la memoria?

_____ la enfermedad de Alzheimer

_____ los problemas de tiroides *(thyroid gland)*

_____ la obesidad

_____ las drogas

_____ la falta de ejercicio

_____ los problemas del corazón

_____ las depresiones

_____ el alcohol

_____ la falta de nutrición

_____ las infecciones

Vamos a leer

P14-12 Mira los factores que seleccionaste en la parte anterior como factores que tienen influencia en la presión sanguínea.

1. Corrige tu lista, según los que menciona el Médico de Familia con un bolígrafo *(pen)* de color diferente.
2. ¿Qué le aconseja el médico al lector que haga para bajar *(to lower)* la presión?

   _____ bajar de peso

   _____ comer sal

   _____ no fumar

   _____ tomar alcohol con moderación

   _____ mantenerse en forma, haciendo ejercicios

P14-13 ¿Qué le preocupa a la persona que escribió la segunda carta?

____

____

P14-14 Mira los factores que seleccionaste en la parte anterior como los que pueden causar la pérdida de memoria.

1. Corrige tu lista, según los que menciona el Médico de Familia con un bolígrafo de color distinto.

   ____

2. Si después de un examen general no se encuentra causa para la pérdida de memoria, ¿a quién debe ver la paciente?

   ____

Nombre ______________________ Fecha ______________

P **Tengo 43 años de edad y en mi último examen clínico una enfermera me comentó que tenía la presión un poco alta. Pero solo me aconsejó que eliminara la sal en las comidas. ¿Qué debo hacer para bajar mi presión alta?**

(Gonzalo Torres)

R La presión sanguínea es determinada por factores genéticos, hormonales, emocionales y relacionados con el tipo de vida del paciente. Los médicos no tienen control sobre todos estos factores, aunque sí pueden ser influenciados. A continuación le damos unos consejos que le ayudarán a bajar su presión sanguínea y a mantenerla normal:

- Elimine el exceso de peso. Guíese por las tablas de talla y peso para que sepa cuál es su peso ideal. Disminuya el consumo de grasas y aumente el de frutas y vegetales.
- Tome alcohol con moderación (no más de dos tragos diarios).
- ¡No fume!
- Haga ejercicios. Si no está "en forma", pregunte al médico qué tipo de ejercicios y qué intensidad es saludable para usted.
- Y, como ya le ha dicho su enfermera, elimine sal en su dieta; restrinja los alimentos preparados con sal (utilice muy poca o ninguna sal en la cocina o en la mesa).

P **Mi madre está perdiendo la memoria y yo estoy muy preocupada por la posibilidad de que tenga la *enfermedad de Alzheimer*. Se sabe muy poco sobre esta enfermedad, pero... ¿qué puedo hacer para ayudarla?**

(Rosario Peñalver)

R Primero que todo, usted no debe presumir que su madre tiene la *enfermedad de Alzheimer*, ni tampoco que la senilidad es una parte inevitable del paso de los años o envejecimiento. Tenga en cuenta que sólo un 10% de las personas mayores de 65 años padecen de senilidad, y que la *enfermedad de Alzheimer* es solamente una de las muchas posibles causas de esta declinación. La pérdida de la memoria, rasgo principal de la senilidad, es a menudo el resultado de condiciones que son reversibles. Es decir, que esta pérdida puede ser efectivamente tratada.

Le sugerimos que lleve a su madre a un buen especialista. La pérdida de la memoria puede ser causada por muchos factores, los cuales incluyen: problemas del corazón, infecciones, mal funcionamiento de la tiroides, nutrición deficiente y depresiones. A esta lista se agrega el consumo de alcohol y ciertos medicamentos utilizados para combatir el insomnio, calmar los nervios, reducir la acidez estomacal o disminuir los temblores. Todas estas sustancias pueden afectar la memoria, especialmente en las personas de edad avanzada.

Si después de un examen general no se encuentran causas físicas o sicológicas de esta pérdida de la memoria, entonces su madre debe ser vista por un neurólogo. Es conveniente que tome algunas notas sobre el patrón de la pérdida de memoria en su madre antes de llevarla al especialista. Tenga en cuenta, al hacerlo, si el cambio ha sido drástico o es la continuación de viejos problemas; si está deprimida o siente soledad; si le faltan estímulos intelectuales; etc. Trate de dar la mayor información posible al médico; su participación será de gran valor en el desarrollo de un plan de tratamiento. ¡Son muchas las cosas que pueden hacerse para mejorar la memoria de una persona!

Nombre ______________________ Fecha ______________

Después de leer

P14-15 Escribe una carta breve al Médico de Familia. Inventa una persona ficticia y una enfermedad. Incluye su edad y cualquier otra información médica que necesite saber el médico.

Querido Médico de Familia...

Nombre ______________________ Fecha ______________

P14-16 Responde a la carta como si fueras el Médico de Familia. Respóndele al (a la) paciente con las recomendaciones apropiadas.

Médico de Familia

Querido (a) Paciente…

Nombre ______________________ Fecha ______________

¡A escribir!

Antes de escribir

P14-17 Completa las siguientes oraciones con información sobre tu juventud.

En mi familia

1. Yo no quería que
 ______________________.
2. Me gustaba que
 ______________________.
3. Era importante que
 ______________________.

En la escuela

4. Los profesores preferían que
 ______________________.
5. Mis amigos no creían que
 ______________________.
6. Yo no estaba seguro(a) de que
 ______________________.

Mis pasatiempos y deportes

7. Mis padres me prohibían que
 ______________________.
8. Para mí era importante que
 ______________________.
9. Mis amigos querían que yo
 ______________________.

Nombre ______________________ Fecha ______________

Vamos a escribir

Phrases: Describing the past; Talking about habitual actions; Talking about past events
Vocabulary: Leisure; Sports; Studies
Grammar: Verbs: preterite & imperfect, subjunctive agreement

P14-18 Escribe en tu diario sobre las emociones, los sentimientos y las opiniones que tenías cuando eras joven sobre la familia, la educación, el país, etc. Incluye la información anterior y agrega otra información apropiada.

Mi diario

Nombre ____________________ Fecha ____________

Después de escribir

P14-19 En tu diario, busca todas las frases que requieren el subjuntivo y haz un círculo alrededor de ellas. Escríbelas en las líneas que aparecen a continuación. Después, haz una lista con todos los verbos que siguen estas frases. ¿Usaste el pasado del subjuntivo? ¿Escribiste correctamente estos verbos? Corrígelos si es necesario.

Las expresiones y frases que requieren el subjuntivo:

Modelo: *Ojalá que mi familia esté junta el año próximo.*

La forma del pasado del subjuntivo correspondiente:

Modelo: *Ojalá que mi familia estuviera junta el año pasado.*

Nombre ____________________ Fecha ____________

Práctica auditiva

En contexto

CD 2-35 **P14-20** **¡Lo siento, pero no me siento bien!** Escucha la siguiente conversación. Decide si las siguientes oraciones son verdaderas **(V)** o falsas **(F)**, o si no hay suficiente información para contestar **(N)**.

____ 1. Mariana siempre come comida del Caribe.

____ 2. A Alicia no le gusta la comida caribeña.

____ 3. A Alicia le duele el estómago desde hace varios días.

____ 4. Mariana quiere llevar a Alicia a su médico.

____ 5. El médico trabaja cerca de la casa de Mariana.

Vocabulario esencial

CD 2-36 **P14-21** **La médica me dijo que me cuidara.** Alicia vio a la médica y luego Mariana le hizo varias preguntas. Escucha la conversación y responde a las siguientes preguntas.

1. ¿Por qué fue Alicia a ver a la médica?

____

2. ¿Qué le recomendó la médica para el dolor de estómago?

____

3. ¿Qué le recomendó la médica que hiciera para el dolor de espalda?

____

CD 2-37 **P14-22** **La Clínica Buena Vista.** La secretaria de la Clínica Buena Vista recibe varias llamadas telefónicas. Escúchalas y luego escribe a continuación lo que dicen los pacientes.

Paciente: Blanca García ____________________

Síntomas: ____________________

____

Mensaje: ____________________

____

Teléfono: ____________________

____

Nombre ______________________ Fecha ______________

Paciente: Señor Perdomo ______________________

Síntomas: ______________________

____

Mensaje: ______________________

____

Teléfono: ______________________

____

Pacient: el hijo de la señora Álvarez ______________________

Síntomas: ______________________

____

Mensaje: ______________________

____

Teléfono: ______________________

____

CD 2-38 **P14-23 Doctor, el (la) paciente dijo que...** Escucha otra vez las conversaciones telefónicas de la Clínica Buena Vista y completa las siguientes frases.

La llamada de la señora García

____ 1. La señora García toma...
   a. aspirinas para el dolor de cabeza.
   b. pastillas para la infección en los oídos.
   c. medicina para el dolor de estómago.

____ 2. La secretaria le dijo a la señora García que...
   a. fuera a la clínica para una cita.
   b. esperara la llamada del doctor Ramírez.
   c. hiciera una cita con el médico.

La llamada del señor Perdomo

____ 3. El señor Perdomo quería que...
a. la secretaria le diera la medicina.
b. el doctor Montiel lo llamara por teléfono.
c. la secretaria le hiciera una cita para ver al doctor.

____ 4. El señor Perdomo dijo que tenía...
a. dolor de espalda.
b. dolor de cabeza y fiebre.
c. dolor de estómago, náuseas y fiebre.

La llamada de la señora Álvarez

____ 5. La señora Álvarez quiere ver al médico para que...
a. le dé unas medicinas para la gripe.
b. vea a su niño.
c. la examine a ella.

____ 6. Al hijo de la señora Álvarez le duele...
a. la garganta.
b. el estómago.
c. los oídos.

Nombre ______________________________ Fecha ______________

LECCIÓN 15 ¿QUÉ PODRÍAMOS HACER NOSOTROS POR NUESTRO MEDIO AMBIENTE?

Práctica esencial

VOCABULARIO ESENCIAL

P15-1 Reacciones. Escribe sobre algunos de los problemas del mundo y de los Estados Unidos. También di cómo te afectan a ti personalmente. Usa las frases y el vocabulario de las siguientes listas.

Siento que...	la delincuencia
Es malo que...	la guerra
Me molesta que...	la pobreza
Es una lástima que...	el terrorismo
Me preocupa que...	la discriminación
Es importante que...	la contaminación del medio ambiente

1. ______________________________
2. ______________________________
3. ______________________________
4. ______________________________
5. ______________________________
6. ______________________________

P15-2 Observaciones personales. Indica dónde viste o ves cada uno de los siguientes problemas. Utiliza los lugares de la lista u otros lugares que conozcas.

Modelo: ver / pobreza
Vi la pobreza en Chicago, en Calcuta y en la Ciudad de México.
Veo pobreza en mi ciudad todos los días.

África	la China	la India
Arabia Saudita	Colombia	Irlanda
Irak	Egipto	el Japón
el Brasil	los Estados Unidos	(otro país o lugar)

1. ver / en la televisión / haber guerra
____
2. ver / haber / deshechos tóxicos
____
3. ver / discriminación racial
____

4. observar / destrucción de la naturaleza

____

5. ver / haber escasez *(scarcity)* de recursos naturales

____

6. ver / contaminación del medio ambiente

____

Gramática esencial

P15-3 ¿Qué harías tú? Completa las siguientes oraciones con información sobre lo que harías si estuvieras en las siguientes situaciones.

Modelo: Si yo fuera presidente de los Estados Unidos, *les daría suficientes fondos a las grandes ciudades para que hubiera más medios de transporte público.*

1. Si yo viviera en un lugar que tuviera mucha contaminación del aire, ____.
2. Si yo fuera multimillonario(a), ____.
3. Si yo fuera a vivir a otro planeta y sólo pudiera llevar cinco cosas, ____.
4. Si yo fuera científico(a), ____.
5. Si yo tuviera la oportunidad de hacer contribuciones humanitarias en este momento, ____.

P15-4 Situaciones. Lee cada situación. Luego completa las oraciones lógicamente, usando los verbos de las listas.

1. volver / tener / regresar

   Ileana se quedaría en Santiago de Compostela si ella no...

   ______________ que terminar sus estudios.

   ______________ a la universidad.

   ______________ a Costa Rica para trabajar.

2. tener / poder / conocer

   Alicia y David harían un viaje a Venezuela si ellos...

   ______________ ahorrar más dinero.

   ______________ un trabajo en Caracas.

   ______________ a muchas personas allí.

Nombre ______________________ Fecha ______________

P15-5 Fin de vacaciones. Ileana y Alicia regresaron a Madison, Wisconsin, para terminar sus estudios y ahora están conversando sobre sus experiencias en México y en España. Completa las siguientes oraciones con la forma correcta del pasado del subjuntivo de los verbos de la lista. Se puede usar un verbo más de una vez.

ir traer pasar ver poder viajar tener

Modelo: Alicia: ¡Qué lástima que David y yo no *fuéramos* a Venezuela!

Ileana: Sí, pero me alegré que ustedes ______________ pasar tres semanas juntos en Chile.

Alicia: Sí, es verdad; estuvimos en Santiago y lo pasamos muy bien. Y a ti, Ileana, ¿no te molestó que no ______________ viajar a Barcelona o Sevilla?

Ileana: No, fue bueno que no ______________ a otros lugares porque así tuve más tiempo con mis primos y mis tíos. Además, mi mamá quería que yo ______________ unas vacaciones tranquilas.

Alicia: De acuerdo, pero mi mamá quería que yo ______________ muchos lugares por si acaso no puedo regresar.

Ileana: Sí, y fue importante que yo te ______________ esta revista para que ______________ los lugares donde puedes trabajar en Latinoamérica con niños.

Alicia: Sí, Ileana, eres una amiga genial. ¡Pura vida!, como dicen en tu país.

P15-6 Especulaciones. ¿Cómo será la vida de los amigos que conocimos en este libro? Especula sobre la vida de ellos.

Modelo: Alicia Benson regresa a los Estados Unidos a terminar sus estudios.
Deseo que *ella tenga la oportunidad de volver a Latinoamérica.*
Ojalá que *ella y David puedan ir algún día a Venezuela.*

1. Luis Chávez no sabe qué quiere hacer cuando termine sus estudios.

   Le aconsejo que ______________________________

   ____

   Espero que ______________________________

   ____

2. David Kerr quiere regresar a Chile para trabajar en el viñedo de los señores Torreón.

   Es bueno que ______________________________

   ____

   Es posible que ______________________________

   ____

3. El señor Gildo Navarro y su hija María Alexandra piensan comprar un mercado más grande en Argentina.

   Estoy seguro(a) que ____

   ____

   Les aconsejo que ____

   ____

4. Enrique y Gloria León van a invertir mucho dinero en la exportación de café colombiano a los Estados Unidos.

   Es probable que ____

   ____

   Me alegro de que ____

   ____

5. Ileana Gamboa quiere regresar a España para trabajar y vivir.

   Es importante que ____

   ____

   Le recomiendo que ____

   ____

Cultura

P15-7 Por el mundo hispano. Contesta las siguientes preguntas sobre las lecturas culturales de la **Lección 15.**

1. ¿Puedes explicar lo que es "La educación sin fronteras"?

   ____

2. ¿Te gustaría participar en este tipo de organización algún día? ¿Por qué sí o por qué no?

   ____

   ____

3. ¿Puedes describir cómo el ruido puede contaminar el ambiente?

   ____

   ____

4. ¿Cuáles son algunos efectos que tiene la contaminación por el ruido?

   ____

   ____

Nombre ______________________________ Fecha ______________

¡A leer!: Veraneantes solidarios

Antes de leer

P15-8 El trabajo de verano. Contesta las preguntas antes de leer el artículo.

1. ¿Qué tipo de trabajo puedes hacer en tus vacaciones de verano?

____

____

2. ¿Te gustaría viajar a un país en vía de desarrollo *(developing country)* y ayudar a estas personas?

____

____

3. Mira las dos fotos en el artículo y lee la descripción de las fotos. ¿Qué tipo de trabajo hacen muchos jóvenes españoles? ¿Te gustaría hacer este tipo de trabajo?

____

____

P15-9 Mira el artículo en la siguiente página mientras haces lo siguiente.

1. Mira el título y las fotos de la lectura de la página siguiente. ¿Quiénes están en las fotos?

____

____

2. ¿Qué trabajo se puede hacer durante las vacaciones de verano?

____

____

3. ¿Qué se requiere para inscribirse en estos programas?

____

____

4. Describe los diferentes trabajos que podrías hacer en estos proyectos.

____

____

Nombre ______________________________ Fecha ______________

Vamos a leer

¿QUIÉNES SON?

Puedes pasar un verano distinto ayudando a los cooperantes del Tercer Mundo.

Cientos de jóvenes españoles pasan sus vacaciones en algún lugar del Tercer Mundo, para echar una mano allí donde los necesitan y, de paso, conocer una realidad muy distinta a la de nuestro país.

Marco Polo

Veraneantes solidarios

Unas vacaciones imborrables

Cada año, durante estos meses de verano, varias organizaciones no gubernamentales (ONG) organizan campos de trabajo y viajes solidarios a diferentes proyectos que ellas mismas u otras organizaciones ya tienen en marcha. Cientos de jóvenes de todo el país se apuntan a estas originales vacaciones, que no son precisamente baratas, ya que si bien la comida y el alojamiento corren a cargo de la organización, el viaje es por cuenta del cooperante. Generalmente se trata de estancias cortas que no superan el mes. Los jóvenes realizan tareas de apoyo a los cooperantes profesionales responsables del proyecto.

¿Qué se requiere para apuntarse?

Como norma general, ser mayor de 21 años, asistir a unos cursos o de preparación y, sobre todo, tener muchas ganas de participar en proyectos de este tipo. Ya a principios de año las organizaciones empiezan a preparar los viajes, no lo dejes para última hora.

¿Dónde informarme?

Estas son algunas de las organizaciones que suelen admitir cooperantes en verano:

- Servei Civil Internacional (SCI): Carmen, 95 bjos. 2a. 08001 Barcelona. Tel. (93) 441 70 79. Organizan campos de trabajo para voluntarios de cualquier punto de la península, Baleares y Canarias.
- Servicio Tercer Mundo (SETEM): St. Antoni Abat, 49 08001 Barcelona. Tel. (93) 441 53 35. Madrid (91) 549 91 28. Granada (958) 81 89 38. Valencia (96) 361 56 51. Vitoria (945) 12 07 46.
- Solidaridad para el desarrollo y la paz (SODEPAZ): Pez, 9 28004 Madrid. Tel. (91) 522 80 91. Barcelona (93) 268 22 02. Logroño (941) 25 45 07. Navarra (948) 24 12 30. Toledo (925) 35 74 86.

Los campos de trabajo son una experiencia original y solidaria en las vacaciones.

Nombre ______________________ Fecha ______________

Después de leer

P15-10 Escríbele una carta a la organización de proyectos de verano y explica a qué lugar te gustaría ir a trabajar, por qué te gustaría ir y las ideas que tienes para ayudar con ese proyecto.

Estimada Organización,

Nombre ______________________ Fecha ____________

¡A escribir!

Antes de escribir

P15-11 Debemos hacer algo para conservar la Tierra. ¿Cuáles son tus metas *(goals)* y planes personales para conservar nuestra Tierra? Llena los espacios en blanco con las cosas que quieres hacer.

Para conservar la Tierra y el medio ambiente, yo...

1. ______________________
2. ______________________
3. ______________________
4. ______________________

Vamos a escribir

Phrases: Animals; Means of transportation; Plants; Working conditions
Grammar: Verbs: conditional, subjunctive agreement

P15-12 Para ti, ¿cómo sería un mundo perfecto? Escribe un ensayo, usando las siguientes preguntas como guía.

- ¿Qué tipo de clima y ambiente tendría el mundo?
- ¿Cómo serían las ciudades, las escuelas y las casas?
- ¿Qué problemas no existirían más?
- ¿Qué haríamos en el trabajo y para divertirnos?

Nombre ______________________ Fecha ______________

Después de escribir

P15-13 Intercambia tu composición con la de un(a) compañero(a) de clase. Lee la nueva composición y compara el mundo de tu compañero(a) con tu mundo. ¿Tienen estos dos mundos algo en común? ¿Cómo son diferentes? Haz una lista de las semejanzas *(similarities)* y las diferencias abajo.

Semejanzas

____

____

____

____

Diferencias

____

____

____

____

Nombre ______________________ Fecha ______________

Práctica auditiva

En contexto

CD 2-39 **P15-14 El planeta Tierra.** Escucha la siguiente conversación. Decide si las siguientes oraciones son verdaderas **(V)** o falsas **(F)**, o si no hay suficiente información para contestar **(N)**.

____ 1. La experiencia de Alicia en Monterrey fue valiosa.

____ 2. Ileana quería quedarse en Santiago de Compostela.

____ 3. Ileana tiene que regresar a Costa Rica para hacer turismo.

____ 4. Alicia quiere trabajar en Latinoamérica toda su vida.

____ 5. Alicia quiere enseñar a los niños latinoamericanos.

Vocabulario esencial

CD 2-40 **P15-15 Las noticias.** Vas a escuchar cinco noticias en la radio. Escribe el número de cada noticia debajo del dibujo a que corresponde.

a. ____________

b. ____________

c. ____________

d. ____________

e. ____________

Nombre ______________________________ Fecha ______________

CD 2-41 **P15-16** **¿Qué oíste en las noticias?** Escucha otra vez las noticias de la última actividad y contesta las siguientes preguntas.

____ 1. En la noticia número uno el locutor *(announcer)* dijo lo siguiente:
a. Se inventó un auto nuevo.
b. Se inventó un motor que usa energía solar.
c. Se creó un laboratorio nuevo en Alemania.

____ 2. En la noticia número dos se mencionó lo siguiente:
a. La selva Amazónica se está quemando.
b. Los árboles en la selva Amazónica están creciendo poco a poco.
c. El río Amazonas está contaminado.

____ 3. En la noticia número tres se reportó que en la ciudad de Santiago de Chile...
a. no hay contaminación ambiental.
b. la ciudad no puede funcionar por cuatro días.
c. el aire está muy contaminado en esta época del verano.

____ 4. En la noticia número cuatro se anunció que se puede comprar...
a. productos biodegradables que ayudan al ambiente.
b. productos biodegradables que no protegen al ambiente.
c. productos biodegradables que son muy económicos.

____ 5. La noticia número cinco anunció que en Venezuela...
a. el agua del Río Orinoco no está contaminada, a pesar de la explotación de recursos renovables.
b. el agua del Río Orinoco está contaminada debido a la explotación de recursos no renovables.
c. el agua del Río Orinoco no está contaminada y ayuda a la vida animal de la zona.

CD 2-42 **P15-17** **¿Qué crees tú?** Vas a oír seis oraciones sobre problemas que afectan el mundo y los Estados Unidos. Indica si estás de acuerdo o no.

Estoy de acuerdo	**No estoy de acuerdo**
1. ____________	____________
2. ____________	____________
3. ____________	____________
4. ____________	____________
5. ____________	____________
6. ____________	____________

Lo suplemental

Nombre ______________________ Fecha ______________

LECCIÓN PRELIMINAR

Prática suplemental

VOCABULARIO SUPLEMENTAL

El mundo y algunas nacionalidades

Centroamericanos

Belice	beliceño(a)

Suramericanos

Guyana	guyanés (guyanesa)
Guayana Francesa	guyanés (guyanesa)
Surinam	surinamés (surinamesa)

Caribeños

Haití	haitiano(a)
Jamaica	jamaiquino(a)
Trinidad y Tobago	trinitario(a)

Europeos

Austria	austríaco(a)
Bélgica	belga
Bulgaria	búlgaro(a)
Dinamarca	danés (danesa)
Finlandia	finlandés (finlandesa)
Holanda	holandés (holandesa)
Hungría	húngaro(a)
Italia	italiano(a)
Noruega	noruego(a)
Polonia	polaco(a)
República Checa	checo(a)
Rumania	rumano(a)
Suecia	sueco(a)
Suiza	suizo(a)

Africanos y asiáticos

África del Sur	africano(a) del sur
Angola	angolés (angolesa)
Argelia	argelino(a)
Corea del Norte/ Sur	coreano(a)
Egipto	egipcio(a)
Etiopía	etiope
Filipinas	filipino(a)
Irán	iranio(a), persa
Israel	israelí
Libia	libio(a)
Nepal	nepalés (nepalesa)
Paquistán	paquistaní
Tailandia	tailandés (tailandesa)
Australia	australiano(a)
Nueva Zelanda	neozelandés (neozelandesa)

Nombre ______________________________ Fecha ______________

Practiquemos

VP-1 Países y nacionalidades. For each national group, identify their country.

Modelo: coreanos
Los coreanos son de Corea del Norte / Sur.

1. italianos
2. austríacos
3. suecos
4. polacos
5. holandeses
6. belgas
7. húngaros
8. daneses
9. argelinos
10. egipcios
11. israelíes
12. filipinos
13. nepaleses
14. persas
15. australianos
16. neozelandeses

Más objetos de la clase

la calculadora	*calculator*
la computadora	*computer*
la grabadora	*tape recorder*
la mesa	*table*
la papelera	*garbage can*
la puerta	*door*
el pupitre	*school desk*
el reloj	*clock*
la ventana	*window*

Practiquemos

VP-2 *¿El o la?* Write the appropriate definite article for the following classroom objects.

Modelo: ___*la*___ mesa

1. __________ puerta
2. __________ ventana
3. __________ grabadora
4. __________ calculadora
5. __________ papelera
6. __________ reloj
7. __________ pupitre
8. __________ computadora

VP-3 Identifique. With a classmate, look around your classroom and identify in Spanish the different things that you see.

Nombre ______________________________ Fecha ______________

GRAMÁTICA SUPLEMENTAL

Some Uses of Definite Articles
The four definite articles in Spanish are **el, los, la,** and **las.** All of these articles mean *the,* and they have a variety of uses.

1. To single out a specific person, place, or thing.

El niño es mi hijo.	*The boy is my son.*
La lección es interesante.	*The lesson is interesting.*

2. To express generalities.

El español es fácil.	*Spanish is easy.*
La vida es muy corta.	*Life is very short.*
Me gustan **los** tamales.	*I like tamales.*
BUT: Estudio español.	*I study Spanish.*

3. To refer to people with titles (except when addressing them directly).

El profesor Vargas es alto.	BUT: Buenas tardes, **profesor Vargas.**
La doctora López es buena.	BUT: **Doctora López,** ¿cómo está usted?

4. To refer to certain countries.

el Brasil	**el** Paraguay	**la** Argentina
el Canadá	**el** Perú	**la** China
el Ecuador	**El** Salvador	**la** India
el Japón	**el** Uruguay	**los** Estados Unidos

5. To express certain time expressions.

Vamos **el** lunes.	*We are going on Monday.*
Vamos **los** miércoles.	*We go on Wednesdays.*
Vamos todos **los** domingos.	*We go every Sunday.*
Es **la** una.	*It's one o'clock.*
Son **las** dos.	*It's two o'clock.*

6. To refer to parts of the body.

—¿Te duelen **los** ojos?	*Do your eyes hurt?*
—No. Me duele **el** estómago.	*No. My stomach hurts.*

7. To refer to articles of clothing.

—Voy a quitarme **la** camisa.	*I'm going to take off my shirt.*
—Ponte **el** pijama, hijo.	*Put on your pajamas, son.*

8. To refer to names of languages.

—Te gusta **el** español?	*Do you like Spanish?*
—Sí, y me gusta **el** japonés también.	*Yes, and I like Japanese, too.*

Nombre ______________________________ Fecha ______________

Practiquemos

GP-4 Los países y sus lenguas. Add the missing definite articles to the following paragraphs.

Se habla inglés en todas partes de __________ Estados Unidos, pero en algunas ciudades se hablan otras lenguas también; por ejemplo, __________ Navaho en Taos en __________ estado de Nuevo México, __________ francés en Nueva Orleans, __________ árabe en Detroit, __________ chino en San Francisco, __________ coreano en Los Ángeles, __________ español en Miami y __________ hebreo en Nueva York.

Se habla español en México y España, en __________ Salvador y en __________ otros países de Centroamérica con excepción de Belice. También se habla español en muchos países sudamericanos; por ejemplo, en __________ Ecuador, __________ Perú, __________ Argentina y __________ Uruguay. En __________ Paraguay se hablan __________ español y __________ guaraní, una lengua indígena del país. En __________ Brasil no se habla __________ español, sino __________ portugués.

En __________ China se hablan varios dialectos y en __________ India se hablan muchos idiomas como, por ejemplo, __________ hindi y __________ urdú.

__________ mundo es muy pequeño, pero hay muchas lenguas, ¿verdad?

GP-5 Una conversación. Write out the following conversation, using definite articles and contractions when needed. Then act it out with a classmate. Some of the lines do not require any article at all.

Doctor Ramos: ¿Cómo van __________ estudios, __________ señorita Pérez?

Señorita Pérez: Muy bien, gracias, __________ doctor Ramos, con excepción de mi clase de inglés. Para mí, __________ inglés es un poco difícil.

Doctor Ramos: Pero __________ profesora Mendoza es buena, ¿verdad?

Señorita Pérez: Sí, muy buena, y __________ textos son interesantes, pero __________ exámenes de la profesora Mendoza son difíciles.

Doctor Ramos: ¿Cuándo es su clase de inglés?

Señorita Pérez: __________ lunes y miércoles a __________ nueve de __________ mañana.

Doctor Ramos: ¿Quiere usted estudiar en un país de habla inglesa? Por ejemplo, ¿en __________ Estados Unidos, __________ Inglaterra o __________ Canadá?

Señorita Pérez: Sí, posiblemente. Quiero estudiar biología en __________ Universidad de Harvard. Me gustan __________ ciencias y para mí son más fáciles que __________ lenguas.

Doctor Ramos: ¡Qué bueno!

Nombre ______________________________ Fecha ______________

PASO 1 Nuevos amigos en México

LECCIÓN 1 ¡BIENVENIDA A MONTERREY!

Práctica suplemental

VOCABULARIO SUPLEMENTAL

Más adjetivos para describir características físicas y de personalidad

agradable	*nice*
alegre	*happy*
callado(a)	*quiet*
cómico(a)	*funny*
desagradable	*unpleasant*
feliz	*happy*
hablador(a)	*talkative*
listo(a)	*smart*
mediano(a)	*average; medium-sized*
nervioso(a)	*nervous*
pobre	*poor*
rico(a)	*rich*
tonto(a)	*silly, foolish*
tranquilo(a)	*calm*

PRACTIQUEMOS

V1-1 Describir. Select the correct form of each adjective to describe the people at the university.

Modelo: Los estudiantes son (agradable / agradables).
Los estudiantes son *agradables.*

1. El profesor es muy (agradables / agradable).

____

2. Vosotros sois (alegre / alegres).

____

3. Las profesoras son (tranquilas / tranquila).

____

4. Mildred es muy (listas / lista).

____

5. Yo soy una persona (nerviosas / nerviosa).

6. Luis y Gloria son (ricos / ricas).

7. José y Gabriela son (pobres / pobre).

8. Julia y yo somos unas personas (feliz / felices).

9. Tú eres muy (cómicos / cómico) y también eres (tontos / tonto).

10. Vosotras sois (habladoras / habladora).

11. Yo soy un(a) estudiante (medianos[as] / mediano[a]).

V1-2 **¿Cómo son?** Write sentences using the adjectives given to describe these people.

Modelo: estudiantes de español / alegre
Los estudiantes de español son alegres.

1. profesora / agradable

2. clases / alegre

3. María y Felipe / hablador

4. nosotras / rico

5. ellos / pobre

6. vosotros / personas / nervioso

7. Mario y Álvaro / mediano / en tamaño

8. yo / listo(a)

Nombre ______________________________ Fecha ________________

9. tú / tranquilo

____

10. vosotras / callado

____

VI-3 Descripción. Complete the following paragraphs to describe your class, your instructor, and your classmates.

Modelo: La clase de español es *grande* y *divertida.*

La clase de español es _________ y divertida. El (La) profesor(a) de español es muy _________ y _________.

Juan es uno de mis compañeros de clase y él es muy _________. Lucero y Alberto son _________, pero Francisco y Rosa son _________. ¡La clase de español es excelente!

VI-4 ¿Cómo eres tú? Pick four or five of the adjectives from the previous list and describe yourself to a classmate. Take turns.

Modelo: *Yo soy hablador(a), listo(a), agradable y... Y tú, ¿cómo eres?*

____

____

____

____

____

____

Nombre ______________________________ Fecha ______________

Gramática suplemental

More uses of *ser*

The English verb *to be* can be expressed in several ways in Spanish, but two very important ways are **ser** and **estar.** The uses of **ser** are described below. The verb is irregular in its conjugation.

	SER
yo	**soy**
tú	**eres**
él/ella/Ud.	**es**
nosotros/nosotras	**somos**
vosotros/vosotras	**sois**
ellos/ellas/Uds.	**son**

1. Used in expressing origin.

   Soy de los Estados Unidos. — *I am from the United States.*

2. Used in expressing possession.

   El libro **es de** Mario. — *The book is Mario's.*

3. Used to show what something is made of.

   La bolsa **es de** cuero. — *The bag is made of leather.*

4. Used before adjectives that express inherent qualities and characteristics (e.g., nationality, physical and personality attributes, color).

   José **es** alto y rubio. — *José is tall and blond.*
   Marcela **es** inteligente. — *Marcela is intelligent.*
   Mis amigos **son** cómicos. — *My friends are funny.*
   La chaqueta **es** azul. — *The jacket is blue.*
   Juana **es** boliviana. — *Juana is Bolivian.*

5. Used to express time, dates, days of the week, and where an event takes place.

   Hoy **es** viernes. — *Today is Friday.*

   —¿Dónde **es** la fiesta? — *—Where is the party?*
   —La fiesta **es** en mi casa. — *—The party is at my house.*
   —¿Qué hora **es**? — *—What time is it?*
   —**Son** las dos. — *—It's two o'clock.*

Practiquemos

G1-5 ¿Quiénes *(Who)* son? Select the appropriate form of the verb **ser** to express who these people are.

Modelo: La señorita Martínez (soy / es) la profesora de español.
La señorita Martínez *es* la profesora de español.

1. Ellos (eres / son) los estudiantes de la clase de español.
2. Yo (soy / somos) la profesora.

3. Vosotras (son / sois) estudiantes de la universidad.
4. Nosotros (somos / es) los amigos de Juan Carlos.
5. Salvador (soy / es) el amigo de Marianela.
6. Tú (es / eres) estudiante de francés.
7. Julia y Francisco (son / somos) estudiantes de español.
8. Nosotros (soy / somos) los profesores de francés.
9. Ellas (somos / son) estudiantes del Tecnológico.
10. Vosotros (sois / somos) profesores de chino.

G1-6 La clase de español. Fill in each blank with the appropriate form of the verb **ser** to express what you know about your Spanish class.

Modelo: Luisa *es* de Portugal; *es* portuguesa.

1. Nosotros __________ de los Estados Unidos.
2. Pierre __________ del Canadá.
3. El profesor Pérez __________ de México; __________ mexicano.
4. Yo __________ estudiante de español.
5. Vosotros __________ de la Argentina; __________ argentinos.
6. Nosotros __________ estudiantes de francés.
7. Tú __________ de Francia; __________ francés.
8. Alicia __________ de Madison, Wisconsin; __________ estadounidense.
9. ¿__________ vosotras estudiantes de español?
10. Alicia y Enrique __________ estudiantes de la universidad.

G1-7 ¿De quién es *(Whose is it)*? Fill in each blank with the appropriate form of the verb **ser** to express possession.

Modelo: La clase *es* de la profesora González.

1. Los textos __________ de los estudiantes.
2. El bolígrafo __________ del profesor.
3. Las tareas __________ de Raúl y Patricia.
4. Los libros __________ de Ramiro.
5. La hoja de papel __________ de la profesora.
6. La clase de francés __________ de los estudiantes de francés.
7. El escritorio __________ del profesor Pérez.
8. Los asientos __________ de los estudiantes de español.
9. El cuaderno __________ de Patricia.
10. Las sillas __________ de la profesora y del profesor.

Práctica comunicativa suplemental I

Tarjeta de identificación. Es el primer día de clase y tú tienes que llenar la tarjeta de identificación de los estudiantes para el (la) profesor(a). Completa la tarjeta de identificación con la información personal de un(a) estudiante.

Vocabulario útil

apellido	*last name*
nombre	*first name*
país de origen	*country of origin*
nacionalidad	*nationality*
estado civil	*marital status*
casado(a)	*married*
divorciado(a)	*divorced*
¿Eres soltero(a)?	*Are you single?*
¿Eres tú de California?	*Are you from California?*
¿Cuáles son tus números de teléfono en casa y de móvil?	*What are your home and cellular phone numbers?*

Tarjeta de identificación	
Apellido	
Nombre	
País de origen	
Nacionalidad	
Estado civil	
Número de teléfono (casa)	
Número de teléfono (móvil)	

Nombre ______________________ Fecha ______________

Práctica comunicativa suplemental II

ESTUDIANTE A

¿Quién es? En parejas, lean la información sobre estas personas famosas y adivinen quiénes son. Pregúntale a tu compañero(a) la información que necesitas para completar tu cuadro.

Vocabulario útil

¿Cuál es su nombre? *What is his/her name?*
¿Cuál es su ocupación? *What is his/her occupation?*
¿De dónde es? *Where is he/she from?*
¿Qué hace? *What does he/she do?*

1. nombre: ______________
   nacionalidad: *chilena*
   ocupación: *escritora*

2. nombre: *Julio Iglesias*
   nacionalidad: ______________
   ocupación: *cantante*

3. nombre: ______________
   nacionalidad: *español / mexicano*
   ocupación: *cantante*

4. nombre: *Daisy Fuentes*
   nacionalidad: *cubana*
   ocupación: ______________

Nombre ______________________________ Fecha ______________

ESTUDIANTE B

¿Quién es? En parejas, lean la información sobre estas personas famosas y adivinen quiénes son. Pregúntale a tu compañero(a) la información que necesitas para completar tu cuadro.

Vocabulario útil

¿Cuál es su nombre? *What is his/her name?*
¿De dónde es? *Where is he/she from?*
¿Cuál es su ocupación? *What is his/her occupation?*
¿Qué hace? *What does he/she do?*

1. nombre: *Isabel Allende*
   nacionalidad: ______________
   ocupación: ______________

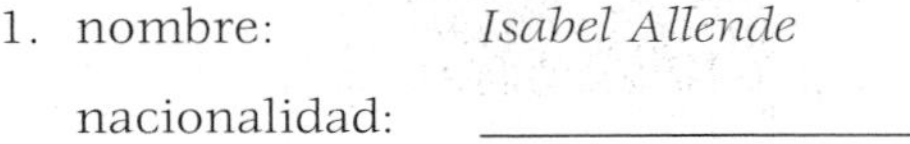

2. nombre: ______________
   nacionalidad: *español*
   ocupación: ______________

3. nombre: *Plácido Domingo*
   nacionalidad: ______________
   ocupación: ______________

4. nombre: ______________
   nacionalidad: ______________
   ocupación: *conductora de televisión; modelo*

Nombre ______________________________ Fecha ______________

LECCIÓN 2 ¿TE GUSTA ESTUDIAR Y TRABAJAR EN LA UNIVERSIDAD?

Práctica suplemental

VOCABULARIO SUPLEMENTAL

¿Qué cursos estudia usted?

Cursos	*Courses*
la anatomía	*anatomy*
el comercio internacional	*international business*
la ética	*ethics*
la filosofía	*philosophy*
las finanzas	*finance*
la física	*physics*
la geografía	*geography*
la química	*chemistry*
Carreras	*Majors*
la enfermería	*nursing*
los estudios para la paz y el desarrollo	*peace and development studies*
las lenguas	*languages*
la odontología	*dentistry*
el turismo	*tourism*
la veterinaria	*veterinary school*

PRACTIQUEMOS

V2-1 El/La consejero(a) ***(counselor).*** You are a counselor at your university; therefore, you have to help students choose the best courses for their majors. Using these lists of majors and courses, in addition to the ones in **Lección 2** (de ***Intercambios***), write the courses that students will have to take for each of these majors.

Enfermería	**Turismo**	**Veterinaria**
________________	________________	________________
________________	________________	________________

Estudios para la paz y el desarrollo	**Lenguas**	**Odontología**
________________	________________	________________
________________	________________	________________

Nombre ______________________ Fecha ______________

V2-2 **¿Qué cursos estudia usted?** It's time for you to select your major and plan the courses you have to take in order to reach your goal. Use these lists of majors (**especializaciones**) and courses in addition to the ones in **Lección 2** to plan your studies.

Facultad de

____

Especialización

____

Cursos

____

____

____

____

Nombre ______________________________ Fecha ______________

Gramática suplemental

Expressions with the verb *tener*
Let's review the expressions that you have used in **Lección 2** of the ***Intercambios*** textbook.

tener... años	*to be . . . years old*
tener calor	*to be hot / warm*
tener frío	*to be cold*
tener hambre	*to be hungry*
tener sed	*to be thirsty*
tener sueño	*to be sleepy*

Practiquemos

G2-3 Expresiones con *tener*. Use these expressions with **tener** to describe how these people feel.

Modelo: Jorge *tiene calor* en la playa *(beach)*.

1. Yo ____________ ____________, y tú, ¿____________ ____________?
2. Después de *(After)* estudiar biología, nosotros ____________ ____________.
3. Ellas ____________ ____________ en las montañas *(mountains)*.
4. José ____________ ____________ en el desierto *(desert)*.
5. Nosotros ____________ ____________ a las ocho de la mañana.
6. Tú ____________ ____________ a las doce de la noche.
7. Nosotros ____________ ____________ en Las Vegas, Nevada, si la temperatura es de 100° F.
8. Ellos ____________ ____________ en Maine si la temperatura es −25° F.
9. Luisa y yo ____________ ____________ a las dos de la madrugada.
10. Beatriz y Carolina ____________ ____________ después de la fiesta.

G2-4 ¿Qué tenemos? Describe what you and your housemate feel at certain times during the day, using the expressions with **tener** that you have learned. Write at least four sentences.

____

____

____

____

____

____

____

____

Nombre ________________________ Fecha ____________

More regular *-ar* verbs

buscar a la profesora en la oficina	***to look for*** *the professor in the office*
conversar con los amigos en un café	***to converse*** *with friends at the café*
entrar a clase a tiempo	***to enter*** *class on time*
mirar la televisión en casa	***to watch*** *TV at home*
practicar español todos los días	***to practice*** *Spanish every day*
tomar apuntes en clase	***to take*** *notes in class*
revisar los apuntes en casa	***to go over*** *the class notes at home*
sacar buenas notas en la universidad	***to get*** *good grades at the university*

Practiquemos

G2-5 En la universidad. Select the appropriate form of the verb to find out what you and your friends do at the university.

Modelo: Mariana (sacan / saca) buenas notas en clase.
Mariana *saca* buenas notas en clase.

1. Nosotros (miro / miramos) un video para la clase de geografía.
2. Ernesto y Juliana (entran / entra) a clase a tiempo todos los martes.
3. Yo (practica / practico) portugués todos los días.
4. Vosotros (sacan / sacáis) buenas notas en español.
5. Ellas (revisan / revisas) los apuntes después de la clase de estadística.
6. Pedro (busco / busca) a la profesora de física.
7. Luis y Patricio (conversamos / conversan) con sus amigos en el parque.
8. Nosotros (sacan / sacamos) un nota regular en química.
9. Marisa (toma / tomas) buenos apuntes en clase.
10. Vosotras (entráis / entra) en la oficina del profesor Peraza a las nueve.
11. La clase de español (mira / miran) la televisión en clase.
12. Marcos (revisan / revisa) las tareas en casa.
13. Tú (practicas / practican) tenis todas las tardes.
14. Nosotros (conversas / conversamos) un poco en español.
15. Ellos (tomas / toman) apuntes en la clase de economía.
16. Yo (busco / busca) a mis amigos para conversar.
17. Lucy (revisa / reviso) los apuntes de la clase de matemáticas.
18. Vosotros (miran / miráis) la tele en casa.

Nombre ______________________________ Fecha ______________

G2-6 La rutina de Alicia. Alicia describes her routine in the following paragraphs. Fill in each blank with the appropriate form of the verb to find out what she does.

Alicia _camina_ (caminar) todos los días a la universidad. Allí *(There)*, ella _trabajadora_ (trabajar) como profesora de inglés y también _estidia_ (estudiar) contabilidad y negocios de México.

Alicia y su amigo Enrique _llegan_ (llegar) a la universidad muy temprano y _entran_ (entrar) a clase a tiempo. Después de clase, ellos _toman_ (tomar) café y _conversan_ (conversar) en la cafetería de la universidad. Luego, Alicia y Enrique _descansan_ (descansar) por una hora y después _revisan_ (revisar) los apuntes de sus clases. Alicia _necesita_ (necesitar) hablar con el profesor Ramírez y por eso _llama_ (llamar) por teléfono al profesor. Alicia siempre *(always)* _visita_ (visitar) a sus profesores en su oficina, así _practica_ (practicar) español con diferentes personas. Alicia siempre _saca_ (sacar) buenas notas en sus cursos de la universidad.

G2-7 Tu vida en la universidad. Now, describe your life at the university by writing five sentences using verbs such as **llegar, entrar, estudiar, hablar, conversar, tomar apuntes, revisar, trabajar,** and **descansar.**

Modelo: *Yo llego a la universidad a las dos de la tarde. Entro a clase a las tres de la tarde y trabajo por la noche...*

Práctica comunicativa suplemental I

¿En quién pienso yo? Piensa en una persona de la clase. Haz cuatro o cinco oraciones sobre la persona. Tus compañeros tienen que adivinar quién es. Si no adivinan, puedes darles una pista *(hint)*.

Modelo: *Es una mujer.*
Es rubia. / Tiene el pelo rubio.
Es estadounidense.
Tiene veinte años más o menos.
Trabaja en la cafetería.

Vocabulario útil

alto(a)	*tall*
atlético(a)	*athletic*
bajo(a)	*short*
intelectual	*intellectual*
más o menos	*more or less*
moreno(a)	*dark-haired*
pelirrojo(a)	*red-haired*
rubio(a)	*blond(e)*
simpático(a)	*nice, friendly*
tímido(a)	*timid, shy*

Nombre ______________________________ Fecha ______________

Práctica comunicativa suplemental II

Entrevistas. Entrevista a tres compañeros de clase y llena las tablas a continuación. Luego, informa a la clase sobre tus compañeros.

Vocabulario útil

la edad	*age*
¿Cuántos años tienes?	*How old are you?*
le gusta	*he likes, she likes*
A Martín le gusta...	*Martín likes....*
A Pati le gusta...	*Pati likes ....*
¿Qué actividades te gustan?	*What activities do you like?*
A él (ella) le gustan	*He (She) likes...*

nombre ______________________________
teléfono ______________________________
edad ______________________________
curso favorito ______________________________
actividades que le gustan ______________________________

Nombre ______________________ Fecha ______________

nombre

____

teléfono

____

edad

____

curso favorito

____

actividades que le gustan

____

nombre

____

teléfono

____

edad

____

curso favorito

____

actividades que le gustan

____

Nombre ______________________ Fecha ______________

LECCIÓN 3 ¡NECESITO UNA PASANTÍA DE TRABAJO PARA JUNIO!

Práctica suplemental

Vocabulario suplemental

Let's review the phrases **Me gusta** / **Me gustaría** from ***Intercambios,*** page X.

¿Qué país le gustaría visitar?	*What country would you like to visit? (you formal)*
Me gustaría visitar...	*I would like to visit . . .*
¿Qué lugar le gustaría visitar?	*What place would you like to visit? (you informal)*
Me gustaría visitar...	*I would like to visit . . .*
el museo de bellas artes	*the fine arts museum*
el teatro de la ópera	*the opera house*
el estadio de béisbol	*the baseball stadium*
las cataratas	*the falls*
las montañas	*the mountains*
la playa	*the beach*
un restaurante tailandés/chino/ruso/alemán	*a Thai/Chinese/Russian/German restaurant*

Practiquemos

V3-1 ¿Qué le gustaría visitar? You are a travel guide and you want to plan a week of activities for some visitors to your city or town. Ask your classmate questions about the places he or she wants to visit or places where he or she wants to eat and at what time. Take note of the itinerary.

Modelo: *¿Qué lugar le gustaría visitar?*
¿Dónde le gustaría comer?
¿A qué hora le gustaría visitar/comer...?

	Lunes	Martes	Miércoles	Jueves	Viernes	Sábado	Domingo
9:00 a.m.							
11:00 a.m.							
1:00 p.m.							
3:00 p.m.							
5:00 p.m.							
7:00 p.m.							
9:00 p.m.							

Nombre ______________________ Fecha ____________

V3-2 ¿Te gustaría... ? Ask your classmates what they would like to do during the weekend.

Modelo: —*¿Te gustaría comer comida italiana el sábado por la noche?*
—*¡Claro que me gustaría!*
—*¿Te gustaría ir a bailar salsa el viernes por la noche?*
—*No, pero me gustaría bailar el sábado.*

V3-3 Otra invitación. Invite your classmate to eat your favorite food with you. Use the following suggestions as a guide for your conversation.

Estudiante A	**Estudiante B**
Greet your friend and ask how he or she is.	Answer appropriately, then ask how your friend is.
Ask: ¿Te gustaría comer comida... ?	Answer the invitation (**Sí** or **no**). Then ask what day and what time.
Answer the question.	
	State your preference for time.
Disagree with the time.	
	Answer, and change the time to go to dinner / lunch.
Agree with this new time.	
	Thank your friend, and say good-bye.
Respond appropriately.	

V3-4 Mis vacaciones favoritas. Write a description of your dream vacation and your favorite restaurant on that vacation. Then describe it to a classmate. Take turns.

Modelo: *Me gustaría visitar Vancouver en Canadá. Me gustaría visitar el mar y la playa y comer comida del mar. Mi restaurante favorito es de comida del mar y comida alemana.*

____
____
____
____
____
____
____
____

Nombre ______________________________ Fecha ____________

Gramática suplemental

More regular *-er* and *-ir* verbs

Review the formation of regular **-er** and **-ir** verbs on page X of ***Intercambios.*** Then study the additional verbs listed here.

depender de los compañeros para estudiar	***to depend on*** *classmates to study*
recoger (recojo) a una persona / una cosa	***to pick up*** *a person / a thing*
romper las gafas / los anteojos	***to break*** *the eyeglasses*
responder al (a la) profesor(a)	***to answer*** *the professor*
vender libros en la librería	***to sell*** *books at the bookstore*
subir al autobús / **subir de** posición en el trabajo	***to get on*** *the bus /* ***to get*** *promoted at work*

Practiquemos

G3-5 ¡A describir! Describe all the activities that you and your classmates do in one week.

Modelo: Yo *bebo* (beber) café por la mañana.

1. Nosotros ______________ (aprender) mucho en clase de política económica.
2. Tomás y Rebeca ______________ (asistir) a la conferencia del escritor mexicano Carlos Fuentes.
3. Berta ______________ (comer) en casa de su padre los sábados.
4. David y yo ______________ (correr) por el parque los domingos por la tarde.
5. La directora ______________ (decidir) nuestros cursos.
6. Tú ______________ (escribir) una carta electrónica todos los días.
7. Nosotras ______________ (discutir) política con la profesora de ciencias políticas.
8. Alicia ______________ (describir) su pasantía a sus amigos.
9. Pedro y Ramón ______________ (abrir) la ventana de la clase todos los días. ¡Ellos siempre tienen calor!
10. Ellas ______________ (recibir) regalos de cumpleaños.
11. Yo ______________ (ver) películas de video los viernes por la noche.
12. Mis compañeros ______________ (vivir) en una casa muy bonita en las montañas.
13. Juan y Lucinda ______________ (comprender) cuando la profesora habla español rápidamente.
14. Nosotros ______________ (deber) descansar después de los exámenes.
15. Marcos ______________ (romper) la ventana de la clase.

Nombre ______________________________ Fecha ______________

G3-6 En la universidad. Select the appropriate form of the verb to find out what these people do at the university.

Modelo: Nosotros (suben / subimos) al autobús por las mañanas.
Nosotros *subimos* al autobús por las mañanas.

1. Los estudiantes (respondo / responden) a las preguntas del profesor.
2. ¿(Subo / Subes) tú al autobús de la universidad a las siete o a las nueve de la mañana?
3. Nosotros (dependes / dependemos) de los compañeros para las actividades en grupo.
4. El profesor (abres / abre) la puerta de la clase temprano *(early)*.
5. José y Lourdes (rompe / rompen) los anteojos de Teresa.
6. Yo (vendo / vende) libros en la librería por la tarde.
7. Marisa (recogen / recoge) a Carolina para ir a la universidad.
8. En la universidad, mi supervisor del departamento (subo / sube) de posición.

G3-7 ¿Qué deciden? You and your friends are going to Tijuana, Mexico this coming weekend. Combine elements from the three columns to tell what each person will do.

Modelo: *Mercedes depende de su hermano para ir a Tijuana.*

A **¿Quién?**	**B**	**C** **¿Qué?**
Juan, Cristóbal y yo	vender	
Kelly y Miguel	abrir	el periódico de Tijuana
tú	recoger	al autobús temprano para México
nosotros	leer	a sus amigos mexicanos
Alejandro	romper	la ventana del auto
yo	subir	

1. ______________________________
2. ______________________________
3. ______________________________
4. ______________________________
5. ______________________________
6. ______________________________

Nombre ______________________________ Fecha ______________

More practice with the verb *querer*

G3-8 **¿Qué quieren?** These people want different things. Form sentences with the appropriate form of the verb **querer.**

Modelo: Marta / aprender portugués perfectamente
Marta quiere aprender portugués perfectamente.

1. Nosotros / asistir a la universidad en España

   ____

2. Raúl y Elena / correr por el parque

   ____

3. Andrea y yo / comer en la cafetería ahora

   ____

4. Yo / comer en el restaurante tailandés

   ____

5. Manuel / escribir una novela en español

   ____

6. Tú / recibir buenas noticias *(good news)*

   ____

G3-9 **Una invitación.** Complete the following conversation using the verb **querer.** Afterward, practice it with a classmate.

Adriana: Arturo y yo ______________ ver una película.

Alicia: ¿Cuándo ______________ ver ustedes una película, hoy o mañana?

Adriana: ______________ ver una película hoy por la tarde. ¿______________ ir con nosotros, Alicia?

Alicia: ¡Lo siento! Necesito estudiar. ¿Qué película ______________ ver ustedes?

Adriana: Bueno, Arturo ______________ ver una comedia y yo ______________ ver un drama.

Alicia: ¡Disfruten de *(Enjoy)* la película!

Nombre ______________________ Fecha ______________

More practice with *ir* and *ir* + infinitive

G3-10 ¿Adónde vas de vacaciones? You and your friends are going on vacation to different world capitals. Select the proper form of each verb to complete the following sentences.

Modelo: Gloria y Tommy (van / vamos) a Bogotá, Colombia.
Gloria y Tommy *van* a Bogotá, Colombia.

1. Tú (vas / voy) a Santiago, Chile.
2. Lucy (vas / va) a Madrid, España.
3. Yo (voy / van) a Quito, Ecuador.
4. Nosotras (van / vamos) a Lima, Perú.
5. Luis (voy / va) a Ciudad de Panamá, Panamá.
6. Enrique y Patricia (vas / van) a San José, Costa Rica.
7. Tú (vas / van) a Ciudad de México, México.
8. Yo (voy / vas) a Caracas, Venezuela.

G3-11 ¿Adónde van? You and your friends are going to different places and have to tell what you are going to do in those places. Write two activities that you and your friends will do at each place.

Modelo: Donovan va a la librería.
a. *Él va a comprar libros.*
b. *Él va a leer.*

1. Anita va a la casa de Sofía.
   a. ______________________
   b. ______________________
2. Yo voy al parque.
   a. ______________________
   b. ______________________
3. Juan y Rosario van al cine.
   a. ______________________
   b. ______________________
4. Nosotros vamos a la universidad.
   a. ______________________
   b. ______________________
5. Tú vas a un restaurante mexicano.
   a. ______________________
   b. ______________________
6. Ellas van a la fiesta.
   a. ______________________
   b. ______________________

Nombre ______________________________ Fecha ______________

Demonstrative adjectives and demonstrative pronouns

Demonstrative adjectives refer to particular persons, places, things, or ideas, as well as to varying distances in space and time from the speaker. To specify who or what is very far from the speaker and the person spoken to, Spanish speakers use a form of the demonstrative adjective **aquel/aquella/aquellos/aquellas.** These adjectives must agree in gender (masculine or feminine) and number (singular or plural) with the nouns to which they refer.

		Masculine	Feminine
Singular	*(that)*	**aquel** niño	**aquella** niña
Plural	*(those)*	**aquellos** niños	**aquellas** niñas

Demonstrative pronouns are used in place of demonstrative adjectives to refer to particular persons, places, things, or ideas that were already mentioned. To specify someone or something that is very far from the speaker and the person spoken to, Spanish speakers use a form of the demonstrative pronoun **aquél/aquélla/aquéllos/aquéllas.** These pronouns must agree in gender (masculine or feminine) and number (singular or plural) with the nouns to which they refer. Demonstrative pronouns are identical in form to demonstrative adjectives, except that the pronouns carry a written accent mark.

		Masculine	Feminine
Singular	*(that one)*	**aquél** niño	**aquélla** niña
Plural	*(those ones)*	**aquéllos** niños	**aquéllas** niñas

PRACTIQUEMOS

G3-12 En mi opinión... The Stuart family likes to buy products from different countries. Express their opinions according to the model.

Modelo: *Aquel* té de Malasia es exquisito.

1. ______________ sopa *(soup)* de Taiwan está rica.
2. ______________ queso *(cheese)* de Holanda es exquisito.
3. ______________ frijoles de México son buenos.
4. ______________ bananas de Guatemala son deliciosas.
5. ______________ bistec de la Argentina está muy rico.
6. ______________ fruta kiwi de Nueva Zelanda es exótica.
7. ______________ café de Colombia es el mejor del mundo.

Nombre ________________________________ Fecha ______________

G3-13 **¿Cómo son?** Describe lo lejos *(far away)* que están las siguientes personas o cosas de ti, según el modelo.

Modelo: una bicicleta
Aquella bicicleta es vieja. Aquélla es vieja.
unos amigos
Aquellos amigos son simpáticos. Aquéllos son simpáticos.

1. un carro
____
____
2. un pueblo
____
____
3. un parque
____
____
4. una playa
____
____
5. una ciudad
____
____
6. unos parientes
____
____
7. una universidad
____
____
8. unas tiendas
____
____

Nombre ______________________ Fecha ____________

Práctica comunicativa suplemental I

Bingo. Completa el cuadro haciéndole preguntas a tus compañeros. Camina por la clase y hazle preguntas a tus compañeros. Escribe el nombre de la persona que responda afirmativamente. Continúa hasta completar una columna en cualquier dirección para poder gritar *(to shout)* "BINGO".

Vocabulario útil

caminar	*to walk*	frecuentemente	*frequently*
cantar	*to sing*	mucho	*a lot*
cocinar	*to cook*	muy	*very*
comprender	*to understand*	poco	*a little*
duchar(se)	*to shower*	el cabello	*hair*
escuchar	*to listen to*	los mensajes electrónicos	*e-mails*
llegar	*to arrive*	el periódico	*newspaper*
salir	*to leave, go out*	los poemas	*poems*
viajar	*to travel*	la química	*chemistry*
a veces	*sometimes*		

Recibe muchos mensajes electrónicos NOMBRE:	Estudia química NOMBRE:	Aprende francés NOMBRE:	Comprende matemáticas NOMBRE:	Trabaja mucho NOMBRE:
Tiene 21años NOMBRE:	Cocina muy bien NOMBRE:	Bebe ocho vasos de agua al día NOMBRE:	Baila salsa y merengue NOMBRE:	Quiere viajar a España NOMBRE:
Lee el periódico todos los días NOMBRE:	Mira mucha televisión NOMBRE:	Sale todos los fines de semana a bailar NOMBRE:	Va al cine mucho NOMBRE:	Habla por teléfono frecuentemente NOMBRE:
Camina a la universidad NOMBRE:	Escribe poemas NOMBRE:	Escucha la radio hispana NOMBRE:	No hace ejercicios NOMBRE:	Llega a clase tarde NOMBRE:
Come en restaurantes los sábados NOMBRE:	Canta al ducharse NOMBRE:	Ve a su familia frecuentemente NOMBRE:	Vive en el dormitorio NOMBRE:	Cambia su color de cabello a veces NOMBRE:

Modelo: ¿Quién recibe muchos mensajes electrónicos?
NOMBRE: Nancy

Nombre ______________________________ Fecha ______________

Práctica comunicativa suplemental II

Planes. Completa tu horario para esta semana y luego haz planes para hacer tres cosas con un(a) compañero(a).

Modelo: **A:** *¿Quieres ir al cine el martes por la tarde?*
B: *No puedo ir porque voy a ir al gimnasio. ¿Quieres ir al cine el miércoles?*
A: *Sí, buena idea.*

Vocabulario útil

cine	*movie theater*
gimnasio	*gym*
por la mañana	*in the morning*
por la noche	*at night*
por la tarde	*in the afternoon*
supermercado	*supermarket*
teatro	*theater*
tengo que + infinitivo	*I have to + infinitive*
voy a ir a + lugar	*I am going to + place*

Lunes	Martes	Miércoles	Jueves	Viernes	Sábado	Domingo

Nombre ______________________ Fecha ______________

PASO 2 Ecoturismo en Centroamérica

LECCIÓN 4 ¡TENEMOS QUE ESTAR DE ACUERDO!

Práctica suplemental

VOCABULARIO SUPLEMENTAL

La familia y los parientes

la bisabuela	*great-grandmother*
el bisabuelo	*great-grandfather*
la comadre	*the female who baptized another person's son or daughter*
el compadre	*the male who baptized another person's son or daughter*
los compadres	*male and female who baptized another person's son or daughter*
la madrina	*godmother*
el padrino	*godfather*
los padrinos	*godparents*
la ahijada	*goddaughter*
el ahijado	*godson*
la suegra	*mother-in-law*
el suegro	*father-in-law*
los suegros	*parents-in-law*
la nuera	*daughter-in-law*
el yerno	*son-in-law*
la compañera	*female partner, companion*
el compañero	*male partner, companion*
la ex-esposa	*ex-wife*
el ex-esposo	*ex-husband*
el hermanastro	*stepbrother*
la hermanastra	*stepsister*
el medio hermano	*half-brother*
la media hermana	*half-sister*

Nombre ______________________ Fecha ____________

Practiquemos

V4-1 Los parientes. Completa las oraciones con el nombre del pariente apropiado. Puedes usar el vocabulario que está en la **Lección 4** del libro.

Modelo: Los abuelos de mi madre son mis *bisabuelos.*

1. La primera esposa de mi padre es ahora su ______________.
2. El hijo de mi madrastra y de mi padre es mi ______________.
3. Los padres de mi esposa son mis ______________.
4. Mi esposa es la ______________ de mis padres.
5. Yo soy el ______________ del hijo de mi hermana. Él es mi ______________ y soy el ______________ de mi hermana.
6. El abuelo de mi papá es mi ______________.
7. Mi comadre Mary Ellen es la ______________ de mi hija.
8. Los ______________ son personas muy especiales en la cultura hispana.
9. La madre de mi abuela es mi ______________.
10. La hija de mi padrastro es mi ______________.

V4-2 ¿Verdadero o falso? Lee la siguiente historia de la telenovela *(soap opera)* sobre la familia Ribadeneira y marca **verdadero** o **falso,** según la historia.

Eduardo Ribadeneira tiene una ex-esposa, Carmen, que es muy descortés y deshonesta con la nueva compañera de él, que se llama Andrea. Andrea es la madrina de la hija de Eduardo, que se llama Ángela, y por eso, además de ser compañeros, ellos son compadres. El abuelo de Eduardo quiere mucho a Ángela y ésta también a él. Ellos siempre caminan juntos por el parque y van a comer a los restaurantes.

	V	F
1. La ex-esposa de Eduardo Ribadeneira se llama Andrea.	________	________
2. Ángela es la ahijada de Andrea.	________	________
3. Andrea y Eduardo son suegros de Carmen.	________	________
4. Andrea y Eduardo son compadres.	________	________
5. Ángela quiere mucho a su bisabuelo.	________	________

Nombre ______________________ Fecha ____________

La casa

la cocina	*kitchen*
los utensilios de cocina	*kitchen utensils*
la olla	*pot*
la sartén	*frying pan*
el cuarto de baño	*bathroom*
la cortina de baño	*bathroom curtain*
el jabón	*soap*
la toalla	*towel*
el cuarto / la habitación	*bedroom*
el aire acondicionado	*air conditioning*
la alfombra	*rug*
la calefacción	*heater*
la cómoda	*dresser*
el espejo	*mirror*
para la cama	*bedding*
la almohada	*pillow*
la cobija / la manta	*blanket*
la sábana	*sheet*
la sala	*living room*
la chimenea	*fireplace*
el jardín	*backyard; garden*
la terraza	*terrace*
la parrilla / la barbacoa	*barbecue*
la piscina / la alberca	*swimming pool*

Nombre ______________________ Fecha ______________

Practiquemos

V4-3 En la casa. Marca en qué lugar de la casa están estas cosas. Descríbele lo que hay en tu casa a tu compañero(a) y díle qué hace en ese lugar. Túrnense *(Take turns)* para hacer la descripción.

Modelo: *En mi jardín, hay una parrilla nueva y pequeña. Invito a mis amigos a comer una parrillada (barbecued meat and vegetables) los fines de semana.*

	La cocina	El baño	El cuarto/ La habitación	La sala	El jardín
la parrilla / la barbacoa					
el aire acondicionado					
el espejo					
la piscina / la alberca					
la chimenea					
la toalla					
la sartén					
la almohada					
la calefacción					
la alfombra					

V4-4 ¿Qué tienes en tu casa? Habla con un(a) compañero(a) de clase y házle las siguientes preguntas.

1. ¿Tienes jardín o terraza en tu casa? ¿Es grande o pequeño(a)?
2. ¿Tienes piscina o alberca en tu jardín?
3. ¿Tienes aire acondicionado, calefacción o chimenea en tu casa?
4. ¿Te gustaría tener una cocina / un cuarto de baño más grande y amplia(o)?
5. ¿Invitas a tus amigos a comer barbacoa los fines de semana?

V4-5 ¿Qué lugar de su casa te gusta más? Descríbele a un(a) compañero(a) de clase el lugar de tu casa que a ti te gusta más y explícale por qué. Puedes escribir tu respuesta.

Modelo: *A mí me gusta el jardín porque tiene una piscina / alberca. Me gusta hacer ejercicio físico.*

____

____

____

Nombre ______________________ Fecha ______________

Gramática suplemental

Estar with adjectives

Estoy **feliz.**	*I am happy.*
Estoy **cansado.**	*I am tired.*
Estás **contento(a).**	*You are content/happy.*
Está **estupendo(a).**	*He/She/It is stupendous/fantastic.*
Estamos **orgullosos.**	*We are proud.*
Estamos **ocupados.**	*We are busy.*
Están **horribles.**	*They are horrible.*
Están **locos.**	*They are crazy.*

Otros adjetivos

arreglado(a)	*arranged*
desarreglado(a)	*disorderly*
limpio(a)	*clean*
listo(a)	*ready*
nervioso(a)	*nervous*
sucio(a)	*dirty*
terrible	*terrible*

Practiquemos

G4-6 **¿Cómo estás?** Escribe una oración con dos adjetivos para describir cómo estás tú en las siguientes situaciones. Luego discute con un(a) compañero(a) de clase y compara sus respuestas.

Modelo: en la universidad
Estoy contento(a) y listo(a) para (in order to) *estudiar.*

1. en una fiesta ______________________
2. en la clase de español ______________________
3. en casa ______________________
4. en un examen ______________________
5. en una entrevista de trabajo ______________________

G4-7 **¿Cómo está la universidad... ?** Escribe una oración con adjetivos para describir cómo están los siguientes lugares. Luego habla con un(a) compañero(a) de clase y compara sus respuestas.

Modelo: la universidad
Está lista para los estudiantes y está limpia.

1. tu casa ______________________
2. tu cuarto de baño ______________________
3. tu trabajo ______________________
4. la cafetería de la universidad ______________________
5. tu restaurante favorito ______________________

Nombre ______________________ Fecha ______________

G4-8 La familia de Luis. Describe los siguientes dibujos usando los siguientes adjetivos con **estar.**

enfermo(a) enojado(a) preocupado(a) contento triste ocupado(a)

1. ______________________

2. ______________________

3. ______________________

4. ______________________

Nombre ______________________________ Fecha ______________

Change of meaning with *ser* and *estar* + adjective
Some adjectives can be used with either **ser** or **estar,** depending on the meaning one intends to express.

Study the meaning of these sentences.

—¿Cómo **es** usted? —**Soy** joven y **soy** inteligente.	—*What are you like?* (appearance, personality) —*I'm young and I'm intelligent.*
—¿Cómo **está** usted? —**Estoy** cansado, pero **estoy** contento.	—*How are you?* (physical or mental health) —*I'm tired, but I'm happy.*
Eres listo, Mario. ¿**Estás** listo, Mario?	*You're smart, Mario.* (personality trait) *Are you ready, Mario?* (conditional state)
Eres guapo, papá. **Estás** guapo, papá.	*You're handsome, Dad.* (inherent trait) *You look handsome, Dad.* (physical state)
Mis abuelos **son** ricos. Sus tacos **están** ricos.	*My grandparents are rich.* (financial status) *Their tacos are delicious.* (conditional state)
Estoy enferma hoy, ¡pero no **soy** enferma!	*I'm sick today,* (physical state) *but I'm not a sickly person!* (inherent trait)
Mi tía **es** aburrida y siempre **está** aburrida.	*My aunt is boring and* (personality trait) *she's always bored.* (emotional state)
Isabel **es** casada. Isabel **está** casada.	*Isabel is a married woman.* (inherent fact) *Isabel is married.* (marital status)
Grisela **es** soltera.	*Grisela is a single woman.* (marital status)

Practiquemos

G4-9 ***¿Ser* o *estar?*** Completa las siguientes conversaciones, usando la forma correcta de **ser** o **estar** según el contexto.

1. —¿Cómo ______________ la familia, Mario?

   —Todos bien, gracias.

   —¿Y tu abuela? ¿Cómo ______________?

   —Todavía un poco enferma.

   —Ay, pobrecita *(poor thing)*.

2. —Quiero conocer a tu amigo, Eduardo. ¿Cómo ______________?

   —Pues, Eduardo ______________ alto, ______________ listo y ______________ generoso.

   —¿También ______________ rico Eduardo?

   —No, no ______________ rico.

   —¿Y ______________ casado tu amigo?

   —No, Eduardo todavía ______________ soltero.

3. —¡Qué bonito ____________ tu auto, Hilda!

—Gracias. Era *(It used to be)* el auto de mi esposo.

—¿Cómo? No comprendo. ¿Qué pasó?

—Jorge y yo ____________ divorciados ahora.

—Ay no, ¡por Dios! ¿Pero por qué, Hilda?

—Él cree que yo ____________ muy aburrida.

—¡Y yo creo que él ____________ aburrido de vivir!

G4-10 Preguntas personales. Contesta las siguientes preguntas con oraciones completas.

1. ¿Cómo está usted hoy?

____

2. ¿Cómo es usted?

____

3. ¿Es usted listo(a) o muy listo(a)?

____

4. ¿Está usted casado(a) o es soltero(a)?

____

5. ¿Quiere usted ser rico(a)?

____

6. ¿Cuándo está usted aburrido(a)?

____

7. ¿Qué hace usted cuando está aburrido(a)?

____

8. ¿Quién es enfermo en su familia?

____

9. ¿Quién está enfermo en su familia?

____

10. ¿Qué hace usted cuando está muy enfermo(a)?

____

Nombre ______________________ Fecha ____________

G4-11 En Ciudad de Guatemala. Tomás Álvarez está en Guatemala para visitar a Luis y a su familia. Luis le escribe un mensaje electrónico *(e-mail)* a su amiga Alicia Benson en Monterrey, México. Completa las ideas de Tomás y escribe la forma de **yo** de los siguientes verbos: **estar, conocer, saber, dar, hacer, poner, traer, salir.**

Modelo: *Doy* paseos por la ciudad por las tardes.
Aquí en Guatemala todos los días yo...

1. ______________ contento de estar aquí en Guatemala.
2. ______________ ejercicio y corro por el parque.
3. ______________ a bailar por las noches.
4. ______________ un restaurante nuevo de comida guatemalteca todas las noches.
5. ______________ hablar un poco más de maya.
6. Les ______________ clases de inglés a los estudiantes de la hermana de Luis.
7. ______________ música de salsa en la radio.
8. Les ______________ regalos a los sobrinos de Luis.

G4-12 ¿Qué hacen? Para saber lo que hacen estas personas, completa los espacios en blanco con la forma apropiada del verbo.

Modelo: Tú *haces* (hacer / salir) la tarea todos los días.

1. Ileana y Tomás ______________ (conocer / saber) una nueva ruina maya todos los fines de semana.
2. ¿______________ (Traer / Dar) Cristina a sus hijos a su casa?
3. Nosotros ______________ (poner / salir) a caminar por la ciudad todas las tardes.
4. Yo ______________ (estar / hacer) lista para conocer la ciudad de Antigua.
5. Ellos ______________ (poner / dar) música guatemalteca todo el día.
6. Tomás ______________ (estar / dar) clases de computación a los sobrinos de Luis.
7. Tú ______________ (conocer / saber) que la familia de Luis ______________ (traer / estar) contenta con tu visita a Guatemala.
8. Yo les ______________ (traer / poner) regalos a la familia de Luis porque son muy amables con nosotros.
9. Nosotros ______________ (hacer / traer) el trabajo en computadoras todas las mañanas.
10. ¿______________ (Salir / Poner) ellos a comer esta noche?

Nombre ______________________ Fecha ______________

Práctica comunicativa suplemental I

La familia. Pregunta a tus compañeros la siguiente información. Escribe el nombre de la persona que responda afirmativamente a tu pregunta. Trata de encontrar *(to find)* una persona diferente para cada pregunta.

Vocabulario útil

abuelo(a)	grandfather/grandmother
cuñado(a)	brother-in-law/sister-in-law
estar casado(a)	to be married
hermanastro(a)	stepbrother/stepsister
hijo(a) único(a)	only child
primos	cousins
sabe	he/she knows
simpático(a)	nice
suegro(a)	father-in-law/mother-in-law

¿Quién... ?	Nombre
1. es hijo(a) único(a)	
2. no tiene primos	
3. conoce a sus abuelos	
4. sabe la edad de su abuelo	
5. tiene un(a) cuñado(a) simpático(a)	
6. tiene hermanastros	
7. está casado(a)	
8. tiene hijos	
9. tiene unos suegros fantásticos	
10. es soltero(a)	

Nombre ______________________________ Fecha ______________

Práctica comunicativa suplemental II

¡Qué problemas! En parejas, lean los problemas de la familia de Ileana y escriban recomendaciones para cada uno *(for each one)*.

Modelo: La prima de Ileana quiere tener más amigos. Está sola.
Ileana *tiene que salir* con su prima.

Vocabulario útil

cansado	*tired*
levantarse temprano	*to wake up early*
perder peso	*to lose weight*
tener que + infinitivo	*to have to + infinitive*

1. La mamá de Ileana quiere perder peso.

   ____

2. El papá está muy cansado. Trabaja diez horas al día.

   ____

3. El tío siempre llega tarde a su trabajo.

   ____

4. La abuela no come nada.

   ____

Ahora, pregúntale a tu compañero(a) qué problemas tiene y dile qué tiene que hacer.

Nombre ______________________ Fecha ____________

LECCIÓN 5 ¿QUÉ CARRERA QUIERES SEGUIR?

Práctica suplemental

VOCABULARIO SUPLEMENTAL

Profesiones y ocupaciones	***Professions and occupations***
el actor / la actriz	*actor/actress*
el ama de casa	*homemaker*
el (la) analista de sistemas	*systems analyst*
la azafata / el sobrecargo	*flight attendant*
el (la) bibliotecario(a)	*librarian*
el (la) bombero(a)	*firefighter*
el (la) carpintero(a)	*carpenter*
el (la) ejecutivo(a)	*executive*
el (la) electricista	*electrician*
el (la) empleado(a)	*employee*
el (la) intérprete	*interpreter; translator*
el (la) juez(a)	*judge*
el (la) obrero(a)	*worker*
el (la) piloto	*pilot*
el (la) técnico(a)	*technician*

PRACTIQUEMOS

V5-1 Cursos y profesiones. Haz una lista con un(a) compañero(a) de clase de los cursos que deben tomar si quieren tener las siguientes profesiones u ocupaciones *(occupations)*. Pueden usar la lista de cursos que sigue o también pueden revisar la **Lección 2** (***WorkFiles,*** página xx) (**actuación** *(acting)*, **ciencias, contabilidad, computación, economía, lenguas, electricidad, matemáticas, informática, ética, finanzas, comercio internacional, historia**).

Modelo: el (la) técnico de computación
computación, matemáticas, informática

1. el (la) electricista ______________________
2. el (la) juez(a) ______________________
3. el (la) analista de sistemas ______________________
4. el (la) ejecutivo(a) ______________________
5. el (la) intérprete ______________________
6. el actor / la actriz ______________________

Nombre ______________________ Fecha ______________

V5-2 **¿Qué hacen estas personas?** Decide con un(a) compañero(a) de clase la profesión de la persona que se describe y los beneficios *(benefits)* que tiene esta profesión.

Modelo: Esta persona trabaja con libros en la universidad.
Es el (la) bibliotecario(a) y ayuda (helps) *a los estudiantes de la universidad.*

1. Esta persona trabaja con máquinas *(machines)* en la industria.

____

____

2. Esta persona trabaja con niños en la casa.

____

____

3. Esta persona ayuda a poner la electricidad en las casas para poder vivir cómodamente.

____

____

4. Esta persona trabaja en un banco o en una compañía grande.

____

____

5. Esta persona trabaja como asistente del (de la) director(a) de un banco, de una universidad o de una compañía.

____

____

6. Estas personas visitan muchos lugares del mundo frecuentemente.

____

____

Nombre ______________________ Fecha ______________

Lugares de trabajo

el aeropuerto	*airport*
la compañía / la empresa	*company*
el consultorio médico	*doctor's office*
la estación de bomberos	*fire station*
la estación de radio	*radio station*
la gasolinera	*gas station*
la industria / la fábrica	*industry/factory*
la oficina de correos	*post office*
la tienda de comestibles	*market*

Practiquemos

V5-3 **¿Dónde trabaja, quién trabaja y qué hace?** Discute con un(a) compañero(a) de clase y llena el cuadro con la información necesaria sobre estas profesiones.

¿Dónde?	¿Quién?	¿Qué hace?
El aeropuerto		
	El (La) empleado(a)	
La fábrica		
		Ayuda a los enfermos
	El (La) bombero(a)	
La compañía / la empresa		
La gasolinera		
	El (La) vendedor(a) en el mercado	

V5-4 **¿Dónde te gustaría trabajar?** Habla con un(a) compañero(a) de clase sobre tu lugar de trabajo ideal y explícale *(explain)* por qué es el trabajo ideal para ti.

Modelo: —¿Dónde te gustaría trabajar?
—*Me gustaría trabajar en el aeropuerto en una línea aérea como azafata / sobrecargo para viajar por todo el mundo.*

Nombre ______________________________ Fecha ______________

Gramática suplemental

Present tense of verbs with stem vowel change
There are three types of vowel changes that occur in the stem of some Spanish infinitives in the present tense. The following verbs change their stem vowel in the **yo, tú, usted/él/ella,** and **ustedes/ellos/ellas** forms.

Stem-Changing *e* → *ie* Verbs		**Stem-Changing *o* → *ue* Verbs**		**Stem-Changing *e* → *i* Verbs**	
cerrar	*to close*	contar	*to tell; to count*	reír	*to laugh*
empezar	*to start, begin*	costar	*to cost*	repetir	*to repeat*
entender	*to understand*	encontrar	*to meet; to find*	sonreír	*to smile*
perder	*to lose*	morir	*to die*		
sentir	*to regret*	recordar	*to remember*		

Practiquemos

G5-5 En clase. Completa las siguientes oraciones con la forma correcta de los verbos adecuados.

cerrar contar empezar entender perder
reír repetir sonreír

Mi clase de español __________ a las diez de la mañana. Mi profesora habla rápidamente, pero yo __________ mucho de lo que ella dice. Muchas veces, yo __________ el libro de español cuando ella __________ sus aventuras en los países de habla española. Sus aventuras son cómicas y, por eso, mis compañeros y yo __________ mucho. A veces (yo) __________ la concentración, pero mi profesora tiene mucha paciencia; ella me __________ las oraciones y las frases que no comprendo. Me gusta mucho mi clase, especialmente mi profesora.

G5-6 Preguntas personales. Contesta las siguientes preguntas con oraciones completas.

1. ¿Cuánto cuestan tus textos de español?
____
2. ¿A qué hora empieza tu clase de español?
____
3. ¿Cuándo empiezas a estudiar para un examen?
____
4. ¿Qué no entiendes muy bien en tu clase de español?
____
5. ¿Qué haces cuando no entiendes a tu profesor(a)?
____
6. ¿Encuentras pocos o muchos problemas para aprender español?
____

Nombre ______________________ Fecha ______________

7. ¿Recuerdas el vocabulario fácilmente o con dificultad?

____

8. ¿Qué haces cuando no recuerdas bien una palabra o una frase?

____

9. ¿De qué te ríes en tu clase de español?

____

10. ¿Qué vas a recordar de tu clase?

____

Present progressive

G5-7 En la clase de español. Completa las oraciones para saber lo que están haciendo ahora estas personas en la clase de español.

Modelo: La profesora *está explicando* (explicar) los verbos irregulares ahora.

1. Los estudiantes ______________ (escuchar) a la profesora ahora.
2. Marcie y Bo ______________ (escribir) notas en el cuaderno.
3. Andy ______________ (hacer) preguntas sobre los verbos.
4. Tú ______________ (leer) las explicaciones en el libro ahora.
5. Yo ______________ (trabajar) con mi compañero(a) de clase.
6. Nosotros ______________ (discutir) las respuestas de los ejercicios en este momento.

G5-8 El domingo. ¿Qué están haciendo estas personas hoy domingo por la mañana?

Modelo: Ernesto / jugar al tenis
Ernesto está jugando al tenis.

1. Luisa y Juan / leer el periódico

____

2. Federico y yo / preparar el almuerzo

____

3. Sofía y tú / estudiar español

____

4. Yo / descansar en casa

____

5. Ana / mirar las noticias en la televisión

____

6. Tú / pedir una pizza por teléfono

____

7. Ileana / dormir la siesta

____

8. Nosotros / escribir mensajes electrónicos a nuestros amigos

____

Nombre ______________________ Fecha ____________

Práctica comunicativa suplemental I

Buscando trabajo. En grupos de tres, encuentren al mejor candidato para el trabajo. Lean la descripción del trabajo y las características de los candidatos y seleccionen a uno. Comparen su selección con la de los otros grupos.

Modelo: *Pienso que X tiene que ser el elegido porque tiene mucha experiencia y...*

Vocabulario útil

ascender	*to climb up the ladder*
buscar	*to look for*
elegido	*chosen*
mercadeo y publicidad	*marketing*
vendedor(a)	*salesperson*
ventas al por mayor	*wholesale*

Gerente para una compañía de ventas

Se necesita a una persona responsable, con experiencia en ventas. Buscamos una persona que pueda trabajar con un grupo con mucha diversidad. La persona tiene que tener capacidad para entrenar a los nuevos vendedores y decidir cómo organizar las campañas de mercadeo.

Candidatos

- Maya Hinojosa. MBA de una universidad muy prestigiosa. Tiene experiencia sólo de un año como voluntaria en una empresa de ventas. Es muy responsable y tiene muy buenas recomendaciones de sus supervisores. Tiene iniciativa.
- Juan Campana. Trabaja en ventas desde el año 2000. Trabajó en una pequeña empresa de ventas al por mayor como gerente por varios años. Ahora quiere más responsabilidades y la oportunidad de ascender en la compañía. No tiene título de especialización en mercadeo y publicidad.
- Julián Martínez. Tiene un MBA de una pequeña universidad no muy conocida. Trabaja independientemente desde hace tres años organizando campañas de mercadeo. Quiere un trabajo más estable. Es muy creativo; tiene ideas revolucionarias sobre ventas.

Nombre ______________________ Fecha __________

Práctica comunicativa suplemental II

El trabajo perfecto. En parejas, busquen un trabajo. ¿Cuál de estas cosas quieren en su trabajo? Lean el cuadro y marquen las actividades que quieren hacer.

Vocabulario útil

ayudar	*to help*
gente	*people*
sueldo	*salary*
al aire libre	*outdoors*
exterior	*foreign country*
mejor	*better*
Me gusta...	*I like . . .*
No me gusta...	*I don't like . . .*
¿Cuál de estas cosas quieres en tu trabajo?	*Which of these things do you want in your job?*
¿Cuál es el mejor trabajo para ti?	*Which is the best job for you?*

Quieres...
hablar con la gente
ayudar a la gente
trabajar en el exterior
actuar frente a la gente
llevar uniforme
usar una computadora
viajar
tener un buen sueldo
trabajar en casa
trabajar de 9 a 5
hablar español
tener compañeros de trabajo
trabajar al aire libre

Pregúntale a tu compañero(a) lo que quiere hacer. Luego deciden cuál es el mejor trabajo para cada uno.

Nombre ______________________ Fecha ____________

LECCIÓN 6 ¡HACE MUCHO CALOR EN PANAMÁ!

Práctica suplemental

VOCABULARIO SUPLEMENTAL

Expressions with *tener*

Spanish speakers use the verb **tener** in many idiomatic expressions, as shown in the following list.

tener... años *to be . . . years old*
tener calor *to be hot*
tener celos *to be jealous*
tener cuidado *to be careful*
tener éxito *to be successful*
tener frío *to be cold*
tener ganas de (+ *infinitive*) *to feel like (doing something)*
tener hambre *to be hungry*
tener miedo *to be afraid*
tener prisa *to be in a hurry*
tener que (+ *infinitive*) *to have to (do something)*
(no) tener razón *to be right (wrong)*
tener sed *to be thirsty*
tener sueño *to be sleepy*
tener suerte *to be lucky*
tener vergüenza *to be ashamed*

—¿Cuántos **años tienes**? *How old are you?*
—**Tengo** treinta **años.** *I am thirty years old.*

—**¿Tienen** ustedes **hambre**? *Are you hungry?*
—No, pero **tenemos sed.** *No, but we're thirsty.*

—¿Qué **tienes que** hacer hoy? *What do you have to do today?*
—**Tengo que** estudiar, pero **tengo ganas de** dormir. *I have to study, but I feel like sleeping.*

How to use these *tener* expressions

1. For emphasis, use the adjective **mucho,** which must match the gender (masculine or feminine) and number (singular or plural) of its noun.

    Tengo **mucha** razón. *I am very right.*
    Tengo **muchos** celos. *I am very jealous.*
    Tengo **mucha** prisa. *I am in a big hurry.*
    Tengo **mucho** frío / calor. *I am very cold/hot.*
    Tengo **mucha** hambre / sed. *I am very hungry/thirsty.*

2. An infinitive follows two of the **tener** expressions above.

    Tengo ganas de comer helado. *I feel like eating ice cream.*
    Tengo que salir ahora. *I have to leave now.*

Nombre ______________________________ Fecha ______________

Practiquemos

V6-1 **¿Qué tienen?** Usando las expresiones **tener frío / calor / hambre / sed / sueño,** completa las oraciones para describir lo que tienen estas personas.

Modelo: Dennis tiene *frío* ya que la temperatura está en –15°F en Wisconsin.

1. Diana y Lisa tienen ______________ después de estudiar ocho horas.
2. Yo tengo ______________ pues no como desde esta mañana.
3. ¡No hay viento y hace mucho sol! Ellas tienen mucho ______________.
4. ¡Hace mucho calor y Luisa corre cinco millas! Ella tiene ______________.
5. En Canadá, durante el invierno, mis primos tienen mucho ______________.
6. Tú tienes ______________ después de levantarte temprano en la mañana.

V6-2 **Para tener éxito...** Completa el párrafo con las expresiones **tener cuidado / prisa / miedo / éxito** para comprender el mensaje.

Modelo: Para tener *éxito* en los negocios, hay que tener mucho *cuidado* al leer el contrato.

Para tener _________ en los estudios en la universidad, es necesario tener _________ cuando estudiamos o hacemos las tareas. Es necesario tener _________ para llegar a las clases a tiempo y tener un poco de _________ de los exámenes para estudiar muchas horas todos los días. Así, vamos a tener mucho _________ en los estudios universitarios.

V6-3 **Cosas del corazón *(heart)*.** Completa el siguiente anuncio con las expresiones **tener razón / suerte / paciencia / celos** para saber qué hay que hacer con el corazón.

En cosas del corazón, hay que tener mucha _________ para poder encontrar a la persona perfecta y tener mucha _________ una vez que usted encuentra al amor *(love)* de su vida. No siempre usted tiene _________ en lo que dice o en lo que piensa y a veces la persona que usted quiere tiene _________ de otras personas sin tener _________.
¡Así que usted necesita mucha _________ para el amor!

Nombre ______________________________ Fecha ______________

V6-4 ¿Qué tienen? Completa las oraciones con las expresiones **tener razón / suerte / paciencia / celos** para saber lo que tienen estas personas.

Modelo: Luis tiene *razón* al decir que estudiar matemáticas es difícil.

1. Michelle tiene ______________ cuando ayuda a Gerard con su tarea de matemáticas. La tarea es muy difícil y complicada.
2. Luis es novio de Michelle y tiene muchos ______________ de Gerard.
3. Luis tiene ______________ de tener una novia como Michelle y Gerard tiene ______________ de tener una amiga como Michelle.
4. Luis no tiene ______________ de tener ______________ de Gerard.
5. Michelle tiene mucha ______________ con Luis y con Gerard.

V6-5 Problemas y soluciones. Escoge las soluciones adecuadas para los problemas.

	Problemas	Soluciones
____	1. Tengo vergüenza.	a. Tome agua.
____	2. Tengo mucha sed.	b. Duerma una siesta.
____	3. No tengo cuidado.	c. Tome un refresco frío.
____	4. Tengo mucho frío.	d. Póngase un suéter.
____	5. Tengo sueño ahora.	e. Tenga más cuidado.
____	6. Tengo mucho calor.	f. Sea más persistente.
____	7. Tengo hambre ahora.	g. Tenga más paciencia.
____	8. Tengo mucha prisa.	h. Coma algo delicioso.
____	9. No tengo razón. ¡Uy!	i. Piense positivamente.
____	10. Tengo celos, a veces.	j. No se preocupe usted.
____	11. Tengo miedo de usted.	k. Hable con un(a) amigo(a).
____	12. No tengo mucho éxito.	l. No tenga miedo de nadie.

V6-6 Preguntas personales. Responde a las siguientes preguntas con oraciones completas.

Mis preferencias

1. ¿Qué bebes cuando tienes mucha sed?

____

2. ¿Qué comes cuando tienes mucha hambre?

____

3. ¿Qué haces cuando tienes sueño pero tienes que trabajar?

____

4. Cuando tienes frío, ¿qué haces? ¿y cuando tienes calor?

____

Nombre ______________________ Fecha ____________

5. ¿Cuándo tienes prisa? ¿Qué problemas te ocurren a ti cuando tienes mucha prisa?

____

6. ¿Qué tienes ganas de hacer mañana? ¿y este fin de semana?

____

Mis emociones

7. ¿En qué tienes éxito? ¿En qué no tienes mucho éxito?

____

8. ¿Qué haces cuando otra persona te dice que no tienes razón?

____

9. ¿Qué ocurrió un día en que tuviste mucha suerte?

____

10. ¿Tienes pocos celos o muchos celos?

____

11. ¿De qué no tienes vergüenza en tu vida?

____

12. ¿De qué o de quién tienes miedo? ¿Cómo puedes resolver ese problema?

____

Nombre ______________________ Fecha ______________

GRAMÁTICA SUPLEMENTAL

More practice with reflexive verbs

Reflexive verbs are usually used to refer to one's daily activities. These verbs have a reflexive pronoun that refers to the same person or thing as the subject. The verb root is conjugated in the same way regular verbs are.

Levantarse			*(to get up)*
(yo)	***me***	**levanto**	*I get up*
(tú)	***te***	**levantas**	*you get up*
(usted, él/ella)	***se***	**levanta**	*you get up, he/she gets up*
(nosotros/nosotras)	***nos***	**levantamos**	*we get up*
(vosotros/vosotras)	***os***	**levantáis**	*you get up*
(ustedes, ellos/ellas)	***se***	**levantan**	*you/they get up*

1. The reflexive pronoun is placed before the conjugated verb or after the infinitive, attached to the verb.

   quedarse *(to stay)*
   Me quiero quedar. o: Quiero queda**rme.** — *I want to stay.*

2. For most reflexive verbs there is a corresponding nonreflexive form. In these cases meaning might change.

   dormir *(to sleep)*
   Siempre **duermo** ocho horas. — *I always sleep eight hours.*

   dormirse *(to fall asleep)*
   Siempre **me duermo** a las ocho. — *I always fall asleep at eight o'clock.*

3. Reflexive verbs can also express a reciprocal action.

   Llamo a mi mamá frecuentemente. — *I call my mother frequently.*
   Mi mamá y yo **nos llamamos** frecuentemente. — *My mother and I call each other frequently.*

4. In most cases, reflexive verbs express an action that the subject does to itself, and nonreflexive verbs indicate an action that the subject does to someone else.

   Me divierto con mis invitados. — *I have fun with my guests.*
   Divierto a mis invitados. — *I entertain my guests.*

Some examples of reflexive verbs:

acostarse (ue)	*to go to bed*	levantarse	*to get up*
afeitarse	*to shave*	maquillarse	*to put on makeup*
atarse los cordones	*to tie one's shoes*	ponerse	*to put on*
cepillarse	*to brush (hair, teeth . . .)*	quemarse	*to get burned*
cortarse el cabello	*to get a haircut*	reunirse (ú)	*to get together*
darse prisa	*to hurry up*	romperse	*to break (a part of one's body)*
desayunarse	*to eat breakfast*		
despertarse (ie)	*to wake up*	sentarse (ie)	*to sit down*
ducharse	*to take a shower*	vestirse (i)	*to get dressed*
lavarse	*to wash (oneself)*		

Nombre ______________________________ Fecha ______________

PRACTIQUEMOS

G6-7 Preguntas personales. ¿Cuál es tu rutina? Contesta las siguientes preguntas sobre tu vida, tu familia y tus amigos. Usa la forma correcta del verbo reflexivo en oraciones completas.

1. ¿A qué hora te despiertas todos los días?

   ____

2. ¿Tus amigos se afeitan todas las mañanas?

   ____

3. ¿Tus amigas se maquillan por la mañana?

   ____

4. ¿A qué hora se acuestan en tu casa?

   ____

5. ¿Cuántas veces a la semana nos reunimos con la clase de español?

   ____

G6-8 ¿Qué van a hacer? Con oraciones completas, indica qué planes tienen estas personas para el futuro.

Modelo: tú / no acostarse temprano / el viernes
Tú no vas a acostarte temprano el viernes.

1. Jane / ducharse / antes de salir

   ____

2. Víctor y José / reunirse con amigos / el sábado

   ____

3. María y José / quedarse en casa / el fin de semana

   ____

4. tú / lavarse el cabello / esta noche

   ____

5. Joaquín / acostarse temprano / el domingo

   ____

Nombre ______________________ Fecha ____________

Reflexive and Nonreflexive Verbs

1. Some Spanish verbs can be used reflexively or nonreflexively, depending on the meaning one intends to express. Study the meaning of the boldfaced verbs in the following sentences.
2. Reflexive pronouns can be used to express *one another* and *each other.*

—Yolanda y Andrés **se conocen** bien. *Yolanda and Andrés know each other well.*
—Sí. Y **se quieren** mucho también. *Yes. And they love each other very much, too.*

Nonreflexive	Reflexive
bañar *to bathe* Yolanda va a **bañar** a su niño Tito.	**bañarse** *to take a bath* Después ella va a **bañarse** también.
despertar *to awaken* Andrés no quiere **despertar** a Tito.	**despertarse** *to wake up* Andrés **se despierta** muy temprano.
dormir *to sleep* Tito **duerme** muy bien toda la noche.	**dormirse** *to fall asleep* Tito **se duerme** mirando televisión.
enojar *to anger* A veces Tito **enoja** a sus padres.	**enojarse** *to get angry* A veces Tito **se enoja** con ellos.
ir *to go* Yolanda y Tito **van** a la tienda pronto.	**irse** *to go away* Ellos **se van** el sábado por la mañana.
lavar *to wash* Yolanda **lava** los platos todos los días.	**lavarse** *to wash (oneself)* Después Yolanda **se lava** las manos.
llamar *to call* Yolanda **llama** por teléfono a su tía.	**llamarse** *to be named* Ella **se llama** María Alicia Ixtamazic.
poner *to put* Andrés **pone** el pijama en la cama.	**ponerse** *to put on (oneself)* Andrés **se pone** el pijama a las once.
quitar *to take (off, away)* Andrés **quita** el suéter de la silla.	**quitarse** *to take off (oneself)* Cuando hace calor, **se quita** el suéter.
vestir *to dress* Yolanda **viste** a Tito por la mañana.	**vestirse** *to get dressed* Luego ella se baña y **se viste.**

Practiquemos

G6-9 Padre e hijo. Completa el siguiente párrafo usando las formas correctas del pretérito de los verbos entre paréntesis.

Hoy Andrés ______________ (despertar / despertarse) a las ocho de la mañana. Esta mañana él y su hijo Tito ______________ (ir / irse) a visitar a sus padres, que se llaman Simón e Irma.

Primero, Andrés ______________ (ir / irse) al dormitorio de Tito, lo ______________ (despertar / despertarse), lo ______________ (bañar / bañarse) y lo ______________ (vestir / vestirse). Luego Andrés ______________ (bañar / bañarse) y ______________ (vestir / vestirse) elegantemente.

Después de comer algo, Andrés ____________ (lavar / lavarse) los dientes y las manos, luego le ____________ (lavar / lavarse) los dientes a Tito. A las nueve los dos ____________ (ir / irse) a Colón, Panamá, donde viven Irma y Simón.

Por la tarde Tito estaba *(was)* muy cansado y ____________ (enojar / enojarse) con su papá cuando él le ____________ (quitar / quitarse) los zapatos. Pero con tiempo, Tito ____________ (dormir / dormirse) la siesta en el sofá de sus abuelos. Luego Andrés ____________ (quitar / quitarse) los zapatos y ____________ (dormir / dormirse) rápidamente al lado de su hijo.

G6-10 Mucho amor. Completa las siguientes oraciones según el modelo.

Modelo: Andrés / conocer / a Yolanda // ellos / conocer / bien
Andrés conoce a Yolanda. Ellos se conocen bien.

1. Yolanda / querer a su hijo Tito // ellos / quererse mucho
____
____
2. Andrés / les escribir a sus padres // ellos / escribirse frecuentemente
____
____
3. Mario / llamar por teléfono a su novia // ellos / llamarse mucho
____
____
4. Juana / ir a visitar / a su hermana mayor // ellas / visitarse los domingos
____
____

More practice talking about the past

PRACTIQUEMOS

G6-11 ¿Qué pasó *(What happened)* el fin de semana pasado? Completa los espacios en blanco para saber lo que pasó en casa de Rodrigo el fin de semana pasado.

Modelo: Rodrigo *invitó* (invitar) a sus amigos a su casa.

1. Rodrigo ____________ (acostarse) a las cuatro de la mañana porque ____________ (ofrecer) una fiesta en su casa.
2. Sus amigos ____________ (comer), ____________ (hablar) y ____________ (bailar) hasta las tres de la mañana.
3. El vecino *(neighbor)* de al lado ____________ (llamar) a la policía por el ruido *(noise)* de la fiesta.
4. Los amigos de Rodrigo ____________ (ayudar) a limpiar la casa y también ____________ (arreglar) la cocina.
5. Ellos ____________ (regresar) a su casa muy contentos pero muy cansados.

Nombre ______________________________ Fecha ______________

G6-12 De viaje. ¿Qué pasó en el viaje a Panamá? Completa las oraciones con las formas correctas de los verbos.

Modelo: Sofía *visitó* (visitar) Panamá y Colón el verano pasado.

1. Federico y Ana ______________ (conocer) Ciudad de Panamá el verano pasado.
2. Santiago ______________ (visitar) el Canal de Panamá en el año 2005.
3. Mis padres ______________ (comprar) boletos para visitar Colón por tren.
4. Yo ______________ (tomar) muchas fotos del canal.
5. Tomás y Gisela ______________ (llegar) al Hotel Paraíso, que es un hotel muy bonito en la ciudad.
6. Cristina y yo ______________ (comer) en el restaurante Bilbao.
7. Tú ______________ (buscar) la dirección del teatro Colón para ir al concierto de Rubén Blades.
8. Nosotros ______________ (discutir) sobre la economía del canal.

G6-13 Mi vitácora de viaje *(travel diary)*. Escribe cuatro o cinco oraciones en tu vitácora de viaje para describir lo que pasó en tu último viaje a....

Luego cuéntale a un(a) compañero(a) de clase lo que pasó.

Nombre ______________________________ Fecha ______________

Práctica comunicativa suplemental I

Línea de vida. Describe la historia de tu vida a uno de tus compañeros. Selecciona los momentos más importantes de tu vida y ordénalos en esta línea. Cuéntale a tu compañero(a) por qué son importantes. Luego escucha a tu compañero(a).

Vocabulario útil

casarse	*to get married*
comprometerse	*to become engaged*
divorciarse	*to get divorced*
graduarse / recibirse	*to graduate*
mudarse	*to move*
nacer	*to be born*
¿Cómo se dice... ?	*How do you say . . . ?*

Modelo: *Yo nací en Venezuela en 1980. Después mi familia se mudó a los Estados Unidos...*

hoy en día

2000

1995

1990

1985

1980

Nombre ________________________________ Fecha ________________

Práctica comunicativa suplemental II

La vieja ***(tic-tac-toe)***. En parejas, completen el cuadro usando verbos en el infinitivo. Luego, formen oraciones por turnos, usando el pretérito de uno de esos verbos. Si la oración está bien formada, puedes marcar el cuadro con tu símbolo (X u O). La persona que primero complete una línea vertical, horizontal o diagonal gana.

Vocabulario útil

afeitarse	*to shave*
despertarse	*to wake up*
dormirse	*to fall asleep*
ducharse	*to take a shower*
lavarse	*to clean, wash*
levantarse	*to get up*
maquillarse	*to put on makeup*
peinarse	*to comb*

Nombre ______________________ Fecha ______________

PASO 3 ¡Buena Onda!

LECCIÓN 7 ¡TENGO GANAS DE IR A LA PLAYA!

Práctica suplemental

VOCABULARIO SUPLEMENTAL

Más pasatiempos

cantar en un coro	*to sing in a chorus*
ir a la ópera	*to go to the opera*
ir al ballet	*to go to the ballet*
ir a un club	*to go to a club*
mirar un espectáculo	*to see a show*
tocar en una banda / orquesta	*to play in a band/an orchestra*

PRACTIQUEMOS

V7-1 ¿Adónde vamos? Si queremos tener ciertos pasatiempos, vamos a ciertos lugares. Escoge el lugar donde pasas el tiempo.

Modelo: Para hablar con los amigos, vamos *a un club*.

1. Para escuchar música clásica, vamos ______________________.
2. Para ver representaciones clásicas con danza o movimiento, vamos ______________.
3. Cuando queremos ver algo sensacional, ______________________.
4. Cuando queremos ser cantantes famosos, ______________________.
5. Para jugar cartas con los amigos, vamos ______________________.
6. Cuando queremos ser famosos en el mundo de la música clásica, ______________.

V7-2 ¿Adónde les gustaría ir? Con un(a) compañero(a) de clase, discutan adónde les gustaría ir el viernes por la noche, qué les gustaría ver y con quién.

Nombre ______________________ Fecha __________

Más deportes	***More sports***
las artes marciales	*martial arts*
el boxeo	*boxing*
el ciclismo	*cycling*
la equitación	*horseback riding*
el esquí acuático	*water skiing*
jugar a las damas	*to play checkers*
jugar al ajedrez	*to play chess*
jugar al boliche	*to go bowling*
jugar al dominó	*to play dominoes*
jugar al hockey sobre hielo	*to play ice hockey*
jugar al hockey sobre hierba	*to play field hockey*

V7-3 ¿Qué deporte practicas en estos lugares? Asocia los deportes con los siguientes lugares.

Modelo: Tengo mi caballo en el club. Allí practico *equitación*.

1. Marcelo y Ricardo van al gimnasio de la universidad en bicicleta para practicar ____________.
2. En el Lago Ginebra, nosotros practicamos ____________.
3. En el gimnasio de la universidad, Luis practica ____________.
4. En el club, las personas pueden practicar el karate, el Tae-Kwon-Do y otras ____________.
5. Elisa tiene un caballo y practica ____________ todos los días en el club.
6. Cuando la familia está junta los domingos, jugamos al ____________, a las ____________ y al ____________.
7. En Connecticut College, las mujeres tienen un buen equipo de hockey. En la primavera ellas juegan ____________.
8. En Buffalo, New York, los Buffalo Sabres juegan ____________ en el invierno.

V7-4 ¿Qué deporte les gustaría practicar? Escribe un párrafo de cuatro oraciones y describe qué deporte te gustaría practicar, dónde y por qué.

____

____

____

____

____

____

Nombre ______________________ Fecha ______________

GRAMÁTICA SUPLEMENTAL

More practice with the preterite tense of irregular verbs

PRACTIQUEMOS

G7-5 Contestador automático *(answering machine).* Luis le dejó este mensaje a su novia, Rita. Completa los espacios en blanco con los verbos en el pretérito para saber lo que le dijo Luis.

Modelo: Yo *estuve* (estar) en tu casa pero no te *encontré* (encontrar).

¡Hola, Rita! Habla Luis. __________ (Ir) a tu casa para invitarte a ir al cine pero no te __________ (poder) encontrar. __________ (Querer) llamarte por teléfono pero no __________ (contestar) el teléfono. También yo __________ (estar) en la biblioteca de la universidad donde __________ (ver) a tus compañeros de clase y ellos me __________ (decir) que tú no __________ (ir) a clases esta mañana. Ahora estoy muy preocupado por ti. Por favor, ¡llama pronto!

G7-6 ¿Qué hicieron ayer? La clase de español lo pasó muy bien ayer. Completa los espacios en blanco para saber lo que ellos hicieron.

Modelo: La profesora *trajo* (traer) música mexicana a la clase.

1. Manuel y Helena ______________ (tener) la idea de hacer una fiesta para el Día de Muertos en la clase de español.
2. Marisa ______________ (hacer) unos postres *(desserts)* muy buenos.
3. Ricardo y yo ______________ (traer) un video del Día de Muertos en Guatemala y México.
4. Tú ______________ (poner) música mexicana en la grabadora.
5. Yo ______________ (querer) invitar a la otra clase de español, pero no ______________ (poder) porque el profesor no ______________ (querer) aceptar la invitación.
6. Vosotros ______________ (ir) a casa contentos después de la clase de español.

Nombre ______________________________ Fecha ____________

More practice with the preterite tense of stem-change verbs

PRACTIQUEMOS

G7-7 Anoche. Forma oraciones para saber lo que hizo la familia Aquino anoche.

Modelo: Gustavo / llegar / temprano a casa
Gustavo llegó temprano a casa.

1. Glenn y María / preferir / salir a comer en un restaurante italiano
 ____
2. ellos / pedir / pasta con salsa de tomates
 ____
3. Glenn / repetir / pasta dos veces
 ____
4. él / sentirse / mal por comer mucho
 ____
5. ellos / ir / a casa para descansar
 ____
6. María / ponerse el pijama y / acostarse rápidamente
 ____
7. Gustavo / preferir / quedarse en casa para mirar la televisión
 ____
8. Glenn / no dormir / muy bien durante la noche
 ____

G7-8 La cena. Al día siguiente los Aquino decidieron quedarse *(to remain)* en casa y preparar ellos la comida. Completa los espacios en blanco para saber lo que hicieron de comida.

Modelo: María y Gustavo *prepararon* (preparar) la comida.

1. María ____________ (preferir) invitar a varios amigos para cenar juntos.
2. Glenn ____________ (servir) las bebidas antes de la comida.
3. Esta vez, Gustavo ____________ (repetir) dos veces la comida.
4. Roberto, uno de los invitados, ____________ (sentirse) mareado *(dizzy)* y ____________ (tener) que regresar a casa antes de comer.
5. Caridad ____________ (pedir) una Margarita para beber y Glenn se la ____________ (servir).
6. La comida ____________ (estar) estupenda y todos se divirtieron mucho.

Nombre ______________________________ Fecha ______________

Other verbs like *gustar*

You can express different emotions by using the following verbs:

encantar	*to love*	interesar	*to interest*
fascinar	*to fascinate*	molestar	*to bother*
importar	*to matter*	parecer	*to seem*

These verbs are used like the verb **gustar,** as shown in the following examples.

1. The verb matches its subject; both must be either singular or plural.

   Me encant**a tu país.** — *I love your country.* (singular subject)
   Me encant**an tus ideas.** — *I love your ideas.* (plural subject)

2. An infinitive is considered a singular subject, no matter what follows it.

   ¿Te import**a afeitarte?** — *Does shaving matter to you?*
   ¿Te gust**a comer** tamales? — *Do you like to eat tamales?*

3. To emphasize or clarify the indirect object pronoun, use an emphatic phrase before it.

   ¡**A mí me** fascina tu casa! — *Your house fascinates **me!*** (emphasis)
   ¡**A nosotros nos** gusta también! — ***We** like it too!* (emphasis)
   A Jaime le interesan los cuentos. — *Stories interest Jaime.* (clarification)
   A él no **le** molestan tus ideas. — *Your ideas don't bother him.* (clarification)

Practiquemos

G7-9 Entre amigos. Completa la siguiente conversación entre Jaime y su amiga Marta, usando la forma correcta de los verbos entre paréntesis.

Marta: ¿Qué te ______________ (parecer) los animales, Jaime?

Jaime: Me ______________ (encantar) y me ______________ (fascinar) jugar con ellos.

Marta: A mí me ______________ (molestar) un poco, a veces.

Jaime: ¿Te ______________ (interesar) jugar con ellos?

Marta: No. No me ______________ (importar) jugar con los animales.

Jaime: Entonces, ¿qué te ______________ (gustar) hacer, Marta?

Marta: Pues, me ______________ (encantar) leer novelas.

Jaime: ¿Qué te ______________ (parecer) la televisión?

Marta: No me ______________ (gustar) porque es aburrida.

Jaime: ¿Te ______________ (molestar) los comerciales?

Marta: Sí. También me ______________ (molestar) la violencia.

Jaime: A ti te ______________ (encantar) la vida tranquila.

Marta: Claro. La tranquilidad me ______________ (importar) mucho.

Nombre ______________________ Fecha ______________

G7-10 Gente feliz. Las siguientes personas están contentas. ¿Qué dicen?

Modelo: Tomás (abuelo): encantar mis nietos porque / parecen simpáticos
Me encantan mis nietos porque me parecen simpáticos.

1. Jorge (agricultor): gustar cuando hace sol y / encantar cuando llueve
____.
2. Cecilia (estudiante): no molestar los exámenes porque / gustar estudiar
____.
3. Daniel (intérprete): fascinar las lenguas y, por eso, / interesar visitar las Naciones Unidas
____.
4. Max (programador): interesar mucho la tecnología, pero / no importar los deportes
____.
5. María Teresa (mujer policía): encantar mi trabajo porque / gustar trabajar con la gente
____.

G7-11 Mis preferencias. Completa las siguientes oraciones, según sus preferencias. Los tres puntos (...) que indican otra posibilidad.

Los cursos / estudios

1. Me parecen fáciles (los idiomas / las ciencias / ...) ______________________.
2. Me parecen difíciles (los / las) ______________________.
3. Me parece interesante (el cálculo / la biología / ...) ______________________.
4. Me parece aburrido(a) (el / la) ______________________.

Los deportes

5. Me fascina (el fútbol / el tenis / ...) ______________________.
6. También me encanta (correr / esquiar / ...) ______________ pero no me interesa ______________.

Los pasatiempos

7. Me interesa ______________, me encanta ______________ y me fascina ______________.
8. Pero no me interesa nada ______________________.

La comida

9. Me (encanta / molesta) ______________ la comida mexicana y la comida italiana, (pero) la comida (china / japonesa) ______________ no me ______________ mucho.

Nombre ______________________________ Fecha ______________

Indirect object pronouns

Indirect object pronouns refer to people **to whom** or **for whom** the action of the verb is performed. They usually answer the question **to whom?** or **for whom?**

Singular		Plural	
me	*to/for me*	**nos**	*to/for us*
te	*to/for you* (informal)	**os**	*to/for you* (informal)
le	*to/for you* (formal), *him, her*	**les**	*to/for you* (formal), *them*

Mis padres **me** dieron una guitarra. — *My parents gave **me** a guitar.*
Quiero comprar**te** un regalo bonito. — *I want to buy **you** a nice present.*
Voy a decir**le** cómo llegar a mi casa. — *I'm going to tell **you** how to get to my house.*
A veces **le** doy flores a mi esposa. — *Sometimes I give my wife flowers.*
Nos preguntó cuándo vamos de compras. — *He asked **us** when we're going shopping.*
Quiero decir**os** que voy a Madrid mañana. — *I want to tell **you** that I'm going to Madrid tomorrow.*
Les hago favores a todos mis parientes. — *I do favors for all my relatives.*
Ayer **les** escribí una carta a mis abuelos. — *Yesterday I wrote a letter to my grandparents.*

Where to place indirect object pronouns

1. Place the pronoun in front of the conjugated verb.

   —¿Silvia **te dio** ese suéter? — *Did Silvia give you that sweater?*
   —Sí. También **me compró** jeans. — *Yes, she also bought me jeans.*

2. In negative sentences, place the **no** in front of the pronoun.

   —**Le** hice una fiesta a mi amiga. — *I threw a party for my friend.*
   —¿Por qué **no nos** hiciste una? — *Why didn't you throw us one?*

3. When the pronoun is used with an infinitive or a present participle, either place it before the conjugated verb or attach it to the infinitive or the present participle. (A written accent is needed to mark the stressed vowel of a present participle when a pronoun is attached to it.)

   Les voy a escribir a mis amigos. — *I'm going to write to my friends.*
   o: Voy a **escribirles** a mis amigos.

   Les estoy escribiendo ahora. — *I'm writing to them now.*
   o: Estoy **escribiéndoles** ahora.

Nombre ______________________________ Fecha ______________

How to clarify or emphasize indirect object pronouns
Because **le** and **les** have several meanings, you may add the expressions **a él, a ella, a usted, a ellos, a ellas,** or **a ustedes** to the sentence for clarification or emphasis.

1. For clarification:

   —¿**Le** dijiste **a él** o a **ella?** — *Did you tell him or her?*
   —**Le** dije **a ella**... a Silvia. — *I told her . . . Silvia.*

2. For emphasis:

   —¿A quién **le** está hablando? — *To whom are you speaking?*

Practiquemos

G7-12 Abuelita, te quiero mucho. En el siguiente párrafo, marca con un círculo los pronombres de complemento indirecto y marque con una flecha *(arrow)* los objetos a que correspondan.

Jaime le dio un poco de dinero a su hijo Pancho. Luego el niño le compró un regalo bonito a su abuela. Después, Pancho le escribió una carta a ella en Valparaíso. Le dijo: «Con esta carta te mando un regalo pequeño». La abuela le respondió a su nieto: «Te mando un beso grande».

G7-13 Entre tía y sobrina. A Silvia le gusta enseñarle a Lucía, su sobrina de cinco años, cómo escribir bien porque a la niña le gusta mandarle cartas a su abuelo. Completa la siguiente conversación, usando pronombres del objeto indirecto.

Lucía: Tía, quiero enseñar ______________ (a ti) cómo escribí mi nombre. Mira.

Silvia: ¡Qué bien! ______________ felicito (a ti), Lucía.

Lucía: Ahora, ¿______________ enseñas (a mí) cómo escribir mi dirección, tía?

Silvia: Sí, y después puedes escribir ______________ una carta a tu abuelito.

Lucía: Y en la carta ______________ voy a mandar (a él) un beso grande.

Silvia: Como él siempre ______________ manda (a nosotras) en sus cartas, ¿no?

Lucía: Sí. Y voy a decir ______________ (a él) en la carta que lo quiero mucho.

G7-14 Quiero mucho a mis compañeros de clase. Robert Owen quiere mucho a sus compañeros de clase. ¿Qué hizo Robert por sus compañeros la semana pasada?

Modelo: comprar algunos libros y programas de computación
Les compró algunos libros y programas de computación a sus compañeros.

1. dar una fiesta para Sharon y Dianita por sus buenas notas

   ____

2. comprar unas flores para la profesora por su cumpleaños

   ____

3. comprar la cena y bebidas a sus compañeros

   ____

Nombre ______________________ Fecha ____________

4. hacer varios favores a Kevin y a Dan

____

5. contestar varias preguntas sobre la computadora a Boji

____

G7-15 Expresiones de cariño. Contesta las siguientes preguntas en oraciones completas.

Modelo: ¿A quién le vas a escribir esta semana?
Voy a escribirle a mi amiga en California.

1. ¿A quiénes les escribes frecuentemente? ¿A quién vas a escribirle esta semana, y por qué?

____

____

2. ¿A quiénes les das regalos a veces? ¿A quién vas a darle un regalo este mes, y por qué?

____

____

3. ¿A quiénes les haces favores con frecuencia? ¿A quién quieres hacerle un favor esta semana, y por qué?

____

____

4. ¿A quiénes les das abrazos? ¿A quién vas a darle un abrazo esta semana, y por qué?

____

____

Nombre ______________________ Fecha ______________

Unintentional incidents with *se*

Spanish speakers use a reflexive construction to describe incidents that happened unintentionally, such as forgetting something or losing something.

1. This construction uses the pronoun **se** + a verb form. The person involved in the incident is indicated by an indirect object pronoun **(me, te, le, nos, os, les).** The verb must agree in number (singular or plural) with its subject (e.g., the thing or things forgotten).

Person	**Verb**	**Subject**	**Person**	**Verb**	**Subject**
Se me	olvidó	el libro.	Se me	olvidaron	los libros.
I	*forgot*	*the book.*	*I*	*forgot*	*the books.*

2. If an infinitive is the subject, the verb is always singular.

Person	**Verb**	**Subject**	**Person**	**Verb**	**Subject**
Se me	olvidó	leer el libro.	Se me	olvidó	leer los libros.
I	*forgot*	*to read the book.*	*I*	*forgot*	*to read the books.*

3. You can clarify or emphasize the person involved in the incident by adding **a** + a noun or pronoun (e.g., **a mi mamá, a ella**) to the sentence.

Person	**Verb**	**Subject**	**Person**	**Verb**	**Subject**
A mi papá se **le**	olvidó	su cámara.	**A él** se **le**	olvidó	su cámara.
My father	*forgot*	*his camera.*	*He*	*forgot*	*his camera.*

4. Spanish speakers often use the following verbs in this construction.

acabarse	*to run out*	perderse	*to get lost*
caerse	*to fall down; to drop*	quedarse	*to be left behind*
escaparse	*to get away*	romperse	*to break*
lastimarse	*to hurt oneself*	olvidarse	*to forget*

Ayer **se nos acabó** la gasolina.	*Yesterday we ran out of gasoline.*
A mi novio **se le cayó** su cámara.	*My boyfriend dropped his camera.*
¡Por Dios! ¡**Se te escapó** el gato!	*Heavens! Your cat got away!*
A mi hijo **se le lastimó** el brazo.	*My son hurt his arm.*
Se me olvidó tomar mi medicina.	*I forgot to take my medicine.*
A mi tía **se le perdió** su dinero.	*My aunt lost her money.*
Se nos quedaron nuestros libros.	*We left our books behind.*
¿Cuándo **se te rompió** el brazo?	*When did you break your arm?*

Nombre ______________________________ Fecha ______________

Practiquemos

G7-16 ¡Qué mala suerte! A las siguientes personas les ocurrió una cosa desafortunada. ¿Qué les pasó exactamente?

Modelo: Mi hermano rompió dos platos. *A mi hermano se le rompieron dos platos.*

1. Mi novio perdió dos libros de microbiología.

   ____.

2. Ayer mi tío rompió un diente mientras comía.

   ____.

3. El otro día olvidé mis libros en el autobús.

   ____.

4. Anoche la mamá de mi novio perdió 400 dólares.

   ____.

5. Mis amigas olvidaron sus tarjetas de crédito.

   ____.

G7-17 Así es la vida. Completa las siguientes oraciones lógicamente.

Modelo: Una vez se me rompió ______________________.
Una vez se me rompió la bicicleta.

1. Una vez sufrí un accidente. Se me rompió (Se me rompieron) ______________________.
   También se me lastimó (se me lastimaron) ______________________.
2. En otra ocasión se me olvidó (se me olvidaron) ______________________ en una de mis clases.
   También se me perdió (se me perdieron) ______________________.
3. Este mes se me acabó (se me acabaron) ______________________.
4. Cuando era niño(a) no era tan responsable como lo soy ahora. Una vez se me cayó (se me cayeron) ______________________.
   Desafortunadamente, se me escapó (se me escaparon) ______________________.

Nombre ______________________________ Fecha ______________

Some uses of *por* and *para*

The prepositions **por** and **para** have many different uses and meanings.

Uses of *por*

In general, **por** conveys the underlying idea of a cause, reason, or source behind an action.

1. Duration of time *(for)*

   Descanso **por una hora** cada día. — *I rest for an hour every day.*

2. Idiomatic expressions

   Me gusta hablar **por teléfono.** — *I like to talk on the telephone.*
   Trabajo mucho **por la noche.** — *I work a lot at night.*
   Estudie un poco más, **por favor.** — *Study a little more, please.*

Uses of *para*

In general, **para** conveys the underlying ideas of purpose, use, and destination.

1. Recipient *(for)*

   Tengo un libro **para usted.** — *I have a book for you.*

2. Purpose (*in order to* [followed by infinitive])

   Estudio español **para viajar y trabajar.** — *I'm studying Spanish in order to travel and work.*

Practiquemos

G7-18 *¿Por o para?* Completa las siguientes oraciones con **por** o **para.**

1. —¿Cuál es su dirección, ______________ favor?

   —Es calle Beltrán, número 2561.

2. —¿Te gusta hablar ______________ teléfono?

   —Sí, especialmente ______________ la noche.

3. —¿Por qué estudias español?

   —Estudio español ______________ hablar la lengua.

4. —¿Cuándo tienes tu clase de español?

   — ______________ la mañana.

   —Ah, ¿sí? Tengo mis clases ______________ la tarde.

5. —Necesito tener un diccionario bilingüe ______________ nuestra clase de español.

   —Este diccionario bilingüe es ______________ usted. Es un regalo *(gift)*.

   —¿______________ mí? ¡Muchas gracias!

Nombre ______________________________ Fecha ______________

G7-19 Preguntas personales. Contesta las siguientes preguntas en oraciones completas.

1. ¿Estudias español para viajar o para tener suficientes créditos en lenguas? ¿Tienes tu clase de español por la mañana, por la tarde o por la noche? ¿Es el español difícil o fácil para ti? ¿Por cuántas horas estudias español todos los días? Para ti, ¿es tu clase interesante o no?

2. ¿Trabajas por la mañana, por la tarde o por la noche? ¿Por cuántas horas trabajas todos los días? Otra pregunta, por favor: ¿Eres trabajador(a) o perezoso(a)?

3. ¿Hablas por teléfono mucho o poco? ¿Hablas por teléfono en inglés o en español? ¿Cuándo hablas por teléfono más: por la mañana, por la tarde o por la noche? ¿Cuál es tu número de teléfono, por favor?

Nombre ______________________ Fecha ______________

Present Perfect Tense

Spanish speakers use the present perfect tense to describe what has and has not happened.

How to form the present perfect

Use the present-tense forms of the auxiliary verb **haber** *(to have)* with the past participle of a verb.

Present of *haber* + past participle			
(yo)	**he**	**comido**	*I have eaten*
(tú)	**has**	**comido**	*you have eaten*
(usted, él/ella)	**ha**	**comido**	*you have, he has/she has eaten*
(nosotros/nosotras)	**hemos**	**comido**	*we have eaten*
(vosotros/vosotras)	**habéis**	**comido**	*you have eaten*
(ustedes, ellos/ellas)	**han**	**comido**	*you have, they have eaten*

How to form past participles

1. Add **-ado** to the stem of **-ar** verbs and **-ido** to the stem of **-er** and **-ir** verbs.

-ar	**-ado**		**-er / -ir**	**-ido**	
hablar	hablado	*spoken*	comer	comido	*eaten*
pensar	pensado	*thought*	vivir	vivido	*lived*
llegar	llegado	*arrived*	dormir	dormido	*slept*

—¿Qué **han pedido** ustedes? *What have you ordered?*
—Nada. Te **hemos esperado.** *Nothing. We've waited for you.*
—¿**Han comido** aquí antes? *Have you eaten here before?*
—No. Nunca **hemos estado** aquí. *No. We've never been here.*

2. Several **-er** and **-ir** verbs have an accent mark on the **i** of their past participles.

creer	creído	*believed*	reír	reído	*laughed*
leer	leído	*read*	traer	traído	*brought*

—Te **he traído** un regalo, Dan. *I've brought a gift for you, Dan.*
—¿Qué me **has traído,** mamá? *What have you brought me, Mom?*
—Un libro que no **has leído.** *A book that you have not read.*

3. Other verbs have irregular past participles.

abrir	**abierto**	*opened*	morir	**muerto**	*died*
decir	**dicho**	*said, told*	poner	**puesto**	*put*
escribir	**escrito**	*written*	ver	**visto**	*seen*
hacer	**hecho**	*done, made*	volver	**vuelto**	*returned*

—¿Qué **han hecho** ustedes hoy? *What have you done today?*
—**Hemos visto** una película. *We have seen a movie.*
—**He escrito** algunas cartas. *I have written some letters.*

Practiquemos

G7-20 Dos amigos. Completa la siguiente conversación entre Kevin y Rob, usando la forma correcta de **haber: he, has, ha, hemos, habéis, han.**

Rob: ¿______________ estado tú en Guadalajara, Kevin?

Kevin: No, pero mi jefe ______________ visitado México.

Rob: Ah, ¿sí? ¿Qué ciudades ______________ conocido él?

Kevin: Pues, Cancún y Cabo San Lucas. ¿______________ estado allí, Rob?

Rob: Sí. Mi jefes y yo ______________ visitado Cancún. ¡Nunca (yo) ______________ visto una ciudad tan organizada!

G7-21 Otras conversaciones. Completa las siguientes conversaciones, usando los participios de los verbos indicados.

1. **escribir / hacer / ver**

   Ángela: ¿Qué has ______________ hoy, Yolanda?

   Yolanda: He ______________ algunas tarjetas postales. ¿Y tú?

   Ángela: Mamá y yo hemos ______________ una película en la televisión.

2. **morir / recibir / pasar**

   Mario: He ______________ malas noticias de mis padres.

   Juana: ¿Qué ha ______________?

   Mario: Mi tío ha ______________.

   Juana: Ay, lo siento mucho, Mario.

3. **ver / leer / comprar**

   Isabel: He ______________ una novela fantástica.

   Ricardo: ¿La has ______________ ya?

   Isabel: No, pero he ______________ el DVD de la película basada en el libro.

G7-22 Recientemente... Describe las actividades que has hecho recientemente y lo que ha pasado, usando las siguientes frases como guía.

1. En clase...

   a. aprender mucho

   ____

   b. (no) estar muy aburrido(a)

   ____

   c. tomar exámenes difíciles (fáciles)

   ____

   d. estudiar con un(a) amigo(a)

   ____

Nombre ______________________ Fecha ______________

2. En casa...
   a. (no) hacer una fiesta

   ____

   b. (no) leer el periódico

   ____

   c. (no) mirar mucho la tele

   ____

   d. (no) ayudar a (mi / su) mamá

   ____

3. Recientemente...
   a. (no) hacer trabajo

   ____

   b. (no) tener problemas

   ____

   c. (no) ganar mucho dinero

   ____

   d. (no) jugar fútbol (tenis)

   ____

4. Esta semana...
   a. (no) dormir mucho

   ____

   b. (no) ver una buena película

   ____

   c. (no) comer en un restaurante

   ____

   d. (no) hacer mucho calor (frío)

   ____

G7-23 **¿Y qué has hecho?** Describe otras cosas que has hecho o que nunca has hecho en tu vida.

Modelo: almorzar en un restaurante japonés
He almorzado en un restaurante japonés. o: *Nunca he almorzado en un restaurante japonés.*

1. escribir muchos mensajes electrónicos
____
2. ver una película en español
____
3. comer un poco de caviar ruso
____
4. visitar un país extranjero
____
5. conocer a una persona de Australia
____
6. correr en un maratón internacional
____
7. tomar una copa de champaña francesa
____
8. almorzar en un restaurante mexicano
____

Nombre ______________________________ Fecha ______________

Práctica comunicativa suplemental I

Historia en cadena.

1. Forma un grupo de cuatro con tus compañeros.
2. Cada uno necesita un pedazo de papel y un lápiz. Todos van a escribir una historia usando la misma frase inicial.
3. Cuando todos hayan terminado la primera línea tienen que pasar su papel a la persona a su izquierda.
4. Luego deben leer el nuevo papel y tienen que escribir la próxima línea para continuar la historia de su compañero(a).
5. Continúa pasando el papel hasta que recibas el tuyo por segunda vez.
6. Todos leen su historia al resto del grupo y eligen cuál es la mejor.

Vocabulario útil

El verano pasado fui a...	*Last summer I went to . . .*
Había una vez...	*There was a time . . .*
Todos fueron a la fiesta excepto...	*Everyone went to the party except . . .*
Una noche de tormenta...	*One stormy night . . .*

Nombre ______________________ Fecha ______________

Práctica comunicativa suplemental II

Un fin de semana de vacaciones. Tú y tres compañeros van a pasar tres días en la costa española, en un hotel de primera clase que ofrece toda clase de diversiones. Planea lo que van a hacer durante estos tres días. Averigua qué les gustaría hacer a tus compañeros cada día. Completa el cuadro.

Nombre	viernes por la noche	sábado por la tarde	sábado por la noche	domingo
1.				
2.				
3.				
4.				

Nombre ______________________________ Fecha ______________

LECCIÓN 8 ¡SALUD Y BUEN PROVECHO!

Práctica suplemental

VOCABULARIO SUPLEMENTAL

Platos principales / Vegetales o verduras / Frutas	***Main courses/ Vegetables/Fruits***
el brécol	*broccoli*
la cebolla	*onion*
las costillas de res / cochino	*ribs/pork ribs*
los huevos	*eggs*
los huevos fritos / revueltos	*fried/scrambled eggs*
la lechuga	*lettuce*
el limón	*lemon*
el maíz	*corn*
la paella	*rice dish with chicken, seafood, and vegetables*
el pan tostado	*toast*
el pepino	*cucumber*
la pera	*pear*
la piña	*pineapple*
la toronja	*grapefruit*
la zanahoria	*carrot*

PRACTIQUEMOS

V8-1 ¿Qué te gusta comer? Escribe lo que a ti te gusta comer para el desayuno, el almuerzo y la cena.

Modelo: Desayuno: *Me gusta desayunar con huevos fritos y con pan tostado.*

Desayuno: ______________________________

Almuerzo: ______________________________

Cena: ______________________________

V8-2 Ensaladas. ¿Qué ingredientes te gustan en una ensalada y en una ensalada de frutas?

Modelo: Ensalada: *tomates, aceite, vinagre...*

Ensalada: ______________________________

Ensalada de frutas: ______________________________

Nombre ______________________________ Fecha ______________

La mesa y los cubiertos | ***The table and silverware***

la copa	*wine glass*
la cuchara	*spoon*
el cuchillo	*knife*
el plato	*plate, dish*
la servilleta	*napkin*
la taza	*cup*
el tenedor	*fork*
el vaso	*glass*

V8-3 Cubiertos. Escribe los cubiertos que usas para comer los siguientes alimentos.

Modelo: La manzana: *el cuchillo*

1. La paella:
____
2. Los huevos revueltos:
____
3. El pan tostado y la mermelada:
____
4. El pepino y la cebolla:
____
5. La toronja:
____
6. La pera y la piña:
____

V8-4 La mesa. Coloca *(place)* los cubiertos (el tenedor, el cuchillo, la cuchara, la servilleta), los platos (principal, de ensalada), la taza, la copa y el vaso.

Nombre ______________________________ Fecha ______________

GRAMÁTICA SUPLEMENTAL

Double-object pronouns

Direct and indirect object pronouns refer to people, things, places, and ideas. Sometimes you may want to use both kinds of pronouns together in the same sentence. Double-object pronouns consist of a direct object pronoun and an indirect object pronoun used together.

How to use double-object pronouns

1. Indirect object pronouns always *precede* direct object pronouns.

Indirect	*before*	**direct**
me		
te		**lo**
le → se		**la**
nos		**los**
os		**las**
les → se		

—¿Compraste mis regalos, mamá?	*Did you buy my presents, Mom?*
—Sí. Acabo de **comprártelos.**	*Yes. I've just bought them for you.*
—Y la torta. ¿**Me la** compraste?	*And the cake. Did you buy it for me?*
—**Te la** compré esta mañana.	*I bought it for you this morning.*
—Mamá, ¡**dámela** ahora mismo!	*Mom, give it to me right now!*
—**Te la doy** en tu fiesta.	*I'll give it to you at your party.*

2. The indirect object pronouns **le** and **les** always change to **se** when they are used together with the direct object pronouns **lo, la, los,** and **las.**

Le compré **dos regalos** a mi hijo.	*I bought two gifts for my son.*
Se los compré en el centro.	*I bought them for him downtown.*
Le compré **botas y una camiseta.**	*I bought him boots and a T-shirt.*
Se las compré para su cumpleaños.	*I bought them for him for his birthday.*

3. To contrast, emphasize, or clarify the meaning of the indirect object pronoun **se,** use **a usted, a él, a ella, a ustedes, a ellos,** or **a ellas,** as shown below.

Los regalos son de buena calidad.	*The gifts are of good quality.*
No **se** los compré **a usted.**	*I didn't buy them for you.*
Tampoco **se** los compré **a ellas.**	*Nor did I buy them for them.*
Se los compré **a mi hijo.**	*I bought them for my son.*
Se los compré **a él.**	*I bought them for him.*

4. In verb phrases, pronouns may be placed before conjugated verbs or attached to infinitives or present participles; they must be attached to affirmative commands. When two pronouns are attached, an accent mark is written over the stressed vowel.

La mamá quiere comprarle dos regalos a su hijo.	*The mother wants to buy two gifts for her son.*
Se los va a comprar hoy.	*She is going to buy them for him today.*
Va a **comprárselos** hoy.	
Se los está comprando ahora.	*She is buying them for him now.*
Está **comprándoselos** ahora.	
No **se los** compre allí.	*Don't buy them for him there.*
Cómpreselos en esa tienda.	*Buy them for him in that store.*

Nombre ______________________ Fecha ______________

PRACTIQUEMOS

G8-5 En el mercado. María Galeano está hablando con un dependiente del mercado. Busca los pronombres en su conversación y dibuja una flecha (→) para indicar los sustantivos a los que se refieren.

Depen.: ¿En qué puedo servirle,→ señora Galeano?

María: Déme 200 gramos de aceitunas, pero las quiero con pimientos.

Depen.: Bueno, aquí las tiene, señora. ¿Algo más?

María: Sí. Quiero cuatro cebollas, pero póngamelas en una bolsa plástica pequeña, por favor! ¡Hoy no traje mi bolso porque mi perro se lo comió!

Depen.: ¡Ja, ja! Bueno, cuatro cebollas en una bolsa plástica. Aquí las tiene. ¿Y tomates? ¿No los quiere? Están muy frescos, señora.

María: No, señor. Ya los compré ayer. Perdón, estas fresas... ¿puedo probar una?

Depen.: Cómo no, señora. Sírvase... ¿Qué le parece la fresa? ¿Le gusta?

María: Mmm. ¡Qué rica! Déme medio kilo de fresas. ¿Me las puede meter en otra bolsa plástica, por favor?

Depen.: Con mucho gusto, señora.

María: Muchas gracias.

G8-6 Para servirles. Completa las siguientes conversaciones, usando pronombres adecuados.

Modelo: **A:** Perdón, ¿me da ese pastel?
B: Sí, señorita. *Se lo* doy ahora.

1. **A:** Me gustaría ver ese reloj. ¿Puede mostrár ______________?

   B: Claro que sí, señor. ______________ ______________ muestro ahora.

2. **A:** Quiero ver la grabadora que se anunció ayer en el periódico. ¿ ______________ ______________ muestra?

   B: Lo siento. Acabo de vender la última. Otra señora se la compró a su hija.

3. **A:** ¿Quiere usted ver otras calculadoras, señora?

   B: Sí, señor. Muéstre ______________, por favor.

4. **A:** A mi hija le gustan esos aretes. Ella quiere probár ______________.

   B: ¡Cómo no, señora! ______________ ______________ puede probar aquí mismo.

Nombre ______________________________ Fecha ______________

G8-7 ¡Qué amiga tan generosa! Imagínate que una de tus amigas les compró varios regalos a sus familiares y amigos. Escribe a quién se los compró.

Modelo: Usted: ¿A quién le compraste ese reloj? (a mi hijo)
Amiga: *Se lo compré a mi hijo.*

Usted	**Amiga**
1. ¿A quién le compraste esos bolígrafos?	(a mi hijo)
2. ¿A quién le compraste esa botella de vino?	(a una amiga)
3. ¿Y esos CDs (discos compactos)?	(a mi esposo)
4. ¿Y esa tarjeta tan bonita?	(a ti, amigo[a])
5. ¿A quién le compraste esos bolígrafos?	(a mi mamá)
6. ¿Y ese papel para cartas?	(a mi abuelita)
7. ¿A quién le compraste el suéter?	(a una sobrina)

G8-8 Entrevista. Pregúntale a otro(a) estudiante.

1. Cuando necesitas dinero para ir de compras, ¿a quiénes se lo pides? ¿Te lo dan? Cuando eras niño(a), ¿a quiénes les pedías dinero? ¿Te lo daban?
2. Cuando vas de compras, ¿a quiénes les compras regalos? ¿Qué cosas les compras? ¿A quiénes les comprabas regalos de niño(a)? ¿Qué les comprabas?
3. ¿Cuándo fue la última vez que fuiste de compras? ¿Con quién fuiste?
4. ¿Qué compraste allí? ¿A quiénes les compraste esa(s) cosa(s)?

Nombre ______________________________ Fecha ______________

G8-9 Unos favores. Conversa con un(a) compañero(a) de clase.

Modelo: **A:** ¿Me das diez dólares hasta la próxima semana?
B: ¿Por qué necesitas el dinero?
A: Lo necesito para comprar comestibles.
B: Bueno, te doy los dólares porque eres mi amigo(a).
o: Lo siento, no puedo dártelos porque no tengo dinero.

1. **A:** ¿Me das (diez dólares / tu cámara) este fin de semana?
2. **B:** ¿Por qué ______________ necesitas?
3. **A:** ______________ necesito para...
4. **B:** Bueno, ______________ ______________ doy porque... (Lo siento, pero...)
5. **A:** ¿Me prestas tu ______________ hasta mañana?
6. **B:** ¿Por qué ______________ necesitas?
7. **A:** ______________ necesito para...
8. **B:** Bueno, ______________ ______________ presto porque... (Lo siento, pero...)

Imperfect tense

The imperfect tense is used to express an indefinite action in the past or a habitual action or state (including descriptions and background information) in the past.

El año pasado **tenía** el pelo largo.	*Last year I had long hair.*
Cuando era niño **vivía** en California.	*When I was a child, I lived in California.*
Siempre **pasaba** mis vacaciones en la playa.	*I always spent/used to spend my vacations at the beach.*

Formation of the imperfect

	***-ar* Verbs**	***-er* Verbs**	***-ir* Verbs**
	cantar	**comer**	**vivir**
	(to sing)	*(to eat)*	*(to live)*
(yo)	cant**aba**	com**ía**	viv**ía**
(tú)	cant**abas**	com**ías**	viv**ías**
(usted, él/ella)	cant**aba**	com**ía**	viv**ía**
(nosotros/nosotras)	cant**ábamos**	com**íamos**	viv**íamos**
(vosotros/vosotras)	cant**abais**	com**íais**	viv**íais**
(ustedes, ellos/ellas)	cant**aban**	com**ían**	viv**ían**

Some irregular verbs

ir: iba, ibas, iba, íbamos, ibais, iban

ser: era, eras, era, éramos, erais, eran

ver: veía, veías, veía, veíamos, veíais, veían

Nombre ______________________________ Fecha ______________

Practiquemos

G8-10 De niña. Alicia está contándole a David algunas cosas que ella hacía de niña. Para saber lo que ella le dice, cambia los verbos indicados en el imperfecto.

Mi familia y yo *vivíamos* (vivir) en una casa pequeña en Milwaukee. Nosotros ______________ (tener) un auto y yo ______________ (tener) una bicicleta. Mi padre ______________ (trabajar) en una compañía de computación. Él ______________ (conocer) bien su trabajo. Mi mamá ______________ (trabajar) en casa y en la universidad. Ella ______________ (dar) clases de español y de inglés. Los sábados y domingos mis hermanos y yo ______________ (divertirse) mucho: ______________ (montar) en bicicleta, mis hermanos ______________ (nadar) en el Lago Michigan y todos los días ______________ (ir) a diferentes partes de Milwaukee para jugar con nuestros amigos. Nosotros nunca ______________ (estar) aburridos porque ______________ (haber) muchas cosas que hacer. Siempre nosotros ______________ (estar) contentos.

G8-11 La infancia de Josefina. Ahora, Josefina nos cuenta su historia. Completa la siguiente narración, usando el imperfecto.

Yo ______________ (vivir) en el Perú con mi familia. ______________ (Ser) la más chica de la familia. ______________ (Ir) al colegio católico. Mis hermanos ______________ (estar) en la universidad. Nosotros ______________ (comer) juntos los fines de semana. Mi mamá ______________ (cocinar) un pescado riquísimo. Mis padres ______________ (ser) muy cariñosos. Siempre ______________ (tener) fiestas de cumpleaños en casa. Nos ______________ (gustar) ir de vacaciones a la sierra. ______________ (Visitar) a mis abuelos que ______________ (vivir) en Cuzco. ¡Qué felices recuerdos!

G8-12 La niñez. ¿Cómo eran las cosas cuando eras niño(a)? Contesta las siguientes preguntas, usando el imperfecto.

1. ¿Dónde vivían tú y tu familia cuando eras niño(a)?

   ____

2. ¿Quién era tu mejor amigo(a)?

   ____

3. ¿Adónde ibas de vacaciones?

   ____

4. ¿A qué jugabas con tus amigos?

   ____

5. ¿Cómo eran tus padres?

   ____

Nombre ______________________ Fecha ______________

Práctica comunicativa suplemental I

ESTUDIANTE A

La receta. Completa tu receta preguntándole a tu compañero(a) la información que te falta. No mires la receta de tu compañero(a); cúbrela con tu cuaderno. Cuando completes toda la información, revísala con tu compañero(a).

Vocabulario útil

aceite	*oil*
batir	*to beat*
carne de res	*beef*
empanado	*breaded*
huevos	*eggs*
pan rallado	*bread crumbs*
sal y pimienta	*salt and pepper*
sartén	*frying pan*
¿Cuánto... necesito?	*How much . . . do I need?*
¿Qué hago después de... ?	*What do I do after . . . ?*

Milanesas

Ingredientes:

____

un paquete de pan rallado

____

aceite sal y pimienta

Instrucciones:

1. ______________________
2. pon el pan rallado en un plato de sopa
3. ______________________
4. luego, bate dos huevos en un plato de sopa y agrégales un poquito de agua
5. pasa el filete empanado por el huevo
6. ______________________, haz lo mismo con el resto de los filetes
7. calienta un poco de aceite (suficiente para cubrir el fondo) en un sartén
8. fríe los filetes empanados de ambos lados hasta que el pan rallado esté color café

Ahora ya tienes las milanesas. Puedes acompañarlas con ensalada o papas fritas.

Nombre ______________________ Fecha ____________

ESTUDIANTE B

La receta. Completa tu receta preguntándole a tu compañero(a) la información que te falta. No mires la receta de tu compañero(a); cúbrela con tu cuaderno. Cuando completes toda la información, revísala con tu compañero(a).

Vocabulario útil

aceite	*oil*
batir	*to beat*
carne de res	*beef*
empanado	*breaded*
huevos	*eggs*
pan rallado	*bread crumbs*
sal y pimienta	*salt and pepper*
sartén	*frying pan*
¿Cuánto... necesito?	*How much . . . do I need?*
¿Qué hago después de... ?	*What do I do after . . . ?*

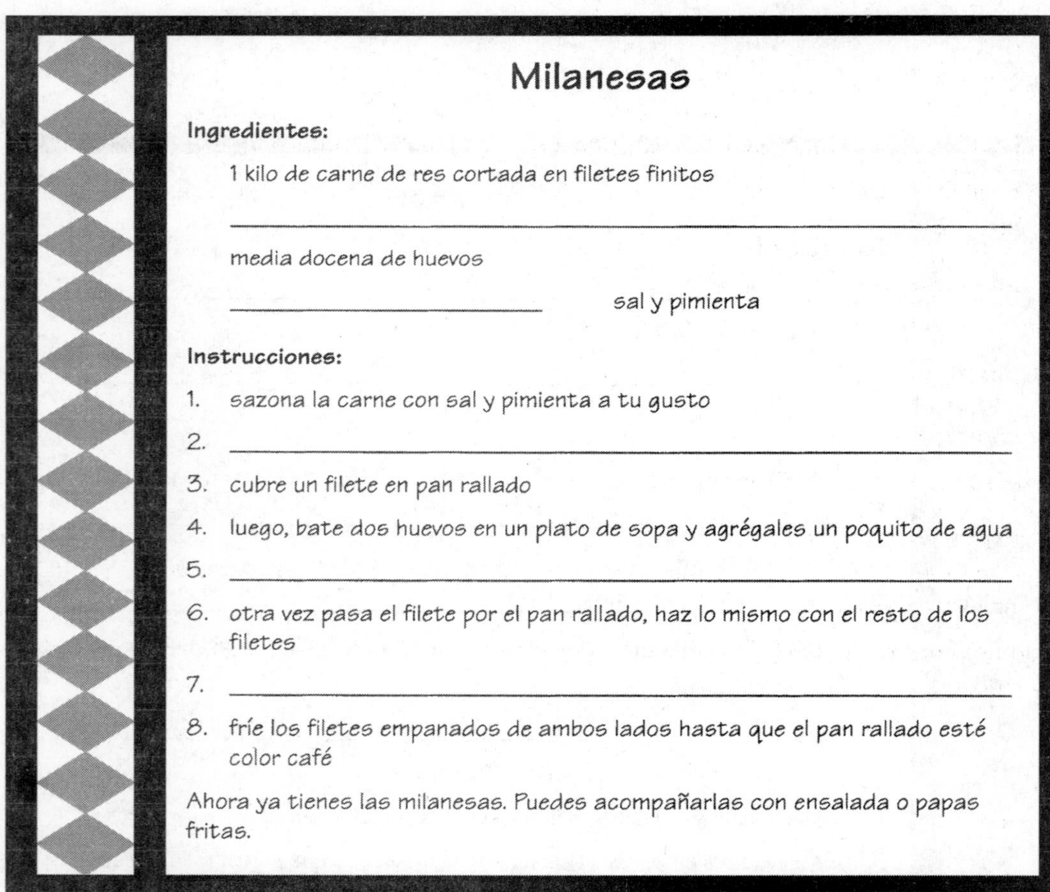

Milanesas

Ingredientes:

1 kilo de carne de res cortada en filetes finitos

____

media docena de huevos

______________ sal y pimienta

Instrucciones:

1. sazona la carne con sal y pimienta a tu gusto
2. ______________________
3. cubre un filete en pan rallado
4. luego, bate dos huevos en un plato de sopa y agrégales un poquito de agua
5. ______________________
6. otra vez pasa el filete por el pan rallado, haz lo mismo con el resto de los filetes
7. ______________________
8. fríe los filetes empanados de ambos lados hasta que el pan rallado esté color café

Ahora ya tienes las milanesas. Puedes acompañarlas con ensalada o papas fritas.

Nombre ____________________ Fecha ____________

Práctica comunicativa suplemental II

ESTUDIANTE A

Memorias. Tu compañero(a) va a escoger una fecha y tú vas a tratar (*to try*) de recordar...

- ¿Dónde estabas en esa fecha?
- ¿Qué hacías?
- ¿Con quién estabas?
- ¿Cuántos años tenías?
- ¿Con quién vivías?

Fechas importantes:

- El 11 de septiembre de 2001 (ataque a las torres gemelas en Nueva York)
- El 31 de agosto de 1997 (la muerte de la Princesa Diana de Inglaterra)
- El 1 de enero de 2002 (el euro es la moneda oficial de 15 países de la Unión Europea)
- El 11 de febrero de 1990 (liberación de Nelson Mandela, líder político en Sur Africa)

ESTUDIANTE B

Memorias. Tu compañero(a) va a escoger una fecha y tú vas a tratar (*to try*) de recordar...

- ¿Dónde estabas en esa fecha?
- ¿Qué hacías?
- ¿Con quién estabas?
- ¿Cuántos años tenías?
- ¿Con quién vivías?

Fechas importantes:

- El 11 de septiembre de 2001 (ataque a las torres gemelas en Nueva York)
- El 20 de abril de 1999 (la tragedia en la escuela secundaria Columbine)
- El 1 de enero de 1994 (Estados Unidos, México y Canadá firman el Tratado de Libre Comercio de Norte América [NAFTA])
- El 2 de noviembre de 2004 (la reelección del Presidente George Bush a la presidencia de los Estados Unidos)

Nombre ______________________ Fecha ______________

LECCIÓN 9 ¿VACACIONES DE VERANO EN DICIEMBRE?

Práctica suplemental

Vocabulario suplemental

Regalos y más regalos

Papelería	*Stationery store*
el álbum para fotos	*photo album*
el papel para cartas	*stationery*
el portarretrato	*picture frame*
el sobre	*envelope*
la tarjeta postal	*postcard*
Equipo electrónico	*Electronic equipment*
el amplificador	*amplifier*
la batería	*drums*
la guitarra eléctrica	*electric guitar*
el piano	*piano*
el teclado electrónico	*electric keyboard*
Equipo deportivo	*Sports equipment*
el bate	*bat*
la(el) cesta(o)	*basket, hoop*
la máquina para hacer ejercicios	*exercise machine*
el palo de golf	*golf club*
la red	*net*

Nombre ______________________ Fecha ______________

Practiquemos

V9-1 Encuesta. Pregúntales a todos tus compañeros qué tipo de regalo les gustaría recibir. Después, haz un gráfico y discute los resultados con el resto de la clase. ¿Son los compañeros de esta clase personas deportivas? ¿Están estos estudiantes más interesados en juegos electrónicos, música, videos, etcétera? ¿Les gustan las joyas a estos compañeros?

	Joyería	Equipo electrónico	Equipo deportivo
Reloj			
Anillos			
Brazaletes/pulseras			
Computadora			
Reproductor de CD portátil			
Cámara de fotografía digital			
Juegos de video			
Radio grabadora			
Juego de pesas			
Caminadora			
Patineta			
Raqueta			
Guante de béisbol			
Más regalos			

Nombre ______________________________ Fecha ______________

V9-2 Deportes. Un(a) compañero(a) de clase va a leer una oración que describe un deporte. Tienes que identificar qué deporte se está describiendo.

1. Los jugadores usan un bate y un guante para poder jugar a este deporte.

   ____

2. Los jugadores meten la pelota en un(a) cesto(a).

   ____

3. Los jugadores usan raquetas y pelotas y pasan la pelota por encima de *(above)* la red.

   ____

4. Los jugadores tienen que caminar muchos kilómetros y usan un palo para este juego.

   ____

5. Las personas juegan a esto en la playa con una pelota y una red.

   ____

V9-3 Música. Pregúntales a tus compañeros de clase si tocan un instrumento, qué instrumento tocan *(they play)* y de qué país es la música.

Instrumento	País de origen de la música

V9-4 Papelería. Pregúntale a un(a) compañero(a) de clase.

1. ¿Te gusta escribir cartas?
2. ¿Qué necesitas para escribir cartas?
3. ¿Escribes tarjetas postales cuando vas de viaje?
4. ¿A quién le escribes tarjetas postales?
5. ¿Te gusta tomar fotografías?
6. ¿Dónde pones las fotografías, en un álbum o en un disco compacto (CD)?

Nombre ______________________ Fecha ______________

GRAMÁTICA SUPLEMENTAL

Preterite versus imperfect tenses

The choice to use the preterite tense or the imperfect tense is not arbitrary; it depends on how a speaker or a writer views the past actions, conditions, and events that he or she describes.

How to use the preterite

The preterite is used to describe past activities and changes in mental or physical states that occurred at a given point in the past. These actions, conditions, and events are viewed as completed.

1. Completed events.

   Brett y Beth Riddle **hicieron** un viaje increíble en canoa. **Comenzaron** su viaje en el Canadá y lo **terminaron** en el Cabo de Horno, Chile.

   Brett and Beth Riddle took an incredible trip by canoe. They began their trip in Canada and ended it in Cape Horn, Chile.

2. Completed actions.

   Los Riddle **salieron** el 8 de junio de 2005 y **siguieron** varios ríos hasta llegar a la Florida. Luego **cruzaron** el Mar Caribe, **entraron** a Venezuela y **continuaron** su viaje por el Brasil, el Paraguay, la Argentina y Chile. **Llegaron** al Cabo de Horno el 1° de marzo de 2006. Ellos **conocieron** a muchas personas interesantes, **visitaron** lugares fascinantes y **sacaron** fotos maravillosas.

   The Riddles left on June 8, 2005, and followed several rivers until they arrived in Florida. Then they crossed the Caribbean Sea, entered Venezuela, and continued their trip through Brazil, Paraguay, Argentina, and Chile. They arrived at Cape Horn on March 1, 2006. They met many interesting people, visited fascinating places, and took marvelous photos.

3. Completed mental and physical states.

   Un día, Beth **se enfermó** de diarrea. Otro día Brett **tuvo** un dolor de estómago.

   One day, Beth became sick with diarrhea. Another day Brett had a stomachache.

How to use the imperfect

1. The imperfect is used to describe past actions and events that were repeated habitually; that is, it describes how people, places, things, events, and conditions were.

   Todos los días antes de comenzar su largo viaje, Brett y Beth **aprendían** algunas palabras nuevas en español, **leían** libros sobre Norteamérica y Suramérica y **estudiaban** el mapa del los continentes.

   Every day before beginning their long trip, Brett and Beth learned some new words in Spanish, read books about North America and South America, and studied a map of the continents.

2. Spanish speakers use the imperfect tense to provide background information about what was going on in the past when something else took place or was taking place.

   Eran las cinco de la mañana y **hacía** buen tiempo para comenzar el viaje en canoa. Mientras Beth **preparaba** el desayuno, Brett **estudiaba** algunos mapas. Los dos **estaban** contentos y **se sentían** felices de la vida.

   It was 5 a.m. and the weather was good for starting the canoe trip. While Beth prepared breakfast, Brett studied some maps. The two of them were happy and felt happy about life.

Nombre ______________________ Fecha ______________

How to use the preterite and imperfect together
Spanish speakers often use the preterite and imperfect tenses together to describe past experiences and to put past actions and events within the framework of what was happening at the time they occurred.

> Cuando los Riddle **terminaron** su viaje, **hicieron** muchas presentaciones audiovisuales sobre sus aventuras. Ellos **querían** describir adónde **fueron** y lo que **hicieron** en sus aventuras por el continente.
>
> *When the Riddles finished their trip, they gave many audiovisual presentations of their adventures. They wanted to describe where they went and what they did on their adventures around the continent.*

Practiquemos

G9-5 Un joven aventurero. Completa la siguiente narración sobre un viaje que hizo un aventurero. Indica las formas correctas de los verbos entre paréntesis.

Cuando James (tuvo / tenía) veinte años, (hizo / hacía) una aventura de autostop *(hitchhiking)* a México porque (quiso / quería) conocer aquel país y a su gente. Él (fue / era) un estudiante dedicado, (supo / sabía) hablar un poco de español y le (gustó / gustaba) viajar.

James (pasó / pasaba) un mes preparándose para el viaje. Por fin, (llegó / llegaba) el día para salir. El joven se (levantó / levantaba) a las seis de la mañana, se (afeitó / afeitaba), se (duchó / duchaba), se (vistió / vestía) de camisa, jeans y zapatos de tenis, (comió / comía) cereal con leche y (bebió / bebía) jugo de naranja.

Luego (fue / iba) al dormitorio de sus padres, que todavía (durmieron / dormían). Los (despertó / despertaba) y se (despidió / despedía) de ellos: (abrazó / abrazaba) a su papá y le (dio / daba) un beso a su mamá.

James se (puso / ponía) la mochila *(backpack)* y (salió / salía) de su casa. Pero, ¡qué horror! (Comenzó / Comenzaba) a llover muy duro. El pobre joven (estuvo / estaba) muy frustrado, pero ¿qué (pudo / podía) hacer? James (pensó / pensaba) un momento. Luego él (tomó / tomaba) una decisión natural: (volvió / volvía) a casa y (salió / salía) el próximo día en que (hizo / hacía) mejor tiempo. ¡(Fue / Era) una decisión excelente!

Nombre ______________________________ Fecha ______________

G9-6 Otros dos aventureros. Mira el mensaje electrónico que está a continuación, que Beth Riddle le mandó a su profesor de español y de portugués. Escríbelo otra vez cambiando los infinitivos en letras oscuras **(bold)** por las formas correctas del pretérito o del imperfecto.

Querido Profesor:

Ayer Brett y yo **llegar** a Manaus, Brasil. ¡Qué bonito día **ser**! **Hacer** mucho calor y **llover** un poco, pero los residentes de la ciudad nos **recibir** bien. (Nosotros) **Estar** muy cansados pero **sentirse** felices porque la gente nos **comprender** cuando (nosotros) les **hablar** en nuestro portugués no muy bueno. Brett y yo **ir** directamente al Hotel Victoria donde **tener** una reservación. ¿Sabe usted qué **ser** la primera cosa que (nosotros) **hacer**? **Acostarnos** y **dormir** por diez horas! Después, **levantarse** y **lavar** toda nuestra ropa que **estar** muy sucia. En la tarde (nosotros) **conocer** al Ministro de Educación, quien nos **invitar** a hacer una presentación sobre nuestro viaje en el famoso teatro de Manaus. **Venir** más de doscientas personas, y la presentación **salir** bien. Cuando (nosotros) **salir** del teatro, dos periodistas nos **decir** que **querer** entrevistarnos *(to interview us)*. Brett y yo **hablar** con ellos por quince minutos, luego **comer** en un café donde se nos **servir** comida típica de la región amazónica.

Hasta pronto,
Beth

G9-7 Un día inolvidable. En algunos párrafos describe una experiencia que nunca vas a olvidar. Usa las siguientes preguntas como guía.

¿Qué tiempo hacía? ¿Qué hora era? ¿Con quién estabas? ¿Qué hacían ustedes? Luego, ¿adónde fuiste? ¿Qué pasó y a quién? ¿Qué hiciste después? ¿Con quién hablaste?

____
____
____
____
____
____
____
____
____
____

Nombre ______________________ Fecha ______________

Práctica comunicativa suplemental I

Un asesinato misterioso en Chile. En grupos de cuatro, tú y tus compañeros tienen una lista de sospechosos *(suspects)*, armas *(weapons)* y lugares *(places)*. También reciben quince pistas *(clues)*. Tienen que descubrir quién mató *(killed)* a Eduardo Woolf. Usando las pistas, traten de resolver el crimen. Luego comparen sus resultados con los otros grupos.

Vocabulario útil

aspiradora	*vacuum cleaner*
culpable	*guilty*
máquina de afeitar	*electric razor*
martillo	*hammer*
secador de cabello / pelo	*blow dryer*
si	*if*

Sospechosos	Armas	Lugares
Carlos	martillo	Santiago de Chile
Renata	equipo de submarinismo	Viña del Mar
Pablo	raqueta	Punta Arenas, Patagonia
Marta	secador de cabello / pelo	Valparaíso
Paco	máquina de afeitar	Iquique
Bárbara		San Antonio

Pistas

1. La raqueta fue la única arma en Iquique.
2. Si el arma del asesinato fue un martillo, el culpable fue Pablo.
3. Carlos tenía el único secador de cabello.
4. El arma del asesinato no fue la raqueta.
5. Si el asesinato ocurrió en San Vicente, Marta es culpable.
6. El secador de cabello fue la única arma en Valparaíso.
7. Paco estaba con Bárbara cuando ocurrió el asesinato.
8. El martillo fue la única arma en Santiago de Chile.
9. Renata fue la única sospechosa en Iquique.
10. El asesinato no ocurrió en Punta Arenas, Patagonia.
11. La única máquina de afeitar estaba en Viña del Mar.
12. Bárbara estaba en Santiago cuando ocurrió el asesinato.
13. El asesinato no ocurrió en Viña del Mar.
14. Sólo había un sospechoso en el lugar donde ocurrió el crimen.
15. El culpable no usó el secador de pelo.
16. Renata nunca aprendió a nadar.
17. El asesinato ocurrió en la playa de San Antonio.

Nombre ______________________________ Fecha ______________

Práctica comunicativa suplemental II

Tu vida en el pasado. En grupos de cuatro, escriban las siguientes expresiones de tiempo en tarjetas (o pedazos de papel), una expresión por tarjeta. Pueden agregar otras expresiones. Hagan una pila con las tarjetas. Saca una tarjeta y di algo acerca de tu vida en el pasado y compárala con tu vida hoy. Luego otra persona del grupo saca una tarjeta y hace lo mismo. Continúen hasta que no haya más tarjetas.

Modelo: *El año pasado iba al cine los fines de semana; este año voy al gimnasio.*

Vocabulario útil

anoche	*last night*
anteayer	*the day before yesterday*
ayer de mañana	*yesterday morning*
el año pasado	*last year*
el fin de semana pasado	*last weekend*
el mes pasado	*last month*
el verano pasado	*last summer*
en 2004	*in 2004*
en los 90	*in the 90s*
hace dos años	*two years ago*

Nombre ______________________ Fecha ______________

PASO 4 De Compras

LECCIÓN 10 ¿DESEA ALGO MÁS?

Práctica suplemental

VOCABULARIO SUPLEMENTAL

Más frutas y vegetales / verduras	***More fruits and vegetables***
el aguacate	*avocado*
la calabaza	*pumpkin*
la espinaca	*spinach*
los guisantes	*peas*
el hongo / el champiñón	*mushroom*
las judías / las vainitas	*green beans*
el mango	*mango*
la mora	*blackberry*
el pepino	*cucumber*
la sandía / la patilla	*watermelon*

PRACTIQUEMOS

V10-1 Descripciones. Lee cada descripción y escoge la fruta o la verdura que mejor se asocie con la descripción.

Modelo: Se usa para hacer pasteles dulces. *la mora*

1. Se usa para preparar el guacamole mexicano. ______
2. Es una fruta tropical. ______
3. Popeye la come para tener fuerza. ______
4. Es una fruta que se come durante el verano en los Estados Unidos. ______
5. Su usa para preparar sopas y también pasteles. Se come durante octubre y noviembre en el Día de Acción de Gracias. ______
6. Se usa para hacer una sopa cremosa *(creamy)*. ______
7. Se usan en las ensaladas. ______

Nombre ______________________________ Fecha ______________

V10-2 Cena del Día de Acción de Gracias. Tú y tu compañero(a) de clase están en Buenos Aires de visita en casa de una familia argentina. Ustedes quieren preparar una cena del Día de Acción de Gracias para esta familia ya que ellos no conocen esta fiesta. ¿Qué ingredientes necesitan? ¿Cuál es el menú? Conversa con tu compañero(a) y decidan lo que van a preparar.

Modelo: —*Necesitamos comprar calabazas.*
—*Sí, podemos preparar una sopa de calabaza o un pastel...*

____

____

____

____

____

____

____

____

V10-3 En el mercado. Después de hacer el menú y la lista de ingredientes que necesitan para la cena del Día de Acción de Gracias, tú y tu compañero(a) van al mercado. Escriban un diálogo usando las expresiones para comprar y preséntenlo a la clase.

Expresiones para comprar
Las siguientes expresiones se usan cuando una persona va al supermercado o al mercado al aire libre a comprar frutas, verduras u otras cosas y quiere ser amable con los vendedores.

¿A cuánto el kilo?	*How much is a kilo?*
Favor de + infinitive.	*Would you please . . . ?*
¿Me da... ?	*Could you give me . . . ?*
¿Me hace el favor de + infinitive?	*Would you please . . . ?*
¿Quiere darme... ?	*Would you give me . . . ?*

Modelo: —*Para la calabaza, ¿cuánto está el kilo?*
—*Está a tres pesos el kilo. ¿Cuántos kilos quiere?*

____

____

____

____

____

____

____

____

Nombre ____________________ Fecha ____________

Gramática suplemental

Informal commands
Spanish speakers use informal commands mainly to tell children, close friends, relatives, and pets to do or not to do something.

How to form affirmative informal commands

1. For most Spanish verbs, use the **él/ella** verb forms of the present tense.

Infinitive	*Él/Ella* Form		*Tú* Command
hablar	habla	→	**habla**
comer	come	→	**come**
escribir	escribe	→	**escribe**
llegar	llega	→	**llega**
volver	vuelve	→	**vuelve**

—¡**Mira** esas uvas grandes! *Look at those big grapes!*
—Sí. **Prueba** una, Laura. *Yes. Try one, Laura.*
—Mmm. ¡**Compra** medio kilo! *Mmm. Buy a half kilo!*

2. Eight verbs have irregular affirmative **tú** commands.

decir	**di**	salir	**sal**
hacer	**haz**	ser	**sé**
ir	**ve**	tener	**ten**
poner	**pon**	venir	**ven**

—**Ven** al mercado conmigo. *Come to the market with me.*
—Sí, pero **sé** paciente. *Yes, but be patient.*

3. Attach pronouns to affirmative **tú** commands. If the command form has two or more syllables, it carries an accent mark over the stressed vowel to retain the stress of the verb.

—**Dime,** ¿es éste mi sándwich? *Tell me, is this my sandwich?*
—Sí. **Siéntate** aquí y **cómelo**. *Yes. Sit here and eat it.*

How to form negative informal commands

1. For all Spanish verbs, use **no** before the **usted** command and add **-s** to it.

Infinitive	*Usted* Command		*Tú* Command
hablar	hable	→	**no hables**
comer	coma	→	**no comas**
escribir	escriba	→	**no escribas**
llegar	llegue	→	**no llegues**
salir	salga	→	**no salgas**
volver	vuelva	→	**no vuelvas**

—**No compres** más zanahorias. *Don't buy more carrots.*
—**No digas** eso. ¡Me gustan! *Don't say that. I like them!*

2. Place pronouns before the verb in negative commands.

—Esa piña... **No la compres.** *That pineapple . . . Don't buy it.*
—Sí, papá. **No te preocupes.** *Yes, Dad. Don't worry.*

Nombre ______________________________________ Fecha ______________

PRACTIQUEMOS

G10-4 Conflictos entre hermanas. Completa la siguiente conversación entre Sara y su hermana Laura usando lógicamente los mandatos de la lista.

sé	dame	llámame	no hables
oye	mira	recuerda	no gastes
ten	toma	no estés	no me pidas

Sara: ______________, Laura. Vamos al cine ahora. ______________ tanto.

Laura: ______________ más paciencia, niña. Estoy hablando con mi novio.

Sara: Sí, pero ______________ que la película comienza en treinta minutos.

Laura: Ay, sí. Bueno, Raúl. ______________ mañana... Chao, mi amor.

Sara: Laura, ______________ 5 dólares, por favor. No tengo dinero.

Laura: ¿Cómo? Nunca tienes dinero. ______________ tanto en ropa, Sara.

Sara: ______________ de mal humor conmigo. Puedes llevar mi suéter nuevo.

Laura: No, gracias. ______________, ______________ este dinero y ______________ más.

Sara: Gracias, Laura. Eres muy amable. Vamos... y ______________ más paciente conmigo, por favor.

G10-5 Consejos de un amigo. Javier González tiene que ir a Tokio, Japón, para hablar con los dueños de su empresa. Su amigo José le dio algunos consejos sobre lo que él debe y no debe hacer en Tokio. ¿Qué le dijo José?

Modelo: cambiar / tu dinero en un banco; no lo / cambiar / en un hotel
Cambia tu dinero en un banco; no lo cambies en un hotel.

1. caminar / en todas partes de Tokio, pero no / caminar / solo de noche
____
2. ir / a Disney Tokio, pero no / ir / con un grupo muy grande
____
3. pasar / más tiempo con tus colegas; no / pasar / mucho tiempo solo
____
4. tomar / agua mineral o un refresco; no / tomar / el agua del hotel
____
5. llevar / ropa conservadora en Tokio; no / llevar / ropa muy exótica
____
6. salir / frecuentemente de tu hotel, pero no / salir / sin tu cámara
____
7. sacar / fotos de tus amigos, pero no las / sacar / sin pedirles permiso
____

Nombre ______________________ Fecha ______________

G10-6 Consejos para Melissa. Melissa Pérez, una amiga de Sara Galeano, va a trabajar como camarera en un restaurante mexicano al este de Los Ángeles. Escribe lo que Sara le dice a su amiga.

Modelo: llegar a tiempo a tu trabajo
Llega a tiempo a tu trabajo.

1. no gastar todas tus propinas
____
2. nunca ofender a tus clientes
____
3. lavarte las manos frecuentemente
____
4. servirles bien a tus clientes
____
5. no acostarte tarde los días de trabajo
____
6. nunca decir malas palabras en tu trabajo
____
7. dormir un mínimo de siete horas al día
____
8. trabajar mucho, pero / divertirte también
____
9. tener paciencia y / ser simpática con todos
____
10. llamarme por teléfono y / decirme cómo te va
____

Nombre ______________________ Fecha ______________

More practice with comparatives and superlatives

G10-7 Tus compañeros(as) y tú. Entrevista *(Interview)* a cuatro de tus compañeros(as), y escribe la información necesaria en el cuadro.

Compañero(a)	¿Qué cursos o materias estudias?	¿Cuántos hermanos tienes?	¿Cuántas horas trabajas?	Pasatiempos

Ahora contesta las siguientes preguntas.

1. ¿Cuántos cursos tienes tú? ¿Tienes más o menos cursos que tus compañeros(as)?

   ____

2. ¿Cuántos hermanos tienes? ¿Tus compañeros(as) tienen más o menos hermanos que tú?

   ____

3. ¿Dónde trabajas? ¿Cuántas horas trabajas? ¿Trabajas más horas, menos horas o tantas horas como tus compañeros(as)?

   ____

4. ¿Qué pasatiempos tienen tus compañeros(as) y tú? ¿Quién practica más o menos deportes?

   ____

G10-8 Los mejores restaurantes de la ciudad. En grupos de cuatro personas, decidan cuáles son los dos mejores restaurantes de la ciudad y cuáles los dos peores y por qué (por ejemplo, la comida es / no es fresca, es / no es económica, es / no es saludable *[healthy]*, el servicio es bueno / malo, etcétera).

Modelo: Compañero(a): *El mejor restaurante de la ciudad es el restaurante español Salud, y el peor restaurante es el de comida rápida, Hamburguesa Lista, porque...*

	Servicio	Frutas, vegetales, ingredientes frescos	Comida saludable	Comida económica
El mejor:				
El mejor:				
El peor:				
El peor:				

Nombre ______________________ Fecha ____________

1. ¿Cuál es el mejor restaurante de los dos mejores? ¿Cuál es el peor restaurante de los dos peores? ¿Por qué?

____

2. ¿Cuál de los restaurantes tiene la comida más saludable / más fresca?

____

3. ¿Cuál de los restaurantes es el menos económico?

____

4. ¿Cuál de los restaurantes tiene el peor servicio?

____

Comenta la información con toda la clase.

G10-9 Mis opiniones personales. Expresa tus opiniones con un(a) compañero(a) de clase.

1. En mi opinión, el mejor restaurante de esta ciudad es ____________. Creo que una de las mejores comidas de ese restaurante es ____________. Al contrario, el peor restaurante por aquí es ____________. ¿Qué crees tú?

2. La mejor música es ____________. Uno de los (las) mejores cantantes del mundo se llama ____________; me gusta mucho escuchar su música. Al contrario, uno de los (las) peores cantantes se llama ____________; su música es horrible.

3. Creo que una de las mejores películas recientes es ____________. Los actores de esa película son ____________ y ____________. En cambio, una de las peores películas recientes se llama ____________; es una película mala.

Formal (usted) commands

Spanish speakers use formal commands when they address people as **usted** or **ustedes.**

How to form affirmative/negative formal commands

Infinitive	**Ud. Command**	**Uds. Command**
hablar	hab**le** / no hab**le**	habl**en** / no habl**en**
comer	co**ma** / no co**ma**	com**an** / no com**an**
escribir	escri**ba** / no escri**ba**	escrib**an** / no escri**ban**
llegar	lleg**ue** / no lleg**ue**	llegu**en** / no llegu**en**
volver	vuel**va** / no vuel**va**	vuelv**an** / no vuelv**an**

Nombre ______________________ Fecha ______________

G10-10 Problemas y consejos. Ahora le vas a dar consejos a las personas que trabajan en el mercado del Sr. Gildo Navarro en Buenos Aires.

Modelo: ¡Sr. Navarro, no *venda* (vender) los productos tan caros!

1. María Alexandra, ______________ (hacer) el pedido de vinos de las Bodegas Etchard.
2. Sr. Peraza, ______________ (ayudar) a María Alexandra con las compras de las frutas y de los vegetales frescos.
3. Sr. Navarro, ______________ (ser) más generoso con el sueldo *(salary)* de sus empleados.
4. María Alexandra, no ______________ (preocuparse) por la contabilidad del mercado.
5. Sr. Peraza, ______________ (llegar) más temprano a la tienda y ______________ (salir) más tarde del trabajo.

G10-11 ¡Mi Buenos Aires querido! Imagínate que vas a ir a vivir con una familia argentina por un mes para practicar español. Tu profesor(a) de español te da cinco consejos sobre lo que debes y no debes hacer en la casa de esta familia. Usa los verbos como **estudiar, salir, pasear, comer, bailar tango, leer, ver, visitar,** etcétera para formar los mandatos formales **(usted).**

Modelo: *No hable inglés con la familia. Hable español.*

1. ____

____

____

2. ____

____

____

3. ____

____

____

4. ____

____

____

5. ____

____

____

Nombre ______________________________ Fecha ______________

Práctica comunicativa suplemental I

Prueba de cultura. En parejas, lean las siguientes preguntas sobre la geografía de Latinoamérica con tu compañero(a) y traten de resolverlas. ¡A ver cuántas pueden resolver!

Geografía de América Latina

1. ¿Cuál es el país más pequeño de Suramérica?

   ____

2. ¿Cuál es el país más grande de Suramérica?

   ____

3. ¿Cómo se llama el río más largo de Suramérica?

   ____

4. ¿A qué país pertenecen *(belong)* las islas Galápagos?

   ____

5. ¿Cuál es la capital de la República Dominicana?

   ____

6. ¿Cuál es la catarata más alta del mundo y dónde está?

   ____

7. ¿Cuál es una de las ciudades más pobladas del mundo que está en Latinoamérica?

   ____

8. ¿Cuál es la mejor estación *(season)* para visitar Costa Rica? ¿Por qué?

   ____

9. ¿En qué país se encuentra la distancia más corta entre el Océano Atlántico y el Océano Pacífico?

   ____

10. ¿Cuál es la montaña más alta en Los Andes latinoamericanos?

    ____

Inventen tres preguntas más y haganlas al resto de la clase. (Puedes encontrar algunas de las respuestas en: http://www.superchicos.net/triviasuramerica.htm.)

____

____

____

Nombre ______________________ Fecha ____________

Práctica comunicativa suplemental II

ESTUDIANTE A

Mapas. Mira tu mapa y pregúntale a tu compañero(a) cómo llegar a los siguientes lugares. No mires el mapa de tu compañero(a). Pídele instrucciones y marca los lugares en tu mapa. Luego dale direcciones de cómo llegar hasta los lugares que él (ella) necesita.

el banco   la farmacia   el supermercado   el cine

Vocabulario útil

Camina dos cuadras.	*Walk two blocks.*
¿Cómo llego a... ?	*How do I get to . . . ?*
Dobla a la derecha.	*Turn right.*
Dobla a la izquierda.	*Turn left.*
¿Dónde está... ?	*Where's . . . ?*
Sigue derecho.	*Go straight.*

Seis

Cinco

Calle Bolívar

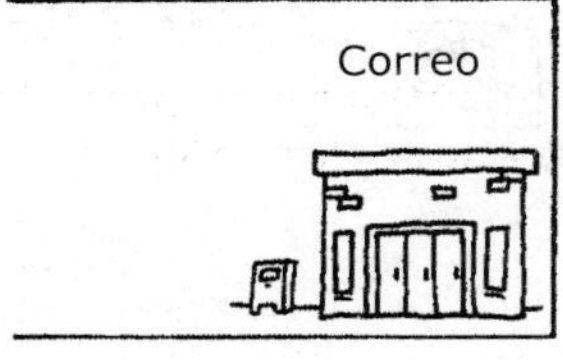

Avenida

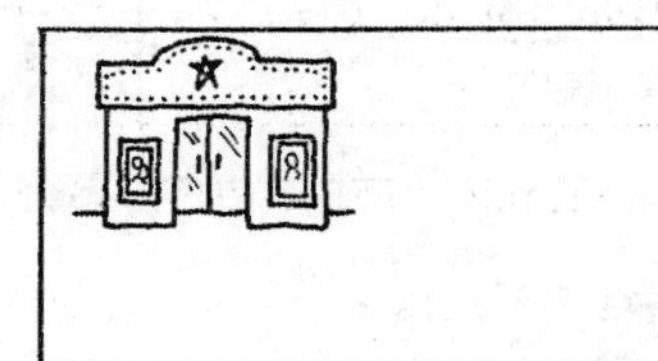

Avenida

Calle Martí

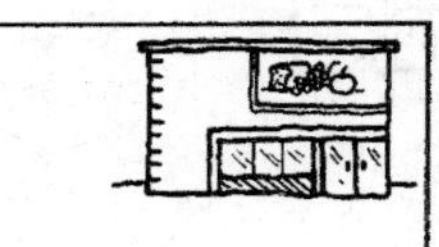

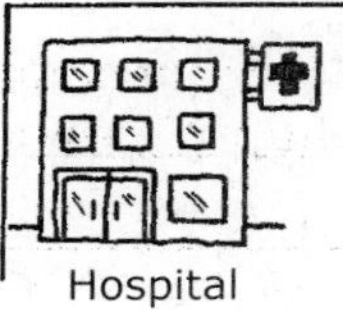

ESTUDIANTE B

Mapas. Mira tu mapa y pregúntale a tu compañero(a) cómo llegar a los siguientes lugares. No mires el mapa de tu compañero(a). Pídele instrucciones y marca los lugares en tu mapa. Luego dale direcciones de cómo llegar hasta los lugares que él (ella) necesita.

la biblioteca   el hospital   la florería   el correo

Vocabulario útil

Camina dos cuadras.	*Walk two blocks.*
¿Cómo llego a... ?	*How do I get to . . . ?*
Dobla a la derecha.	*Turn right.*
Dobla a la izquierda.	*Turn left.*
¿Dónde está... ?	*Where's . . . ?*
Sigue derecho.	*Go straight.*

Banco

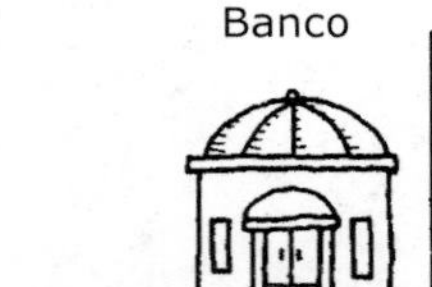

Seis

Cinco

Farmacia

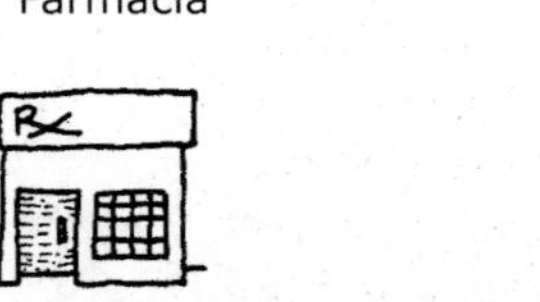

Calle Bolívar

Avenida

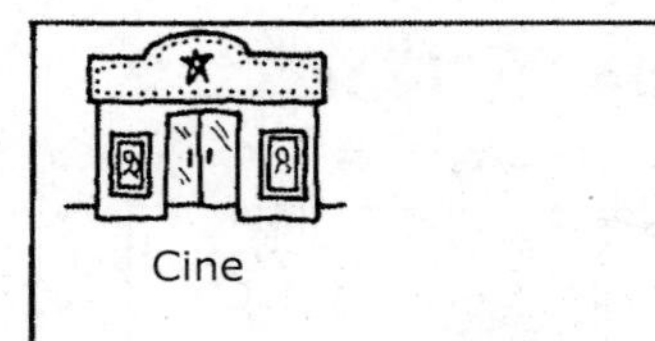

Cine

Avenida

Calle Martí

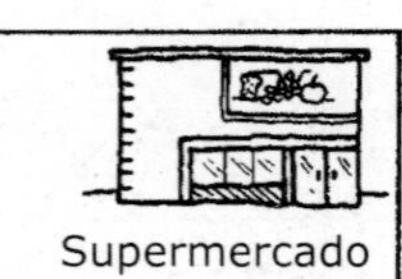

Supermercado

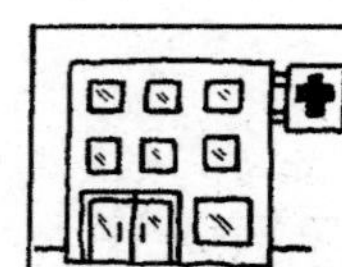

Nombre ______________________ Fecha ______________

LECCIÓN 11 ¡VAMOS DE COMPRAS! ¡QUÉ CHÉVERE!

Práctica suplemental

VOCABULARIO SUPLEMENTAL

La ropa y los colores

Ropa	*Clothing*
la bata de baño	*robe*
los calzoncillos	*boxer shorts*
la chaqueta	*jacket*
los pantalones cortos	*shorts*
la ropa interior	*underwear*
el saco	*blazer*
la sudadera	*jogging suit, sweatshirt*
los vaqueros / los jeans	*blue jeans*
Colores	*Colors*
azul claro	*light blue*
azul marino	*navy blue*
azul oscuro	*dark blue*
beige	*beige*
de cuadros	*plaid*
de rayas	*striped*
unicolor	*solid color*
Para describir la ropa	*To describe clothing*
ancho(a)	*wide*
¿Cómo me queda?	*How does it fit me?*
Te queda bien / mal.	*It fits you fine/poorly.*
estrecho(a) / angosto(a)	*narrow, tight*
rebajado(a)	*on sale*
estar de moda	*to be fashionable/in style*

PRACTIQUEMOS

V11-1 ¿Cuándo usas... ? Asocia un lugar o una situación de la columna A con las prendas de vestir de la columna B.

Modelo: Se usa en la piscina / alberca: *traje de baño*

A

1. Cuando vas a la playa en el verano usas ______________.
2. Beatriz usa una cuando sale a correr ______________.
3. Antes de vestirnos, nos ponemos la ______________.
4. Roberto saldrá esta noche a una cena elegante, así que se pondrá un ______________.
5. Al salir del baño, Alicia usa su ______________.
6. Elizabeth va a montar a caballo, así que se pondrá sus ______________.
7. Kay tiene un almuerzo de negocios, así que necesita llevar una ______________.

B

ropa interior
saco
pantalones cortos
vaqueros / jeans
sudadera
chaqueta
bata de baño
traje de baño

Nombre ______________________________ Fecha ______________

VI1-2 **¿Cómo me queda?** Elizabeth, Beatriz y Graciela fueron de compras pero encontraron varios problemas con las prendas de vestir. Estudia cada problema con tu compañero(a) y escribe una solución.

Prenda de vestir	Problema	Solución
falda	Me queda ancha.	Busca una más pequeña.
pantalones cortos	Me quedan anchos y no me gustan las rayas.	
chaqueta	Ya tengo una unicolor.	
sudadera	Es muy cara.	
vaqueros grises	No están de moda en ese color.	
ropa interior	Me queda estrecha.	
saco	No me gusta a cuadros.	
vestido	No me gusta el color claro y me queda estrecho.	
camiseta	Es muy cara y no me gusta unicolor.	

VI1-3 **Situaciones.** Tú y tu amigo(a) irán a Venezuela de vacaciones en agosto. Es verano, aunque en las montañas hace frío. Hagan una lista de las prendas de vestir que necesitan para las siguientes actividades.

Modelo: las montañas de los Andes donde hace mucho frío
Vamos a llevar abrigos, guantes, pañuelos y botas.

1. las playas de Río Chico en el centro del país
2. un restaurante de comida típica venezolana para comer arepas *(round cornbread)* y pabellón criollo *(sheared beef, rice, and fried plantains).*
3. una fiesta muy elegante en el Hotel Tamanaco de Caracas
4. el Pico Espejo, una montaña en los Andes venezolanos
5. ir de compras al centro comercial San Bill

____

____

____

____

____

Nombre ______________________ Fecha ______________

GRAMÁTICA SUPLEMENTAL

The future tense
You have learned to use the present indicative forms of **ir a** + infinitive to express actions, conditions, and events that are going to take place (e.g., **Voy a viajar a Venezuela este verano.** *I'm going to travel to Venezuela this summer*).

- Spanish speakers use this construction frequently in everyday conversation.
- Another way to express future ideas in Spanish is to use the future tense.

How to form the future tense

1. Add these personal endings to the infinitive of most verbs: **-é, -ás, -á, -emos, -éis, -án.**

viajar	**volver**	**vivir**	**ir**
viajar**é**	volver**é**	vivir**é**	ir**é**
viajar**ás**	volver**ás**	vivir**ás**	ir**ás**
viajar**á**	volver**á**	vivir**á**	ir**á**
viajar**emos**	volver**emos**	vivir**emos**	ir**emos**
viajar**éis**	volver**éis**	vivir**éis**	ir**éis**
viajar**án**	volver**án**	vivir**án**	ir**án**

—¿Cuándo **llegaremos** a Los Andes? *When will we get to the Andes?*
—**Estaremos** allí en ocho horas. *We'll be there in eight hours.*
—Bien. Luego **iré** a subir las montañas. *Good. Later, I'll climb the mountains.*
—Sí, y los niños **se divertirán.** *And the children will have fun.*

2. Add the future endings to the irregular stems of these verbs.

Verb	**Stem**		**Ending**	**Example**
decir	**dir**			
hacer	**har**	→	-é	diré
poder	**podr**	→	-ás	dirás
poner	**pondr**	→	-á	dirá
querer	**querr**	→	-emos	diremos
saber	**sabr**	→	-éis	diréis
salir	**saldr**	→	-án	dirán
tener	**tendr**			
venir	**vendr**			

Note: The future tense of **hay** is **habrá** *(there will be)*.

—¿**Habrá** tiempo para nadar? *Will there be time to swim?*
—Claro. **Tendrás** dos horas. *Sure. You'll have two hours.*
—¿Qué otras cosas **haremos**? *What other things will we do?*
—Te lo **diré** cuando lleguemos. *I'll tell you when we arrive.*
—¿**Podremos** visitar un museo? *Will we be able to visit a museum?*
—Cómo no. **Tendremos** tiempo. *Of course. We'll have time.*

Nombre ______________________________ Fecha ______________

How to use the future tense

Spanish speakers use the future tense to express actions, conditions, and events that will take place, particularly at a distant future time.

Su excursión por Los Andes **comenzará** en Mérida donde su guía lo **recibirá** en el aeropuerto. Allí usted **conocerá** a sus compañeros de viaje, luego **irán** en autobús a su hotel. **Pasarán** tres días en la ciudad de Mérida, luego...

Your tour through the Andes will begin in Mérida where your guide will meet you in the airport. There you will meet your traveling companions, then you will go by bus to your hotel. You will spend three days in the city of Mérida, then . . .

Practiquemos

G11-4 Opiniones. ¿Eres optimista o pesimista? Léele las siguientes ideas a otro(a) estudiante, quien debe decirte cómo opina él o ella.

Modelo: Algún día todos hablaremos más de una lengua.
A: *Algún día todos hablaremos más de una lengua.*
B: *Estoy de acuerdo.* o: *No estoy de acuerdo. Hablaremos sólo el inglés.*

1. Casi todos viviremos por más de 100 años.
2. Se aprenderán idiomas tomando una pastilla.
3. Se aprenderá a conservar más la naturaleza.
4. La gente se vestirá diferente.
5. Hará más calor en el planeta en el próximo siglo.
6. Más personas estarán sin comida que en este siglo.
7. Habrá más conflictos mundiales antes del siglo XXII.

G11-5 ¿Qué pasará? Completa las siguientes oraciones, usando los verbos adecuados de las listas.

1. ¿Qué harán Elizabeth y Graciela después de salir de su cuarto en el hotel de la Isla de Margarita en Venezuela?

   bajar caminar ir meter pagar salir

   Ellas *bajarán* en el ascensor desde el tercer piso hasta la planta baja del hotel. __________ a la recepción donde __________ la cuenta de su cuarto. Después, __________ a su auto en que __________ sus maletas. Luego, __________ para la playa de la Restinga.

2. ¿Qué hará una empleada del hotel ahora en el cuarto de Elizabeth y Graciela ya que ellas se fueron del hotel?

   hacer lavar limpiar pasar poner sacar

   La empleada __________ el cuarto. Por ejemplo, ella __________ la aspiradora *(vacuum cleaner)*, __________ las camas y __________ la basura *(garbage)*. Después, __________ la ducha y __________ jabón y toallas limpias en el baño.

Nombre ______________________________ Fecha ______________

G11-6 Juego en ronda. Forma un grupo pequeño con otros tres o cuatro estudiantes. Luego una persona comienza, diciendo una actividad que hará en el futuro. Entonces otro(a) estudiante repite lo que dijo la primera persona, luego dice lo que él o ella hará en el futuro. Así sigue este juego.

Modelo: **Pete:** Buscaré otro trabajo.
Beth: *Pete buscará otro trabajo y yo daré una fiesta.*
Judy: *Pete buscará otro trabajo, Beth dará una fiesta y yo haré un viaje.*

G11-7 Algunas predicciones. ¿Cómo será tu situación en el año 2008 o 2010? Contesta las siguientes preguntas usando el tiempo del futuro.

1. ¿Cuántos años tendrás? ______________________________

2. ¿Cómo serás físicamente? ______________________________

3. ¿Cuál será tu estado civil? ______________________________

4. ¿Dónde y con quién(es) vivirás? ______________________________

5. ¿Dónde trabajarás y qué tipo de trabajo harás? ______________________________

Ahora escribe otras cuatro o cinco acciones, condiciones o eventos interesantes que tendrán lugar en tu futuro dentro de los próximos cinco años.

____

Nombre ________________________ Fecha ____________

G11-8 Una oferta fabulosa. Imagínate que tú y un(a) compañero(a) de clase quieren ir al Hotel Villa Linda. Primero, lean el anuncio; luego contesten las preguntas que siguen.

Hotel Villa Linda

ACAPULCO

4 + 4 + 4x480 mil pesos

4 DIAS ¡TODO INCLUIDO! *
4 PERSONAS
4a. NOCHE GRATIS

Por sólo 480 mil pesos todo incluido:

* 6 alimentos: desayuno y comida o cena, suites con cocineta, refrigerador, ventiladores, agua caliente, alberca, estacionamiento, descuento en Yates Fiesta y Mágico Mundo Marino, (servicio cancha de tenis). A sólo 3 calles del famoso Acapulco Plaza, en la zona dorada de Acapulco. Habitación sin cocina 100 mil pesos por persona.

Promoción válida excepto vacaciones y festividades. Su anfitriona Hilda Saavedra Velázquez

RESERVACIONES:

ACAPULCO: 91 (74) 87-44-12, Fax 82-30-06

1. ¿A qué ciudad y a qué país irán ustedes?

____

2. ¿Cuántas personas podrán acompañarlos(las)? ¿Quiénes serán?

____

3. ¿Cuándo saldrán ustedes? ¿Cómo llegarán allí?

____

4. ¿En qué hotel se alojarán? ¿Por cuánto tiempo?

____

5. ¿Cuánto costará el viaje? ¿Quién lo pagará?

____

6. ¿Dónde comerán ustedes?

____

7. ¿Qué harán allí?

____

8. ¿Cuándo volverán a casa? Y luego, ¿qué harán?

____

Nombre ______________________________ Fecha ______________

More practice with the subjunctive

G11-9 En la clase de español. ¿Qué quieren los profesores de español que los estudiantes hagan durante su clase?

Modelo: El profesor González quiere que Roberto *haga* (hacer) su tarea a tiempo.

1. La profesora Artigas quiere que los estudiantes __________ (hablar) solamente español en su clase.
2. El profesor Moreno quiere que nosotros __________ (practicar) la conversación con nuestros amigos hispanos.
3. La profesora Guinand quiere que vosotros __________ (escribir) las composiciones en la computadora.
4. El profesor Zuloaga quiere que Rosario y Gisela __________ (buscar) información sobre Venezuela en la red.
5. La profesora Vegas quiere que tú __________ (leer) una historia sobre el Salto Ángel y que la __________ (explicar) en clase.
6. El profesor Cadenas quiere que yo __________ (traer) fotografías de Caracas a la clase para una presentación.
7. La profesora Camacho quiere que Rebeca __________ (completar) todos los ejercicios de esta lección para mañana.
8. El profesor Leo quiere que vosotras __________ (estudiar) dos horas todos los días.
9. La profesora Bermúdez quiere que nosotros __________ (hacer) una comida española para la clase.
10. El profesor Berrizbeitia quiere que tú __________ (llegar) a clase a tiempo.

Nombre ______________________________ Fecha ______________

G11-10 ¡De compras! Graciela y Beatriz quieren que Eli lleve mucha ropa de regreso a los Estados Unidos. Completa los espacios en blanco con el presente del subjuntivo para saber lo que ellas quieren que Eli compre en Caracas.

Modelo: Graciela: Eli, quiero que *compres* (comprar) esta blusa azul oscuro y esta falda azul claro.

1. Beatriz: Eli, quiero que te __________ (llevar) estos lentes de sol para el verano en California.
2. Graciela: Eli, quiero que __________ (probarse) este traje sastre color café, con el pañuelo anaranjado. ¡Te queda muy bien!
3. Beatriz: Eli, quiero que __________ (preguntar) el precio de estos zapatos negros.
4. Graciela: Eli, quiero que __________ (comprar) este abrigo, este maletín y este paraguas para ir a trabajar vestida elegantemente.
5. Beatriz: Eli, quiero que __________ (ver) los descuentos en los trajes de baño.

Elizabeth: ¡Déjenme en paz! *(Leave me alone!)* ¡No me digan más cosas que ustedes quieren que haga o compre! ¡No tengo mucho dinero y la maleta ya está llena *(full)*!

G11-11 Aspiraciones. Primero, dile a un(a) compañero(a) de clase lo que quieres lograr *(achieve)*. Luego, dile lo que quieren que logres *(that you achieve)* tus padres, tu esposo(a), tu novio(a) o tus profesores.

Modelo: terminar mis estudios en la universidad
Yo quiero terminar mis estudios en la universidad.
Mis padres quieren que yo termine mis estudios en la universidad.

1. estudiar mucho
2. hacer más ejercicio
3. descansar mucho más
4. encontrar un buen trabajo
5. dormir más horas todas las noches
6. llegar a mis clases a tiempo
7. pagar todas mis cuentas a tiempo
8. aprender a hablar español bien
9. vivir en un país de habla española
10. visitar a mi familia frecuentemente

Nombre ______________________ Fecha ____________

G11-12 **¿Qué dices tú?** Imagínate que eres amigo(a) de Elizabeth. Primero, escribe una lista de algunos consejos adecuados para Eli, basándote en tu experiencia. Luego, escribe un mensaje electrónico para expresar sus consejos.

Modelo: (lista)

- *que tenga cuidado al ir de compras*
- *que salga a divertirse pero no hasta muy tarde*
- *que les escriba a los amigos*

Modelo: (mensaje)
Eli, quiero que tengas cuidado al ir de compras y que encuentres los mejores precios. Quiero que salgas a divertirte mucho, a comer, a bailar, a subir montañas pero que no estés fuera hasta muy tarde porque... Quiero que me escribas mensajes electrónicos para saber cómo estás en Caracas.

A: Eli

De: ____________

Tema: Te aconsejo

Nombre ______________________ Fecha ______________

Práctica comunicativa suplemental I

¿Quién lo hace? Necesitas ayuda con las tareas de la casa. En parejas, decidan quién hace cada tarea, el hombre o la mujer. Si quieren, pueden decidir que ambos *(both)* deben hacer la tarea. Completen el cuadro con sus opiniones. Luego, comparen sus respuestas con las de un(a) compañero(a) y explíquenle por qué decidieron eso.

Modelo: *Quiero que el hombre saque la basura porque es muy pesada.*
No quiero que el hombre planche porque los hombres no son tan cuidadosos como las mujeres.

Vocabulario útil

Me parece que...	*I believe that . . .*
(No) Estoy de acuerdo.	*I (don't) agree.*
Pienso que...	*I think that . . .*

Tarea	Hombre	Mujer	Ambos
cocinar			
lavar los platos			
pasar la aspiradora			
decorar la casa			
cuidar el jardín			
sacar la basura			
hacer las compras			
pagar las cuentas			
lavar la ropa			
planchar			
limpiar el baño			

Nombre ____________________ Fecha ____________

Práctica comunicativa suplemental II

El futuro. En grupos, decidan qué quieren que cambie en los próximos diez años. Hagan una lista de los cambios que quieren y las razones. Después comparen su lista con las de los otros grupos. Usen el subjuntivo.

Modelo: *Queremos que haya una mujer presidente porque las mujeres son menos violentas que los hombres.*

Vocabulario útil

Deseamos que...
Esperamos que...
Queremos que...
Será bueno que...

____

____

____

____

____

____

____

____

LECCIÓN 12 ¡QUÉ DELICIOSO EL CAFÉ!

Práctica suplemental

VOCABULARIO SUPLEMENTAL

Más expresiones bancarias	***More banking expressions***
el billete	*paper money*
la moneda	*coin (money)*
el sencillo	*change*
No tengo sencillo.	*I don't have any change.*
cobrar un cheque	*to cash a check*
depositar un cheque	*to deposit a check*
firmar un cheque	*to sign a check*

PRACTIQUEMOS

V12-1 En el banco. ¿Qué actividades bancarias hacen las personas cuando necesitan o tienen dinero? Con un(a) compañero(a) de clase, decidan lo que tienen que hacer estas personas o entidades. Repasen el vocabulario de la **Lección 12** de ***Intercambios***.

¿Qué hacen?	**Actividad bancaria**
Cuando escribo un cheque, tengo que...	*firmar el cheque*
El cajero automático solamente tiene... , pero no tiene...	
Cuando una tienda recibe muchos cheques, tiene que...	
Todas las personas deben hacer un...	
Cuando una persona recibe un cheque por su trabajo, va al banco para...	
Cuando una persona va de viaje, es mejor comprar...	
Para escribir cheques personales, las personas deben tener...	
Las compañías y las personas deben abrir una cuenta de... para el futuro y para invertir en otras compañías.	

Nombre ______________________________ Fecha ______________

VI2-2 Anuncio bancario. En parejas, lean el siguiente anuncio bancario y contesten las preguntas a continuación.

> **BANCO CAFETALERO COLOMBIANO**
>
> Estimado cliente(a): Si está interesado(a) en invertir en el mercado de exportación del café, hable con nosotros, pues le ofrecemos los siguientes servicios:
>
> - Cuenta corriente
> - Cuenta de ahorros
> - Chequera personal
> - Inversiones directas en el mercado del café
> - Crédito
> - Tarjeta de crédito con un interés del 8%
> - Servicio de cajero automático las 24 horas del día
> - Puede depositar y cobrar cheques por una caja directa sin tener que hacer fila *(without having to be in line)* por más de 10 minutos.
>
> ¡Es mejor que usted venga a hablar con nosotros y cuanto antes mejor!

1. ¿Qué tipo de banco es éste?

   ____

2. ¿Qué tipo de servicios ofrece el banco?

   ____

3. ¿Qué servicios se pueden hacer por una caja directa?

   ____

4. ¿Cuál es el servicio que a ustedes les interesa más de un banco?

   ____

5. En el cuadro que se encuentra en la página siguiente, escriban otro aviso bancario para el Banco de Santander de Medellín. Revisen el vocabulario de la **Lección 12** del libro de texto para ofrecer diferentes servicios.

Nombre ______________________ Fecha ______________

V12-3 Tarjetas postales. Estás en Barranquilla, Colombia, y quieres mandarles varias postales a tus amigos en los Estados Unidos. Habla con el (la) dependiente(a) del kiosko; compra tarjetas postales y pregúntale si tiene estampillas o sellos. Luego, con un(a) compañero(a) preséntenle su conversación a la clase.

Usted:

____

Dependiente(a):

____

Usted:

____

Dependiente(a):

____

Usted:

____

Nombre ______________________ Fecha ______________

Gramática suplemental

More on the subjunctive with verbs of volition

aconsejar	*to advise*	preferir (e → ie)	*to prefer*
desear	*to desire, to wish*	prohibir	*to forbid*
insistir (en)	*to insist (on)*	recomendar (e → ie)	*to recommend*
pedir (e → i)	*to request*	rogar (o → ue)	*to beg, to implore*
permitir	*to permit*	sugerir (e → ie)	*to suggest*

G12-4 Consejos para la clase de español. Los (las) profesores(as) de español les dan consejos a los estudiantes de su clase. ¿Qué les dicen? Completa la oración con la forma correcta del verbo, usando el presente del subjuntivo. Recuerda que cuando no hay cambio de sujeto, no se usa el subjuntivo sino el infinitivo.

Modelo: El profesor Vergara no permite que sus estudiantes *hablen* (hablar) en inglés durante su clase.

1. La profesora Gutiérrez le aconseja a Roberto que ______________ (estudiar) el subjuntivo.
2. El profesor Rosser les pide a sus estudiantes que ______________ (practicar) español por las calles de Boston.
3. La profesora Vegas insiste en que yo ______________ (ir) de viaje a Colombia con la universidad.
4. La profesora Blanco desea ______________ (viajar) a España.
5. El profesor Morán desea que sus estudiantes ______________ (asistir) a la conferencia del escritor colombiano Gabriel García Márquez.
6. La profesora Pérez te pide que no ______________ (llegar) tarde a clase.
7. El profesor Delgado os aconseja que vosotras ______________ (hacer) la tarea a tiempo.
8. La profesora González prohíbe que nosotros ______________ (comer) en clase.
9. El profesor Berrizbeitia prefiere ______________ (conocer) Latinoamérica.
10. El profesor Arvelo recomienda que tú ______________ (leer) el cuento en español.
11. La profesora Maldonado les ruega a los estudiantes que ______________ (escribir) muy claro en el examen.
12. El profesor Camacho le sugiere a Marisa que ______________ (estudiar) más y que ______________ (trabajar) menos horas.

G12-5 Consejos. Tu amigo(a) irá a Cali, Colombia, el mes que viene así que le das algunos consejos.

Modelo: cambiar dólares por pesos colombianos
José, te aconsejo que cambies dólares por pesos colombianos.

1. ir al banco y comprar cheques de viajero

____

2. pedir un número personal para el cajero automático en Colombia

____

3. leer las últimas noticias sobre el país

____

4. estudiar el vocabulario en español

____

5. llevar un diccionario pequeño

____

6. hacer una maleta pequeña también

____

More on the subjunctive with verbs of emotion and impersonal expressions

Verbs of emotion		Impersonal expressions	
alegrarse (de)	*to be glad (about)*	es bueno / malo	*it's good/bad*
esperar	*to hope*	es importante	*it's important*
gustar	*to be pleasing, to like*	es (im)posible	*it's (im)possible*
molestar	*to bother*	es (una) lástima	*it's too bad*
preocuparse (de)	*to worry (about)*	es lógico	*it's logical*
quejarse (de)	*to complain (about)*	es mejor	*it's better*
sentir (e → ie, i)	*to be sorry*	es ridículo	*it's ridiculous*

G12-6 Emociones. Karen y Femi están de viaje por toda Colombia y sienten muchas emociones buenas y malas. Forma oraciones con las siguientes frases.

Modelo: Karen / espera / que Femi / pagar todas las comidas
Karen espera que Femi pague todas las comidas.

1. Femi / alegrarse / de que Karen / conocer / Bogotá

____

2. Karen / quejarse / de que Femi / dormir mucho

____

3. a Femi / le gusta / que Karen / hablar español

____

4. a Karen / le molesta / que Femi / comer muchísimo

____

5. Femi / preocuparse / de que Karen / salir sola de noche

____

6. Femi y Karen / sentir / que la gente colombiana / tener muchos problemas económicos

____

Nombre ______________________________ Fecha ______________

G12-7 En un banco colombiano. Femi y Karen no tienen dinero y tienen que ir a un banco en Cartagena de Indias. Completa lo que hacen en el banco con la forma adecuada de los verbos en paréntesis.

Modelo: Es importante que Femi y Karen *encuentren* (encontrar) un banco.

1. Es bueno que Karen ______________ (llevar) su pasaporte al banco.
2. Es imposible que Femi no ______________ (tener) una tarjeta para el cajero automático.
3. Es una lástima que el banco ______________ (estar) cerrado al mediodía.
4. Es lógico que ellos ______________ (querer) sacar dinero. ¡Ya llevan un mes viajando!
5. Es mejor que Karen ______________ (firmar) un cheque personal en el banco con su pasaporte.
6. Es ridículo ______________ (tener) que esperar más de veinte minutos en el banco.

G12-8 ¡Ojalá! ¿Qué deseas para tu familia el próximo año? Forma oraciones usando **ojalá** con los elementos de las siguientes columnas.

Modelo: *Ojalá que mi padre descanse en la playa.*

A	B	C
mi padre	comprar	ejercicio
mis hermanos	tener	una casa nueva
mi mamá	hacer	en una nueva compañía
yo	trabajar	un contrato nuevo de trabajo
mi novio(a)	firmar	en la playa
mi esposo(a)	descansar	un auto nuevo
mis primos	asistir / a	montar en bicicleta
tú	aprender	a la universidad

____

____

____

____

____

____

____

____

____

____

____

____

Nombre ______________________________ Fecha ______________

Práctica comunicativa suplemental I

Las Naciones Unidas. Tú y tus compañeros son miembros de la Organización de las Naciones Unidas. En grupos de cuatro personas, den sus recomendaciones de cómo cumplir con los siguientes objetivos de la organización. Expliquen sus decisiones y luego compartan sus decisiones con el resto de la clase.

Vocabulario útil

Es importante que...	Es ridículo que...
Es lógico que...	Es ilógico que...
Es mejor que...	Es una lástima que...
Es normal que...	Es terrible que...

Posibles usos de las riquezas:

- Administración del estado
- Reducción de los impuestos
- Construcción de viviendas *(housing)*
- Salud
- Defensa
- Transporte
- Educación
- Pagar la deuda al FMI (Fondo Monetario Internacional)

Los objetivos de la organización:

- Erradicar la pobreza extrema y el hambre
- Lograr la enseñaza primaria universal
- Promover la igualdad entre los géneros y la autonomía de la mujer
- Reducir la mortalidad infantil
- Mejorar la salud materna
- Combatir el VIH/SIDA, el paludismo, y otras enfermedades
- Garantizar la sostenibilidad del medio ambiente
- Fomentar una asociación mundial para el desarrollo

Modelo: ¿Qué harían ustedes para erradicar (terminar) la pobreza extrema y el hambre en los países latinoamericanos o africanos?

Nombre ______________________________ Fecha ______________

Práctica comunicativa suplemental II

Predicciones. Lee las predicciones que se hicieron al comienzo del siglo XX. ¿Estuvieron acertadas? *(Were they right?)* Comenta esta información con tu compañero(a).

Vocabulario útil

delfines	*dolphins*
envejecimiento	*aging*
Es cierto que...	*It's true that . . .*
No es cierto que...	*It's not true that . . .*
Ojalá (que)...	*I wish that . . .*

Predicciones para el siglo pasado:

- comunicación con los delfines
- cura contra el envejecimiento
- tener una presidente mujer
- viaje a Marte

Ahora, hagan predicciones para el siglo XXI. ¿Qué quieren ustedes que ocurra en el siglo XXI?

Predicciones para el siglo XXI

1. Ojalá ______________________________
____
2. ______________________________
____
3. ______________________________
____
4. ______________________________
____

Compartan sus predicciones con el resto de la clase. ¿Cuáles son las más probables?

Nombre ______________________ Fecha ______________

PASO 5 ¡Buen Viaje!

LECCIÓN 13 ¡TE ESPERAMOS EN GALICIA!

Práctica suplemental

VOCABULARIO SUPLEMENTAL

Mas direcciones	***More directions***		
a la derecha	*to the right*	detrás de	*behind*
a la izquierda	*to the left*	doblar	*to turn*
la avenida	*avenue*	enfrente de	*in front of*
la calle	*street*	la esquina	*corner*
la cuadra	*city block*	recto	*straight*

PRACTIQUEMOS

V13-1 ¿Dónde está... ? Ileana está en Madrid y quiere ir a la estación de tren porque es hora de ir a Santiago de Compostela en Galicia. Ella le pide instrucciones a la recepcionista. Completa el diálogo con las siguientes instrucciones.

esquina recto cuadra(s)
a la derecha a la izquierda detrás de delante de

Ileana: Señorita, ¿cómo llego a la estación de tren desde el hotel?

Recepcionista: Siga ______________ por la Avenida Mariño y pase cuatro ______________. En la quinta ______________, doble a la ______________ en la ______________. La estación de tren está ______________ del Hotel Plaza Mayor y ______________ de la Biblioteca Principal.

Ileana: ¡Gracias, señorita!

V13-2 En la ciudad. Usando el vocabulario de la ciudad, pídele a un(a) compañero(a) de clase que te dé instrucciones de cómo llegar a los siguientes lugares.

Modelo: Tú estás en la piscina y quieres ir al aeropuerto.
Sal de la piscina, dobla a la izquierda y en la esquina dobla a la derecha y sigue...

1. Estás en la universidad y quieres ir al parque.
2. Estás en la oficina de correos y quieres ir al hospital.
3. Estás en la farmacia y quieres ir a la biblioteca de la ciudad.
4. Estás en la estación de tren y quieres ir al hotel de la ciudad.

Nombre ______________________________ Fecha ______________

Más de los hoteles | ***More on hotels***

el (la) botones	*bellhop*
la caja fuerte	*safe*
el (la) conserje	*concierge*
el hotel de cuatro estrellas	*four-star hotel*
el (la) huésped	*guest*
la propina	*tip*
el servicio de lavandería	*laundry*
el servicio de oficina	*office service (fax, photocopies, teleconferencing)*
el servicio de películas de video	*video service*

V13-3 Asociaciones. ¿Qué asocias con las siguientes actividades en el Gran Hotel?

servicio de lavandería	huésped	botones
servicio de oficina	conserje	caja fuerte
servicio de películas de video	propina	

Modelo: Luis necesita lavar su ropa. *servicio de lavandería*

1. Los Rodríguez necesitan guardar muchos cheques de viajero. ______________.
2. Necesito que el (la) ______________ me lleve las maletas a la habitación.
3. ¿Tienes cambio para darle la ______________ al botones por las maletas?
4. Los niños quieren ver películas en el cuarto; ojalá el hotel tenga ______________.
5. El gerente de la compañía necesita hacer copias y mandarles faxes a los clientes. Menos mal que el hotel tiene ______________.
6. El (La) ______________ del hotel siempre sabe de los espectáculos que hay en la ciudad.
7. La abuela de Teresa da muy buenas propinas y por eso los botones piensan que ella es una buena.

V13-4 Hotel de cuatro estrellas. En un hotel de cuatro estrellas debe haber muchos servicios. Conversa con un(a) compañero(a) de clase sobre qué servicios hacen que un hotel tenga cuatro estrellas. Luego escribe sus opiniones.

____

____

____

____

____

Nombre ______________________________ Fecha ______________

GRAMÁTICA SUPLEMENTAL

More on the subjunctive with verbs and expressions of uncertainty

dudar	*to doubt*	no creer	*to disbelieve*
es dudoso	*it's doubtful*	no estar seguro(a)	*to be unsure*
no es cierto	*it's not true*	no es verdad	*it's not true*

G13-5 ¡No lo cree! El primo de Ileana, Ernesto, no cree en nada ni en nadie. Usa las expresiones anteriores para completar estas ideas, usando el subjuntivo.

Modelo: Ernesto duda que su prima Ileana *venga* (venir) a visitarlos.

1. Ernesto no cree que Ileana lo ______________ (invitar) a comer en un buen restaurante.
2. Es dudoso que Ernesto e Ileana ______________ (ir) de marcha por las calles de Santiago.
3. No es verdad que Ernesto ______________ (pensar) que su prima ______________ (ser) simpática y amable con él.
4. No es cierto que los tíos de Ileana ______________ (estar) tristes porque ella ______________ (venir) a visitarlos.
5. Ileana no está segura de que sus primos ______________ (ser) cariñosos con ella.
6. Ernesto duda que su prima ______________ (divertirse) con él.

G13-6 Es dudoso. Habla con un(a) compañero(a) de clase sobre las actividades que dudas que tengan lugar en la universidad.

Modelo: es dudoso / que los profesores / no trabajar los fines de semana
Es dudoso que los profesores no trabajen los fines de semana.

1. Luisa y Nina no creer / que los estudiantes / hacer la tarea con tiempo

   ____

2. yo dudar / que el profesor de francés / dar un examen difícil

   ____

3. no es verdad / que la clase de química / ser fácil

   ____

4. no es cierto / que nuestros compañeros de clase / estudiar poco

   ____

5. es dudoso / los administradores / comprender todos nuestros problemas

   ____

Nombre ______________________________ Fecha ______________

Con estas expresiones usamos el indicativo, ya que no tenemos duda de nada.

Expresiones de seguridad	Expressions of certainty
creer	*to believe*
es cierto	*it's true*
es verdad	*it's true*
no dudar	*not to doubt*

G13-7 **Sí lo cree.** La prima de Ileana, Ana, sí cree en todo. Usa las expresiones anteriores para completar estas ideas, usando el indicativo porque no hay duda.

Modelo: Ana cree que Ileana *es* (ser) muy simpática.

1. Ana no duda que Ileana ______________ (divertirse) con ella en Santiago.
2. Es cierto que Ana e Ileana ______________ (salir) de marcha todas las noches por las calles de Santiago.
3. Ileana no duda que sus tíos ______________ (estar) felices con su visita.
4. Ana cree que Ileana ______________ (querer) aprender a hablar gallego.
5. Ana no duda que Ileana y los tíos ______________ (comer) en un buen restaurante gallego.
6. Los tíos creen que Ana e Ileana lo ______________ (pasar) muy bien todo el tiempo.

G13-8 **Sus opiniones.** Con un(a) compañero(a) de clase, reaccionen a las siguientes ideas sobre España. Usen las siguientes expresiones.

creer	no creer	dudar	no dudar
es verdad	no es verdad	es dudoso	

Modelo: España es un país muy interesante y lleno de historia.
Yo creo que España es un país muy interesante y lleno de historia.

1. En España no hay verano y llueve todos los días.
____
2. Las fiestas de Santiago de Compostela son en junio.
____
3. La gente se divierte mucho con las fiestas de Santiago.
____
4. La Universidad de Santiago de Compostela es una universidad muy nueva.
____
5. En España el sistema de trenes no funciona rápidamente.
____
6. Los paradores españoles no están en lugares famosos y la comida que sirven no es muy buena.
____
7. En los hoteles en España le piden el pasaporte a los turistas cuando se registran.
____
8. En España no hay muchos lugares como albergues u hoteles para pasar las vacaciones.
____

Nombre ______________________ Fecha ______________

More practice with the conjunctions of purpose

para que	*so (that)*	en caso (de) que	*in case (of)*
sin que	*without*	con tal (de) que	*provided (that)*
a menos que	*unless*		

G13-9 Consejos de la tía Victoria. La tía Victoria les da consejos a Ileana y a Ana. ¿Cuáles fueron estos consejos? Completa la idea usando una conjunción y cambia el verbo al subjuntivo.

para que   en caso (de) que   con tal (de) que   a menos que   sin que

Modelo: Ileana, llama por teléfono, *en caso que tengas* (tener) un problema por la calle.

1. Ileana, toma mi teléfono celular ______________ (llamar) cuando quieras.
2. Ileana y Ana, podéis caminar solas por las calles por la noche ______________ Ernesto ______________ (ir) con vosotras.
3. No se queden hasta muy tarde en la calle ______________ los amigos ______________ (estar) con vosotras.
4. Ileana, no pases más días ______________ (hablar) con tus padres en Costa Rica.
5. Ileana y Ana, llevaos la tarjeta de crédito ______________ el restaurante y la comida ______________ (ser) más caros de lo que vosotras pensáis.
6. Ana, cuida a tu prima ______________ ella ______________ (querer) regresar a Galicia a visitarnos.

Nombre ______________________ Fecha ______________

More practice with the conjunctions of time

antes (de) que	*before*	cuando	*when*
después (de) que	*after*	hasta que	*until*
tan pronto como	*as soon as*		

G13-10 De viaje por España. Tú y un(a) amigo(a) están de viaje por España. Completa las oraciones con una conjunción de tiempo y la forma adecuada del verbo que aparece entre paréntesis. Recuerda que puedes usar el indicativo o el subjuntivo, dependiendo de si la oración indica una acción habitual o una acción que no ha sucedido todavía *(pending in the future)*.

Modelo: José sacará su pasaporte *tan pronto como sepa* (saber) si él va a viajar.

1. Yo voy a sacar mi pasaporte ______________ (saber) si viajaré con José.
2. José y yo siempre compramos maletas nuevas ______________ (decidir) ir de viaje.
3. ______________ (llegar) a Madrid, José y yo alquilaremos un auto por una semana.
4. José sacará muchas fotos con su cámara digital nueva ______________ (visitar) la Plaza Mayor y el Museo del Prado.
5. Yo espero viajar por España ______________ (tener) dinero.
6. ______________ (conocer) Madrid, nosotros queremos visitar Toledo.
7. ______________ (llegar) a Toledo, compraré artesanía toledana.
8. Le mandaremos una tarjeta postal a nuestro(a) profesor(a) ______________ (comprar) sellos o estampillas.

Nombre ______________________ Fecha ______________

Práctica comunicativa suplemental I

La pensión. Tú y tu compañero(a) están en España de vacaciones. Se están quedando en una pensión muy barata para ahorrar *(save)* dinero. La habitación que les han dado tiene algunos problemas. Comenta con tu compañero(a) tu opinión sobre la habitación. Mira el dibujo y expresa tu opinión utilizando expresiones de duda, incredulidad *(disbelief)*, etcétera.

Modelo: *No creo que limpien esta habitación muy seguido.*

Vocabulario útil

alfombra	*carpet*	roto	*broken*
almohadas	*pillows*	sábanas	*sheets*
cama	*bed*	Dudo que...	*I doubt that . . .*
espejo	*mirror*	Es dudoso que...	*It's doubtful that . . .*
manchado	*stained*	No creo que...	*I don't believe that . . .*
muerto	*dead*	No estoy seguro de que...	*I'm not sure that . . .*

Nombre ______________________________ Fecha ______________

Práctica comunicativa suplemental II

ESTUDIANTE A

El itinerario. Tú y tu compañero(a) están planeando un itinerario para un amigo que va a venir de visita a España. Cada uno tiene una lista de las actividades que quiere hacer con él. Ponte de acuerdo con tu compañero(a) para decidir el itinerario final. No mires el itinerario de tu compañero(a).

Modelo: *Tan pronto como llegue vamos a visitar Segovia.*

Vocabulario útil

a menos que	*unless*
antes (de) que	*before*
aunque	*even though*
castillos	*castles*
cercana	*near*
cuando	*when*
después (de) que	*after*
en caso (de) que	*in case*
hasta que	*until*
por los alrededores	*around the places nearby*
tan pronto como	*as soon as*

Itinerario

1. Ir al Museo del Prado
2. Pasear por el centro
3. Sacar fotos en la Puerta del Sol
4. Viajar en tren a una ciudad cercana
5. Ir de compras al Corte Inglés
6. ______________________

Nombre ______________________________ Fecha ______________

ESTUDIANTE B

El itinerario. Tú y tu compañero(a) están planeando un itinerario para un amigo que va a venir de visita a España. Cada uno tiene una lista de las actividades que quiere hacer con él. Ponte de acuerdo con tu compañero(a) para decidir el itinerario final. No mires el itinerario de tu compañero(a).

Modelo: *Tan pronto como llegue vamos a visitar Segovia.*

Vocabulario útil

a menos que	*unless*
antes (de) que	*before*
aunque	*even though*
castillos	*castles*
cercana	*near*
cuando	*when*
después (de) que	*after*
en caso (de) que	*in case*
hasta que	*until*
por los alrededores	*around the places nearby*
tan pronto como	*as soon as*

Itinerario

1. Ir al teatro
2. Pasear por el barrio bohemio
3. Visitar castillos y monumentos
4. Comer en restaurantes españoles y visitar los bares de tapas
5. Alquilar un coche para viajar por los alrededores
6. ______________________________

Nombre ______________________ Fecha ______________

LECCIÓN 14 ¡LO SIENTO, PERO NO ME SIENTO BIEN!

Práctica suplemental

VOCABULARIO SUPLEMENTAL

El cuerpo y las enfermedades	***The body and illnesses***
El cuerpo humano	*The human body*
la cadera	*hip*
la cintura	*waist*
el corazón	*heart*
el dedo	*finger*
el pecho	*chest*
el tobillo	*ankle*
La cara	*The face*
la ceja	*eyebrow*
la frente	*forehead*
los labios	*lips*
la lengua	*tongue*
la mejilla	*cheek*
la pestaña	*eyelash*
Las enfermedades	*Illnesses*
¿Qué te pasa?	*What's wrong with you?*
enfermar(se)	*to become sick*
Me enfermé con un resfriado.	*I became sick with a cold.*
torcer(se) (o→ ue)	*to twist*
Me torcí el tobillo.	*I twisted my ankle.*
fracturar(se)	*to fracture, to break*
Me fracturé un brazo / una pierna.	*I fractured my arm/leg.*
El tratamiento médico	*Medical treatment*
la aspirina	*aspirin*
la inyección	*injection*
la pastilla	*pill*
el termómetro	*thermometer*
el yeso	*cast*

Nombre ______________________________ Fecha ______________

Practiquemos

V14-1 Definiciones. Lee las definiciones y decide la parte del cuerpo que mejor describe.

Modelo: Sirve para hablar. *la lengua*

1. Sirven para conversar o besar. ______________
2. Sirve para bailar salsa muy bien. Hay que moverla. ______________
3. Sirven para usar anillos. ______________
4. Sirven para proteger *(to protect)* los ojos. ______________
5. Sirve para regular las actividades del cuerpo. ______________

el corazón
los dedos
la cintura
los labios
las pestañas
la lengua
las cejas

V14-2 Los doctores del Hospital General. Con un(a) compañero(a) de clase, llenen el siguiente cuadro. Ustedes encontrarán las enfermedades y tendrán que decidir el mejor tratamiento.

Enfermedades	Tratamientos
Brian se torció el tobillo.	Que tome dos aspirinas y guarde cama *(stay in bed)* por tres días
Heather se fracturó el brazo derecho.	
Bernardo se enfermó con gripe.	
Steve se fracturó un dedo.	
Julie se enfermó con tos, fiebre y dolor de oídos.	
Jo tiene un dolor de espalda horrible.	
Stuart se torció la mano izquierda.	

Nombre ______________________________ Fecha ______________

V14-3 En la clínica. Habla con otro(a) estudiante: una persona es el(la) médico(a) y la otra persona es el(la) paciente.

Médico(a)	**Paciente**
1. Buenos días.	2. Buenos días, doctor(a). ¿Cómo está usted?
3. ¿Qué tiene usted?	4. Pues, me duele(n) _____, doctor(a).
5. ¿Dónde le duele(n) exactamente?	6. Aquí... Ay, ¡me duele(n) mucho!
7. ¿Hace cuánto tiempo que tiene ese dolor?	8. Más o menos por ____________.
9. ¿Tiene usted fiebre o náuseas?	10. Pues, ____________.
11. Siéntese aquí, (señor/señorita/señora).	12. ¿Es algo grave? Estoy preocupado(a).
13. Voy a examinarlo(la).	14. ¿Qué tengo, doctor(a)?
15. Creo que tiene ______________. Tome ______________.	16. Gracias, doctor(a). Ya me siento mejor.

V14-4 Por teléfono. Habla con otro(a) estudiante, imaginándote que ustedes están hablando por teléfono.

Amigo(a) A	**Amigo(a) B**
1. Hola, ______________, ¿qué tal?	2. Ay, no me siento bien.
3. ¿Cómo? ¿Por que? ¿Qué tienes?	4. Pues, tengo ______________.
5. Ay, lo siento. ¿Fuiste a ______________?	6. Sí, ______________, pero...
7. Pues, espero que te sientas mejor.	8. Ahora tengo que ______________.
9. Cuídate mucho, ¿eh? Adiós.	10. Sí, gracias. Chao.

Nombre ______________________________ Fecha ______________

Gramática suplemental

More on the past (imperfect) subjunctive
Spanish speakers use the past subjunctive to express wishes, emotions, opinions, uncertainty, and indefiniteness about the past, just as they use the present subjunctive to discuss such feelings about the present or future.

How to form the past subjunctive
For *all* Spanish verbs, drop the **-ron** ending from the **ustedes** form of the preterite tense, and then add these personal endings: habla**ra,** habla**ras,** habla**ra,** hablá**ramos,** habla**rais,** habla**ran.**

The **nosotros** form always has an accent mark.

Practiquemos

G14-5 En Phoenix. Alicia y Mariana querían hacer muchas cosas en Phoenix. Completa la oración, usando el imperfecto del subjuntivo para saber lo que ellas querían hacer.

Modelo: Mariana quería que Alicia *se sintiera* (sentirse) bien para poder pasear.

1. Alicia quería que Mariana la ______________ (llevar) a conocer el museo de Phoenix.
2. Mariana quería que Alicia ______________ (visitar) el nuevo estadio de béisbol ParkOne.
3. Mariana se alegraba que a Alicia le ______________ (gustar) su ciudad.
4. Alicia esperaba que Mariana ______________ (tener) tiempo para ir a Sedona.
5. Mariana deseaba que ellas ______________ (caminar) por las montañas rojas de Sedona.
6. Mariana quería que Alicia ______________ (conocer) a todos sus amigos.
7. Era posible que ellas ______________ (comer) en restaurantes españoles en Phoenix.
8. Era importante que Alicia ______________ (ir) al Departamento de Economía de Arizona State University para conocer a otros estudiantes y a los profesores.
9. Era lógico que Mariana y Alicia ______________ (pasear) por las galerías de arte de Scottsdale.
10. Después de todo esto, Mariana quería que su amiga ______________ (descansar) un poco.

Nombre ______________________________ Fecha ____________

G14-6 Eres el(la) doctor(a) del Hospital General. ¿Qué les dijiste a estos pacientes? Escribe la oración completa usando el imperfecto del subjuntivo.

Modelo: A la Sra. Corona le duele mucho la rodilla.
Tú le dijiste que: a. (no) descansar en cama por varios días
descansara en cama por varios días
b. (no) hacer ejercicios fuertes con la rodilla
no hiciera ejercicios fuertes con la rodilla
c. (no) tomar dos aspirinas
tomara dos aspirinas

1. Al Sr. Miller le duele la espalda porque tiene un lumbago.

   Tú le dijiste que: a. (no) nadar dos horas todos los días

   ____

   b. (no) descansar y tomar pastillas de relajante muscular

   ____

   c. (no) ir a su trabajo

   ____

2. La Srta. Silva le duele la garganta y tiene fiebre.

   Tú le dijiste que: a. (no) tomar aspirinas y tomar mucho agua

   ____

   b. (no) descansar en casa

   ____

   c. (no) salir por la noche

   ____

3. A Rodrigo, un niño de once años, se le fracturó la pierna jugando al fútbol.

   Tú le dijiste que: a. (no) jugar más al fútbol por dos meses

   ____

   b. (no) llevar el yeso por dos meses

   ____

   c. (no) mirar fútbol por la televisiónp

   ____

4. A la niña Mildred se le torció el tobillo.

   Tú le dijiste que: a. (no) caminar por tres semanas

   ____

   b. (no) llevar yeso por tres semanas

   ____

   c. (no) salir y descansar

   ____

Nombre ______________________ Fecha ____________

Additional uses of the past subjunctive

1. Spanish speakers use the past subjunctive of the verbs **querer, saber,** and **poder** to soften requests, to make polite suggestions, and to persuade gently.

   —¿**Quisieran** ustedes acompañarnos al teatro?
   —*Would you like to accompany us to the theater?*

   —Gracias, pero **deberíamos** volver.
   —*Thank you, but we should return.*

   —Quizás **pudiéramos** ir otra noche.
   —*Maybe we could go another night.*

2. Spanish speakers use the past subjunctive after the expression **como si** *(as if, as though)* to express actions or conditions that are contrary to fact.

   —¡Uy! ¡Tengo un dolor de cabeza horrible!
   —*Ugh! I have a horrible headache!*

   —Hablas **como si fueras** a morirte.
   —*You're talking as if you were going to die.*

Practiquemos

G14-7 La cortesía. Imagínate que estás de vacaciones en España. Deseas ser cortés con los españoles y, por eso, usas el imperfecto del subjuntivo de los verbos **querer, deber** y **poder.** ¿Qué les dirías a las siguientes personas?

Modelo: You want a friend to tell you how to pronounce a word.
¿Pudieras decirme cómo decir esta palabra?

1. You ask a fellow passenger on a train to help you with your suitcase.

   ____

2. At a restaurant one of your Spanish friends ordered *gambas*, a word you don't understand. Ask for an explanation.

   ____

3. A housekeeper knocks at your hotel room door and asks if she may clean your room. Because you just got up, you ask her to come back in an hour.

   ____

4. You telephone a friend to persuade him or her to go shopping with you tomorrow.

   ____

5. You can't understand a police officer because he's speaking too fast.

   ____

6. While sightseeing in Madrid, you and a friend meet a young couple whom you invite to dinner.

   ____

7. You meet two university students who want to study law in your country. Suggest several good schools that they might contact.

   ____

Nombre ______________________ Fecha ______________

G14-8 **¡Qué exageraciones!** En Santiago de Compostela, Ileana e Isabel conocen a un grupo de niños que les dicen cosas exageradas. Lee lo que dice cada niño(a), luego escribe una oración que dirías **como si** fueras Ileana e Isabel.

Modelo: **Niño:** ¡Ay! ¡Qué auto más bonito tiene usted, señora!
Ileana: *Gracias, pero hablas como si yo fuera rica.*

Niño: ¿Desde Madrid hasta Santiago viajan ustedes? Pues, ¡ustedes son grandes viajeras!
Isabel: ______________________

Niña: Tengo siete años. ¿Y ustedes? Pues, creo que ya son viejas.
Ileana: ______________________

Niño: ¿Siempre duermen ustedes en hoteles? ¡Debe costarles una fortuna!
Isabel: ______________________

Niña: ¿Por qué llevan ustedes cuatro maletas, señora? ¡Parece que viajan alrededor del mundo por un año!
Ileana: ______________________

G14-9 **¿Qué dices tú?** Para expresar tus opiniones francamente, completa las siguientes oraciones, usando la expresión **como si** con el imperfecto del subjuntivo.

Modelo: Hay estudiantes que no vienen a clase...
Hay estudiantes que no vienen a clase como si supieran todo.

1. Hay personas que trabajan día y noche...

   ____

2. Los turistas ricos gastan dinero...

   ____

3. Muchos políticos hablan con la gente...

   ____

4. Algunos médicos malos practican la medicina...

   ____

5. Conozco a profesores que dan tanta tarea...

   ____

6. Algunos de mis amigos me hablan por el teléfono celular...

   ____

Nombre ______________________________ Fecha ______________

More on the conditional

How to form the conditional

1. Add these personal endings to the infinitive of most verbs: **ía, ías, ía, íamos, íais, ían.**
2. Add the conditional endings to the irregular stems of these verbs:

   decir (diría)
   hacer (haría)
   poder (podría)
   poner (pondría)
   querer (querría)
   saber (sabría)
   salir (saldría)
   tener (tendría)
   venir (vendría)

Practiquemos

G14-10 El fin de semana. ¿A ti qué te gustaría hacer el fin de semana si tuvieras tiempo? Completa las oraciones para saber lo que estas personas querrían hacer el fin de semana, usando la forma correcta del condicional.

Modelo: Si tuviera tiempo, *saldría* (salir) con mis amigos.

1. Julie y Heather ______________ (dormir) si tuvieran tiempo.
2. Steve ______________ (ir) a Flagstaff si tuviera tiempo.
3. Bernardo y Jo ______________ (salir) a bailar el sábado por la noche si no tuvieran exámenes el lunes.
4. Stuart y tú ______________ (viajar) a New York el viernes por la tarde si tuvieran dinero.
5. Mike ______________ (hacer) las composiciones de español si no tuviera sueño.
6. Nicole ______________ (venir) a visitarme si tuviera tiempo y dinero.
7. Eric y yo ______________ (estudiar) más español si no tuviéramos examen de economía política internacional.
8. Yo ______________ (comer) en el mejor restaurante de la ciudad si tuviera dinero.
9. Nosotros ______________ (pasear) más por Arizona si no tuviéramos tanto trabajo.
10. Tú ______________ (nadar) todos los días si no tuvieras que trabajar hasta las diez de la noche.

Nombre _______________________________ Fecha _______________

G14-11 **¿Qué harías tú si... ?** Completa las siguientes oraciones con el condicional. Léele tus respuestas a un(a) compañero(a) de clase y discutan sus respuestas.

Modelos: Si estuviera enfermo(a), *descansaría en cama todo el día.*
Descansaría en cama todo el día, si estuviera enfermo(a).

1. Si tuviera tiempo, _______________________________.
2. Si tuviera dinero, _______________________________.
3. Si viviera en Latinoamérica, _______________________________.
4. Si no estudiara en la universidad, _______________________________.
5. Si tuviera un trabajo, _______________________________.
6. _______________________________, si fuera a España.
7. _______________________________, si viajara a Los Ángeles.
8. _______________________________, si viajara a visitar a mis amigos.
9. _______________________________, si comprara un auto nuevo.
10. _______________________________, si me mudara de casa.

Nombre ______________________ Fecha ______________

Práctica comunicativa suplemental I

La máquina del tiempo. Entrevista a tu compañero(a) y averigua qué haría si estuviera en estas épocas. Luego tu compañero(a) te entrevistará a ti. ¿Tienen respuestas similares?

Modelo: **A:** *¿Qué serías y qué harías si estuvieras en el siglo XVI?*
B: *Si estuviéramos en el siglo XVI sería un explorador y viajaría por los océanos.*

Épocas posibles:
La prehistoria
La Edad Media
Los años sesenta
El Renacimiento
La Colonia
El siglo XXII

Vocabulario útil

colonizador	*colonizer*
cura	*priest*
hombre prehistórico	*prehistoric man*
reina	*queen*
rey	*king*
siglo	*century*

Nombre ____ Fecha ____________________

Práctica comunicativa suplemental II

Un mundo perfecto. En grupos, decidan qué quisieran cambiar para hacer un mundo mejor o perfecto. Hagan una lista y luego compárenla con la de los otros grupos.

Modelo: *No debiera haber fronteras entre los países.*

Vocabulario útil

Debiera haber...	*There should be . . .*
Quisiéramos que...	*We would like . . .*
Si pensara...	*If I thought . . .*
Si pudiera...	*If I could . . .*
Si tuviera...	*If I had . . .*

Nombre ______________________________ Fecha ______________

LECCIÓN 15 ¿QUÉ PODRÍAMOS HACER NOSOTROS POR NUESTRO MEDIO AMBIENTE?

Práctica suplemental

VOCABULARIO SUPLEMENTAL

Más sobre el medio ambiente	***More about the environment***
las armas nucleares	*nuclear arms*
los bosques tropicales	*tropical forests*
la conservación	*conservation*
el daño	*damage*
la guerra biológica	*biological war*
el medio ambiente	*environment*
la reserva	*reserve*
la selva	*jungle*

PRACTIQUEMOS

V15-1 Asociaciones. Decide cuál de estos asuntos ambientales corresponde a las afirmaciones *(statements)* que aparecen en las oraciones siguientes.

Modelo: El gobierno del Brasil está tratando de cuidar parte de la selva amazónica en una *reserva.*

el daño / la selva / las reservas naturales / las armas nucleares / el medio ambiente / la guerra biológica / la conservación

1. ______________ del medio ambiente debe ser lo primero que se les debe enseñar a los niños en la escuela.
2. Los Estados Unidos tiene cuidado con ______________, que es una amenaza por parte de los terroristas.
3. ______________ amazónica es uno de los pulmones *(lungs)* más importantes del planeta.
4. Todos debemos reciclar y cuidar las plantas y los animales para así conservar ______________.
5. Uno de los problemas más graves que tiene la Tierra es que varios países no firmaron el acuerdo para detener *(to stop)* el uso de ______________.
6. Todos debemos estar conscientes de que ______________ que le hagamos al medio ambiente a veces no se puede reparar *(to fix).*

Nombre ______________________ Fecha ______________

V15-2 **¿Qué harían ustedes?** Con un(a) compañero(a) de clase, hablen sobre los siguientes asuntos globales. Digan qué problemas pueden suceder y qué podrían hacer ustedes.

Asuntos globales	Problemas	¿Qué podrían hacer Uds.?
La conservación		
La guerra biológica		
Los bosques tropicales		
Las reservas de animales o plantas		

V15-3 **Si tú fueras . . .** Escribe cuatro oraciones diciendo lo que harías si fueras las siguientes personas. Comparte tus ideas con un(a) compañero(a) de clase.

Modelo: *Si yo fuera el(la) ministro(a) del Medio Ambiente, escribiría una ley* (law) *para la mejor conservación del medio ambiente.*

1. Si yo fuera el(la) ministro(a) del Medio Ambiente, ______________________.
2. Si yo fuera el(la) presidente(a) de Exxon, ______________________.
3. Si yo fuera el(la) presidente(a) del Brasil, ______________________.
4. Si yo fuera el(la) vicepresidente(a) de los Estados Unidos, ______________________.

Nombre ______________________________ Fecha ______________

Gramática suplemental

More on *if* clauses

1. To imply that a situation is factual or is likely to occur, use **si** *(if)* with an indicative verb form in both the *if* (dependent) clause and the conclusion (independent) clause.

Factual situation

Si **seguimos** usando los recursos naturales no renovables sin control, **continuaremos** contaminando el aire.

If we continue to use nonrenewable natural resources without control, we will continue polluting the air.

Likely to occur

—Si **conservamos** los recursos naturales, **vamos a tener / tendremos** suficientes recursos para el futuro.
—Creo que tienes razón.

—If we conserve natural resources, we are going to have enough resources for the future.
—I think you're right.

2. To imply that a situation is contrary to fact or is unlikely to occur, use **si** *(if)* with a past subjunctive verb in the *if* clause and a conditional verb in the conclusion.

Contrary to fact

—Si **usáramos** más la energía solar, **ahorraríamos** dinero, ¿verdad?
—¡Sí, claro que sí!

—If we used more solar energy, we would save money, wouldn't we?
—Yes, of course!

Unlikely to occur

—Si **fueras** el presidente, ¿**podrías** eliminar la delincuencia?
—Creo que sería imposible.

—If you were president, would you be able to eliminate crime?
—I think it would be impossible.

Como si... *(As if . . .)*

After **como si** the imperfect subjunctive is used when the verb in the main clause is either in the present or in the past.

David habla de la contaminación **como si fuera** un experto.

David talks about pollution as if he were an expert.

Nombre ______________________ Fecha ______________

Practiquemos

G15-4 En la universidad. Tú y tus compañeros quieren conservar los recursos naturales en su universidad. ¿Qué pueden hacer? Todas estas situaciones son posibles. Discuten estas situaciones y escriban cuatro oraciones.

Modelo: Si apagamos *(we turn off)* el aire acondicionado, *ahorramos electricidad.*

1. Vamos a conservar el agua si
______________________________.
2. Si caminamos a la universidad,
______________________________.
3. No le haremos ningún daño al medio ambiente si
______________________________.
4. Si cuidamos la reserva de árboles (el arboretum) de la universidad,
______________________________.

G15-5 En la comunidad. Tú y tus compañeros quieren reciclar más papel, botellas y latas en su comunidad. ¿Qué podrían hacer? Estas situaciones no son totalmente posibles. Conversen sobre estas situaciones y escriban cuatro oraciones.

Modelo: Si tuviéramos dinero, *compraríamos más potes de basura* (garbage cans) *para reciclar.*

1. Si tuviéramos tiempo, ______________________________
______________________________.
2. Si pudiéramos hablar con el alcalde *(mayor)* de la ciudad, ______________________________
______________________________.
3. Tendríamos más potes para reciclar si ______________________________
______________________________.
4. Conservaríamos más los recursos naturales en la comunidad si ______________________________
______________________________.

Nombre ______________________ Fecha ______________

G15-6 En el mundo. A ti y a tus compañeros les gustaría solucionar varios asuntos globales. ¿Qué podrían hacer si ustedes tuvieran un trabajo con el gobierno? Estas situaciones son totalmente imposibles. Hablen sobre estas situaciones y escriban cuatro oraciones.

Modelo: Si fuera el (la) presidente(a) de Exxon, *pagaría la multa por derramar* (to spill) *petróleo en la costa de Alaska.*

1. Si fuera el (la) alcalde de mi ciudad, ______________________________.
2. Si fuera el (la) presidente(a) de Laboratorios de Medicinas Merck, ______________________________.
3. Si fuera el (la) presidente de Ford, ______________________________.
4. Si fuera el (la) senador(a) de mi estado, ______________________________.

G15-7 Como si... Con tus compañeros, hablen sobre las acciones de los otros compañeros de clase y escriban cuatro oraciones describiendo estas actitudes.

Modelo: José habla como si *supiera mucho de los métodos de conservación.*

1. Louise discute como si ______________________________.
2. Jenny y Steve piensan como si ______________________________.
3. Heather y tú hablan como si ______________________________.
4. Tú actúas *(act)* como si ______________________________.

Infinitive versus subjunctive

Use an infinitive . . .

1. after verbs of volition when there is only one subject in a sentence.
   Ileana quiere **conservar** energía.
   Ileana wants to conserve energy.
2. after verbs of emotion when there is only one subject in a sentence.
   David espera **reciclar** más en Chile.
   David hopes to recycle more in Chile.
3. after impersonal expressions when there is no personal subject in a sentence.
   Es bueno conservar la energía.
   It's good to conserve energy.

Use a subjunctive verb form . . .

1. after verbs of volition when there is a change of subject in a sentence.
   Ileana quiere que **nosotros** la **conservemos.**
   Ileana wants us to conserve it.
2. after verbs of emotion when there is a change of subject in a sentence.
   David espera que **usted recicle** más.
   David hopes that you recycle more.
3. after impersonal expressions when there is a personal subject in a sentence.
   Es bueno que **usted** la **conserve**.
   It's good that you conserve it.

Nombre ______________________________ Fecha ______________

Practiquemos

G15-8 Problemas mundiales. Escoge la forma del verbo correcta según las situaciones.

Modelo: Es importante *reciclar* el plástico.
El gobernador quiere que la comunidad *recicle* más y de manera más eficiente.

1. En Chile, David quiere que los Srs. Torreón ______________ (reciclar) mejor el número de botellas que usan.
2. En México, Alicia desea que la universidad ______________ (usar) más potes de basura para reciclar.
3. Es importante ______________ (conservar) el agua en el Canal de Panamá, ya que es el medio de transporte del canal.
4. En Costa Rica, Ileana espera que el gobierno ______________ (proteger) los bosques naturales.
5. Es necesario ______________ (plantar) más árboles todos los años.
6. En Guatemala, Luis desea que la gobernadora del estado ______________ (multar) a las compañías que contaminen.
7. Es dudoso que a la comunidad no le ______________ (preocupar) el medio ambiente.
8. Es una lástima ______________ (dañar) los recursos naturales.

G15-9 Limpiar sin contaminar. Lee el siguiente artículo sobre la limpieza y escoge la forma correcta del verbo según la situación.

Modelo: ¿Qué (hacer / haría) para (limpiar / limpiara) la casa sin contaminar?

Limpiar sin contaminar

Los productos que (usar / usamos) en la casa para limpiar tienen sustancias químicas que dañan al medio ambiente. Es importante (conocer / conozcamos) los productos que usan las abuelas para limpiar. Las abuelas desean (tener / tuviéramos) unas casas muy limpias y al mismo tiempo no usan productos contaminantes. Por ejemplo, las abuelas quieren que en sus casas la cocina y el baño (ser / sean) los lugares más limpios, y por eso usan limón porque limpia y deja un olor *(smell)* muy agradable. Otro producto importante es la leche. Es bueno que usted (saber / sepa) que la leche caliente sirve para limpiar muebles de madera *(wood furniture)*. También usted puede usar la cebolla si usted desea (tener / tenga) ventanas muy limpias.

Estoy seguro(a) de que si usted (seguir / sigue) nuestros consejos *(advice)*, tendrá una casa muy limpia y sin elementos contaminantes.

Nombre ______________________ Fecha ______________

Práctica comunicativa suplemental I

El medio ambiente. Los han contratado para colaborar con el grupo de defensa del medio ambiente del Amazonas. Tú estás encargado(a) de dar sugerencias y decir qué es necesario hacer. Como defensor(a) del medio ambiente tienes que dar ideas que protejan al medio ambiente y a la comunidad. Lee los problemas que el grupo quiere resolver. Decide con tu compañero(a) qué hacer y luego comparte tus respuestas con los otros grupos.

Modelo: *Es necesario que protestemos en contra de las compañías que contaminan.*

Vocabulario útil

fábrica	*factory*
ganaderos	*cattle ranchers*
ganado	*cattle*
gobierno	*government*
minas	*mines*
petróleo	*oil*
químicos	*chemicals*
se han estado enfermando	*have been getting sick*
tratados	*treaties*
yacimiento	*ore*
Es necesario que...	*It is necessary that . . .*
Se debe...	*It must be/One must be . . .*
Tenemos que...	*We have to . . .*

Problemas:

1. Una compañía quiere extraer minerales preciosos *(precious minerals)* en el Amazonas.
2. Los ganaderos de la región quieren quemar árboles para sembrar pasto *(pasture)* para su ganado.
3. Han descubierto un yacimiento de petróleo en el área y una compañía extranjera quiere explotarlo.
4. Los pobladores de la región se han estado enfermando por tomar agua contaminada con productos químicos usados en las minas.
5. El gobierno no ha respetado los tratados que declaran parte de la región como parque natural.

Nombre ______________________ Fecha ______________

Práctica comunicativa suplemental II

Debate. En grupos de cuatro, preparen sus argumentos para defender las opiniones que ustedes favorecen. Luego intercambien dos miembros de su grupo por dos miembros de otro grupo. Cada pareja debe dar sus opiniones y dar sus razones en el nuevo grupo. Cuando terminen, decidan quién ganó. (No necesitan discutir todos los temas.)

Modelo: *No es bueno experimentar con animales porque sufren mucho.*

Vocabulario útil

consumo	*consumption*
proveniente de	*originating from*
Creo que...	*I believe (I think) that . . .*
Es bueno que...	*It's good that . . .*
Es injusto que...	*It is unfair that . . .*
Es malo que...	*It's bad that . . .*
(No) Estoy de acuerdo	*I (don't) agree*
Si dejáramos...	*If we let . . .*
Si permitiéramos...	*If we permitted . . .*
Si usáramos...	*If we used . . .*

Asuntos:

1. No se debe experimentar con animales.
2. Los menores de dieciocho años deben ser tratados como adultos si cometen crímenes.
3. Las drogas deben legalizarse para reducir su consumo.
4. Debemos usar energía nuclear si es más barata que el petróleo.
5. Los terroristas deben ser tratados humanamente.

REALIDADES en video

Nombre ______________________________ Fecha ______________

REALIDADES en VIDEO

LECCIÓN 1

*In **Intercambios,** Fifth Edition, you will meet five young people from Spain, the United States, and different parts of Latin America who come to live together for a month in the beautiful* **Hacienda Vista Alegre** *in San Juan, Puerto Rico. You will notice that these five people have different accents and different ways of addressing one another, depending on which country they are from.*

In this episode, the new roommates meet each other for the first time and explore the new house.

Expresiones

The following are expressions that you will encounter in the video:

Encantado(a) en conocerte	*Nice to meet you*
Vengo desde...	*I come from. . .*
¿Qué tal?	*How's it going?*
¿Cómo te va?	*How's it going?*

ANTES DE VER REALIDADES

1. Write some other expressions in Spanish that you can use to introduce yourself and greet other people.

   Modelo: ¡Hola! Me llamo....

   ____

   ____

   ____

2. Can you use any of the new **expresiones**? Introduce yourself to two of your classmates and greet one another using the phrases from the list above.
3. Do you kiss a person when you meet him or her for the first time?

Nombre ______________________ Fecha ______________

Nota Cultural: Notice what the Spaniard and the Latin Americans do when they meet each other for the first time.

DESPUÉS DE VER REALIDADES

1. Since these young people come from different countries, they have different ways of introducing themselves and greeting one another. In the following chart, check off the expressions they use to introduce themselves or greet each other.

	Javier	**Alejandra**	**Antonio**	**Sofía**	**Valeria**
Saludos					
Hola					
Me llamo					
Mi nombre es...					
Soy					
¿Qué tal?					
¿Cómo te va?					
Respuestas					
Encantado(a)					
Mucho gusto					
¡Bienvenido(a)!					
Muy bien, gracias					

Nombre ______________________ Fecha ______________

2. Where are these five young people from?
   a. ¿De dónde es Javier? ______________________
   b. ¿De dónde es Alejandra? ______________________
   c. ¿De dónde es Antonio? ______________________
   d. ¿De dónde es Sofía? ______________________
   e. ¿De dónde es Valeria? ______________________
3. What did you notice about the roommates' way of greeting one another? How many kisses did Sofía give to her new friends? How many kisses did Alejandra, Javier, Antonio, and Valeria give to their new friends? Do you kiss people that you meet for the first time? If not, what do you do?

____

____

____

____

Nota Cultural: When greeting one another in Spain, as well as in Brazil, people tend to kiss both cheeks, but in the rest of Latin America people give only one kiss on the cheek.

4. Could you hear differences in accents among the new roommates? Can you describe some of these differences?

____

____

TU PROPIA REALIDAD

Discuss with your classmates:

a. Would you like to be on a reality show? Why?

b. Would you like to live in a foreign country? If so, in which country and why?

c. What type of roommates would you like to have?

Nombre ______________________ Fecha ______________

REALIDADES en VIDEO

LECCIÓN 2

In this episode, the five roommates continue to get to know one another, asking about interests, hobbies, and studies at the university. They also share their first impressions with us.

Expresiones

The following are expressions that you will encounter in the video:

personas corrientes	*ordinary people*
Me gusta / No me gusta	*It is pleasing to me/It is not pleasing to me*
Me parece	*It seems to me*
¡Qué aburrido!	*How boring!*
¿A qué te dedicas?	*What do you do?*
Me interesa / No me interesa	*It is interesting to me/It is not interesting to me*
pasatiempo	*hobby*
Me encanta	*It is fascinating to me*
¡Qué gracioso!	*How funny!*
¡Es una broma!	*It's a joke!*
¡Pero tío(a)!	*Spanish expression meaning young guy (woman)*

ANTES DE VER REALIDADES

1. Make a list of the subjects you study at school.

   Modelo: Sofía estudia filología (*philology [language & literature]*) española.

   ____

   ____

   ____

Nombre ____ Fecha __________________

2. Ask your classmate what classes he or she is taking and if he or she enjoys them.

   Modelo: ¿Te gusta la clase de español? ¿Te gusta la clase de biología?

3. Choose three **expresiones** and write a sentence. Then, share each of the sentences with two of your classmates, observing whether they understand.

   Modelo: Take your classmate's book and say: ¡Pero tío(a), qué es una broma!

   ____

   ____

   ____

Después de ver REALIDADES

1. Let's summarize what we know about our friends in Puerto Rico. Complete their descriptions using the following words:

España	Argentina	Venezuela	Texas	Colombia
medicina	diseño	bailarina *(dancer)*	tomar fotos	filología española
naturaleza *(nature)*	escritora *(writer)*		administración de empresas	

   a. Antonio es de ______________ y estudia ______________.

   b. Javier es de ______________. No quiere *(does not want)* estudiar ______________, y a él le gusta la ______________.

   c. Alejandra es de ______________, le gusta ______________ y también es ______________.

   d. Sofía es de ______________, estudia ______________ y quiere ser ______________.

   e. Valeria es de ______________, y estudia ______________en Italia.

2. Personalities. How do Valeria and Antonio describe their roommates' personalities?

guapo(a)	arrogante	corriente(s)	atractivo(a)
vanidoso(a)	raro(a)	aburrido(a)	sexi

   a. Valeria dice *(says)* que Sofía y Alejandra son ______________, y que todo el grupo es ______________, que Antonio es ______________ pero *(but)* ______________ y que Javier es ______________.

   b. Antonio dice que Valeria es ______________ y ______________, pero ______________ y hace comentarios pesados.

Nota Cultural:

In Spain, at the end of the fifteenth century, *vos* was used as the formal singular pronoun and *tú* as the informal one. In later years, *vos* disappeared from the dialects of Spain but remained in use throughout much of Latin America.

Today, in Central America as well as in Argentina, Uruguay and Paraguay, *vos* is used instead of *tú*. The *vos* form is so widely used in Argentina in private and public settings that if a person from Argentina tries to use the form *tú* with another Argentinean, he or she will be criticized.

3. In the video, we heard Javier say the following to Alejandra: "Alejandra, ¿y vos...? ... Digo, ¿y tú? Eres de Colombia ¿verdad?"

   a. ¿De dónde es Javier? Javier es de ______________.

   b. Why do you think Javier first addresses Alejandra using the *vos* form and then suddenly changes to the *tú* form? Discuss with your classmates.

TU PROPIA REALIDAD

Discuss with your classmates:

a. What would you do if you had to study a career because someone else wanted you to do so? Would you do it? Why?

b. Do you have a future project that you would like to accomplish? (For example, Sofía wants to write a book about . . .)

c. Describe to your classmates your pastimes or hobbies.

Nombre ______________________ Fecha __________

REALIDADES en VIDEO

LECCIÓN 3

In this episode, the five new friends decide to visit the old section of San Juan. They need to be ready at nine o'clock sharp, but someone is in the bathroom and does not want to leave. The other roommates know that they are late and try to hurry the person in the bathroom along.

Once they leave, four of the roommates decide to visit the Castle San Felipe del Morro, the Plaza de la Rogativa, the Paseo de la Princesa and Old San Juan; one of them decides to go shopping.

Expresiones

The following are expressions that you will encounter in the video:

estar listos	*to be ready*
estar de acuerdo	*to be in agreement*
Vale la pena / No vale la pena	*It's worth it/It is not worth it*
hora para vernos	*a certain time to meet*
¡No se pierdan!	*Do not get lost!*
¡No te preocupes por mí!	*Do not worry about me!*
chavo(a)	*In Mexico, young man (woman)*
¿Adónde te metiste todo el día?	*Where were you all day long?*

Nombre ______________________ Fecha ______________

ANTES DE VER REALIDADES

1. Discuss with your classmates:
   a. Who do think is taking too much time in the bathroom? ______________
   b. Who do you think is going to go shopping in Old San Juan? ______________ Why?
   ____

2. Write three questions asking a classmate what time he or she does particular activities. Then, prepare to answer his or her questions.

   Modelo: ¿A qué hora estudias? ¿A qué hora miras la televisión?

   a. ____
   b. ____
   c. ____

3. Review the **expresiones:**
   a. *Vale la pena / No vale la pena* Discuss with your classmates what you think is worth it and what is not worth it.
   b. *No te preocupes por mí* Discuss with your classmates when and with whom you might use this expression.

DESPUÉS DE VER REALIDADES

1. All the friends want to do something different; do you remember what each wants to do?
   a. ¿Qué quiere hacer Alejandra? ______________________________.
   b. ¿Qué quiere hacer Sofía? ______________________________.
   c. ¿Qué quiere hacer Antonio? ______________________________.
   d. ¿Qué quiere hacer Valeria? ______________________________.

2. In the end, they decide to split up; do you remember who goes where?
   a. ¿Por dónde pasean Sofía y Javier? ______________________________.
   b. ¿Por dónde pasean Alejandra y Antonio? ______________________________.
   c. ¿Adónde va Valeria? ______________________________.

Nombre ______________________ Fecha ______________

3. After reading the **Nota Cultural** and seeing the sites that the roommates visit in Old San Juan, what would like to do if you were there? Discuss with your classmates.

Nota Cultural:

Castillo San Felipe del Morro: This is one of the largest forts built by the Spaniards in the Caribbean. Spanish engineers started its construction in 1539, although it was not completed until 1787. This fort suffered countless attacks from pirates, such as Sir Francis Drake in 1595 and the Dutch fleet in 1625. In 1898, American ships fired on it during the Spanish-American War, destroying its lighthouse, which was later restored. During World War II, the U.S. government added an annex of its own design on top of the fort. El Morro is both a UNESCO World Heritage Site and a National Historic Site in the U.S. National Park Service.

Paseo de la Princesa: Located at the southern tip of Old San Juan, this stylish promenade hosted a former Spanish prison, which now houses the Puerto Rico Tourism Company. It offers breathtaking views of the San Juan Bay and is bordered by a huge colonial wall. The Paseo is the place for an afternoon "piragua", a traditional Puerto Rican sweet concoction made from ice and tropical fruit syrups.

La Plaza de la Rogativa: This is a small plaza with a bronze sculpture that commemorates the day a bishop and his companions, carrying torches and chanting, scared off British troops during a 1797 attack on the city. The enemies thought the procession was local troop reinforcements.

Tu propia REALIDAD

Discuss with your classmates:

a. What would you have done/seen if you went to Old San Juan?

b. What is the most important thing or place to visit in a foreign city or country?

c. What would you do to prepare yourself for the place you will visit?

Nombre ______________________ Fecha ______________

REALIDADES en VIDEO

LECCIÓN 4

En este episodio, los cinco amigos dividen sus habitaciones y describen los muebles que tienen. Además, ellos hablan de sus familias y describen lo que hacen sus padres y sus hermanos. Al final del episodio, los personajes (characters) *hablan de lo que ellos piensan de sus otros compañeros de casa.*

Expresiones

Las siguientes expresiones están en el video:

¿No te da miedo?	*Aren't you afraid?*
pelo negro	*dark hair*
bajito(a)	*small in height*
hermano mayor	*older brother*
hermana menor	*younger sister*
modelo jubilada	*retired model*
¡Extraño a mi familia!	*I miss my family!*
¡Es insoportable!	*It's unbearable!*
¡Se trae un rollo!	*He (She) has such a big problem!*
¡Un día movido!	*A very active day!*

Nombre ______________________________ Fecha ______________

ANTES DE VER REALIDADES

1. Con un(a) compañero(a) de clase, describan a sus papás, mamás, hermanos y hermanas.

   ¿Cuántos hermanos tienes? ¿Cómo se llaman? ¿Qué trabajo tiene tu papá? ¿Qué trabajo tiene tu mamá? ¿Qué estudian tus hermanos? ¿Dónde estudian?

2. Ahora usa adjetivos para describir a tu familia (puedes revisar el vocabulario de la **Lección 4** de tu libro de texto):

   Mi papá es ______________

   Mi mamá es ______________

   Mi hermano es ______________

   Mi hermana es ______________

   Yo soy ______________

3. Describe los muebles que hay en tu habitación:

   ____

   ____

   Y los que hay en tu casa:

   ____

   ____

DESPUÉS DE VER REALIDADES

1. Completa las siguientes oraciones de lo que pasa en este episodio usando las **expresiones** (página 347):

   a. La mamá de Alejandra es ______________ y tiene el ______________.

   b. Antonio camina de noche dormido y su habitación está al lado de la de Valeria. Antonio pregunta: Valeria, ¿ ______________?

   c. Javier tiene dos hermanos. Un hermano ______________ que tiene 29 años y que estudia medicina y una ______________ de 18 años que también estudia medicina.

   d. Javier no quiere estudiar medicina y por eso ______________ un ______________ con su padre, que también es médico.

   e. Valeria es modelo y su mamá es una ______________.

   f. Valeria es bonita pero ______________, según *(according to)* Sofía.

   g. Para todos los amigos es un día largo y con muchas actividades; Sofía describe el día como un ______________.

Nombre ______________________________ Fecha ______________

2. ¿Extrañas a tu familia? ¿A quién extrañas de tu familia? ¿Dónde está tu familia? ¿Extrañas a tus amigos? ¿Dónde están tus amigos?

____

____

____

____

3. Al final del episodio, los amigos describen a sus compañeros de cuarto. ¿Qué dicen?

a. Valeria: Antonio cree *(believes)* que es muy gracioso, pero me parece muy ______________.

b. Alejandra: Sofía es muy ______________ y ______________.

c. Sofía: Alejandra es ______________ y ______________. ¡Valeria es ______________ pero es insoportable!

d. Javier: Vivir con cuatro personas que no conoces es ______________ pero también ______________.

TU PROPIA REALIDAD

Discute con tus compañeros:

a. Tú deseas vivir con cuatro personas que no conoces. ¿Cómo van a ser estas personas? ¿Dónde van a vivir tú y estas personas? ¿Cuántos días o meses van a vivir juntos? ¿Cuál va a ser la razón de vivir juntos?

b. ¿Tienen tradiciones familiares en tu familia? ¿Cuáles son estas tradiciones? ¿Te gustan o no? ¿Por qué?

Nombre ______________________________ Fecha ______________

REALIDADES en VIDEO

LECCIÓN 5

En este episodio, los cinco amigos van a aprender a bailar una danza típica de Puerto Rico que se llama **la bomba.** *Y por supuesto Sofía y Valeria tienen una discusión porque a Sofía le gusta mucho el folclor pero a Valeria no le gusta. Además, uno de los amigos no puede bailar porque le duele el tobillo* (ankle).

¿Quién no está en esta foto? ¿Por qué no quiere bailar?

Expresiones

Las siguientes expresiones están en el video:

cambiar el ánimo	*change the mood*
¡No seas tan presumido(a)!	*Do not be so arrogant!*
antepasado(a)(s)	*ancestor(s)*
Esta vez sí me pasé.	*This time I went too far.*
No tengo tiempo para esos desplantes.	*I do not have time for unpleasant incidents.*
¿Te duele la rodilla?	*Does your knee hurt?*
yeso	*cast*
muletas	*crutches*

Nombre ______________________________ Fecha ______________

ANTES DE VER REALIDADES

1. Con tus compañeros(as) de clase, discute: ¿Quién no está en la foto (página 350)? ¿Por qué no quiere bailar esta persona?
2. Describan y escriban todas las actividades que ven en la siguiente foto.

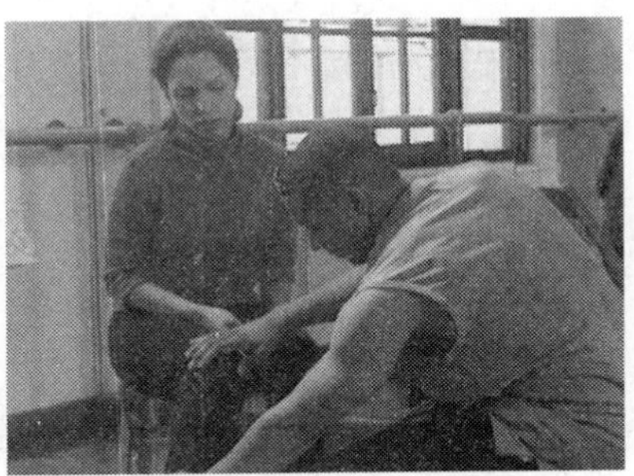

¿Qué están haciendo Alejandra y el instructor?

____

____

____

3. ¿Cuáles son las profesiones y ocupaciones de nuestros amigos?

ingeniero(a)	guía de turismo	agente de viajes
médico(a)	escritor(a)	abogado(a)
fotógrafo(a)	hombre (mujer) de negocios	músico(a)
programador(a)	bailarín (bailarina)	diseñador(a)

a. Sofía quiere ser ______________.
b. Alejandra quiere ser ______________.
c. Valeria quiere ser ______________.
d. Antonio quiere ser ______________.
e. Javier quiere ser ______________.

Nombre ______________________________ Fecha ______________

DESPUÉS DE VER REALIDADES

1. Lean las siguientes oraciones con respecto a este episodio y decidan si las oraciones son verdaderas (V) o falsas (F); si son falsas reescríbanlas para ser verdaderas:

   a. Sofía les da buenas noticias a Alejandra y a Valeria. Ella les va a cambiar el ánimo a las muchachas. ______________________________

   b. Ellos van a aprender a bailar un baile puertorriqueño. ______________________________

   c. A Valeria le gusta la música clásica. ______________________________

   d. Todos los amigos bailan en la clase de baile. ______________________________

   e. A Sofía le duele el tobillo. ______________________________

   f. Alejandra quiere salir con el instructor de baile. ______________________________

2. Decide qué **expresiones** de la lista anterior (página 350) se usan en las siguientes situaciones. Discute las respuestas con tus compañeros.

   a. Tu compañero(a) de cuarto estudia mucho, tienen buenas notas A, A+, A, etc. y siempre habla de sus buenas notas... ______________________________

   b. Haces muchas bromas a tus compañeros de casa y un día uno(a) de tus compañeros está muy enojado(a) contigo. Sabes que es demasiado mala la broma o el chiste *(joke)*. ______________________________

   c. Tu amigo no se siente bien y se toma una aspirina para el dolor de cabeza. ______________

   d. Eres muy paciente y tu amigo no es simpático contigo. Le dices a tu amigo: ______________________________

TU PROPIA REALIDAD

Discute con tus compañeros:

a. ¿Es importante el folclor para ti? ¿Qué es muy importante de una cultura para ti?

b. ¿Te gusta la música y el baile? ¿Te gusta saber sobre la historia de la música en tu país o en otro país?

c. ¿Quién tiene razón *(to be right)* sobre el folclor, Sofía o Valeria?

REALIDADES en VIDEO

LECCIÓN 6

En este episodio, Valeria habla con su ex novio por teléfono y Antonio escucha la conversación. Entonces Valeria se pone furiosa porque piensa que él la está espiando (he is spying on her). *Luego vamos a conocer los planes futuros de Sofía y Javier.*

Expresiones

Las siguientes expresiones están en el video:

¡Ay pero no digas estupideces!	*Don't say such silly things!*
¡Es el colmo!	*This is the limit!*
¿Le diste motivos para ser celoso(a)?	*Did you give him (her) reason to be jealous?*
¡Ella se enamoró! (enamorarse)	*She fell in love! (to fall in love)*
¡Eres un(a) mentiroso(a)!	*You're a liar!*

ANTES DE VER REALIDADES

1. Discute los siguientes temas con los compañeros de clase:
   a. ¿Te gusta la privacidad? ¿Cuándo te gusta estar solo(a) *(alone)*?
   b. ¿Te gusta compartir *(to share)* tus planes para el futuro? ¿Con quién compartes tus planes?
   c. En nuestro programa **REALIDADES** en video, ¿quiénes creen ustedes que pueden ser más que amigos? ¿Creen ustedes que Valeria y Antonio y Sofía y Javier pueden ser más que amigos? ¿Por qué sí o no?

Nombre ______________________ Fecha ______________

DESPUÉS DE VER REALIDADES

1. Usa las **expresiones** de la lista anterior (página 353) y decide lo que dicen los amigos de la hacienda:

   a. Sofía le dice a Javier que está buscando los números de la lotería. Pero ella está buscando un apartamento. Entonces, Javier le dice a Sofía: "______________________".

   b. La ex novia de Antonio se fue *(left)* con su mejor amigo. Antonio le dice a Valeria que: "______________________ de mi amigo".

   c. Antonio no piensa que una muchacha puede ser bonita y fiel. Antonio le pregunta a Valeria: "¿ ______________________?" a tu novio.

   d. Valeria está furiosa porque no tiene privacidad y no puede hablar por teléfono. Ella dice: "______________________ ya no puedo hablar en esta casa sin que alguien escuche mi conversación".

2. Lean las siguientes oraciones con respecto a este episodio y decidan si las oraciones son verdaderas (V) o falsas (F); si son falsas reescríbanlas para ser verdaderas.

   a. Sofía quiere escribir un libro sobre comida puertorriqueña. ______________________

   b. Sofía busca un apartamento. ______________________

   c. Sofía quiere trabajar en la universidad. ______________________

   d. Javier quiere ser un médico en Argentina. ______________________

   e. Sofía es la inspiración de Javier. ______________________

3. En el video, vemos a Javier beber algo. ¿Qué bebe Javier? ¿Qué es ese recipiente donde bebe Javier?

Nota Cultural: Javier es de Argentina y toma *mate*. El mate es una infusión que se toma en Argentina, Uruguay, Paraguay y al sur de Brasil durante la tarde como el té. El nombre de *mate* viene de la palabra quechua *matí* que es el nombre del recipiente donde se toma el *mate*. Las hojas secas *(dry leaves)* se ponen en el recipiente con agua muy caliente y se toma por medio de la *bombilla (straw)* que tiene un colador *(strainer)* al final para prevenir *(to prevent)* que las hojas suban por la bombilla. (En la **Lección 10** de tu libro ***Intercambios*** hay una explicación más completa de lo que es *mate*.)

Nombre ______________________ Fecha ______________

TU PROPIA REALIDAD

Discute con tus compañeros:

a. ¿Te gustaría beber mate? ¿Te gusta la tradición de tomar mate o té por la tarde? ¿Tomas café o té con tus amigos? ¿Cuándo?

b. ¿Cuáles son algunas de tus metas *(goals)* ? ¿Qué haces para alcanzar *(to reach)* tus metas? ¿Qué piensas sobre los planes futuros de Sofía de quedarse *(to remain)* en Puerto Rico para escribir un libro sobre la cultura puertorriqueña?

Nombre ______________________ Fecha ______________

REALIDADES en VIDEO

LECCIÓN 7

En este episodio, todos los amigos de la ***Hacienda Vista Alegre*** *van a nadar, a tomar el sol y hacer esnórkeling en la playa. También ellos discuten las actividades que les gustan hacer durante su tiempo libre.*

¿Dónde están los amigos?

¿Qué hacen los muchachos en el yate?

¿Qué están haciendo los muchachos?

Expresiones

Las siguientes expresiones están en el video:

tener tiempo libre	*to have free time*
mucha suerte	*good luck*
Fui porrista.	*I was a cheerleader.*
ir de compras	*to go shopping*
¡A mí me encanta(n)!	*It's delightful to me!/I love it!*
¡Me da miedo! (darme)	*It scares me.*
(No) estoy acostumbrado(a)	*I'm (not) used to (something)*
zarpar	*to cast off*
chiquilla	*In Spain, means "little girl"*

ANTES DE VER REALIDADES

1. Discute con un(a) compañero(a) las siguientes preguntas usando las **expresiones** de la lista anterior:
   a. ¿Qué haces en tu tiempo libre? ¿Estás acostumbrado(a) a hacer mucho / poco deporte? ¿Qué deporte practicas?
   b. ¿Te gusta el mar? ¿Te gustan las actividades en el mar? ¿Te da miedo el mar?
   c. ¿Te encantan los deportes al aire libre *(outdoors)*? ¿Te encanta tomar el sol? ¿O prefieres ir de compras? ¿Qué deporte te da miedo?
   d. ¿Quiénes, creen ustedes, van a nadar en este episodio?

Nombre ______________________ Fecha ______________

DESPUÉS DE VER REALIDADES

1. Ya vimos lo que hicieron nuestros amigos en su tiempo libre. Completa el siguiente relato usando los verbos en el pretérito para describir sus actividades.

   Ayer los muchachos ______________ (ir) a la playa en San Juan. ______________ (navegar) en yate por la costa y luego ______________ (decidir) hacer esnórkeling. Sofía ______________ (nadar) muy bien aunque no está acostumbrada al mar. Javier ______________ (estar) feliz de poder nadar y bucear en la playa. La pobre Valeria ______________ (querer) nadar, pero no ______________ (poder) porque no sabe nadar. Alejandra y Antonio ______________ (ver) muchos peces de colores debajo del mar. ______________ (ser) un día increíble que los muchachos no van a olvidar *(to forget)*.

2. Ahora sabemos los deportes que practican nuestros amigos. Completa las oraciones usando el verbo **gustar.** Recuerda que este verbo se usa:

   En singular: *Me gusta el fútbol.*
   En plural: *Me gustan los deportes.*

   a. A Sofía le ______________ el vóleibol.
   b. A Alejandra no le ______________ los deportes. A ella sólo le ______________ bailar.
   c. A Antonio le ______________ muchos deportes como el baloncesto y el hockey sobre hielo.
   d. A Javier le ______________ todos los deportes al aire libre y por eso quiere tener su agencia de viajes de aventuras para hacer alpinismo, esnórkeling, buceo, etc.
   e. A Valeria le ______________ el tenis y practica el yoga. ¡Pero no sabe nadar!

TU PROPIA REALIDAD

Discute con tus compañeros:

a. ¿Qué deportes te gustan a ti? ¿Qué deporte te gusta ver en la tele? ¿Qué deporte no te gusta ver en la tele pero te gusta practicar?

b. ¿Sabes nadar? ¿Te gustaría aprender o no te gusta el agua? ¿Crees que Valeria debe ser sincera con sus amigos y explicarles que no le gusta el agua y que le da miedo porque no sabe nadar?

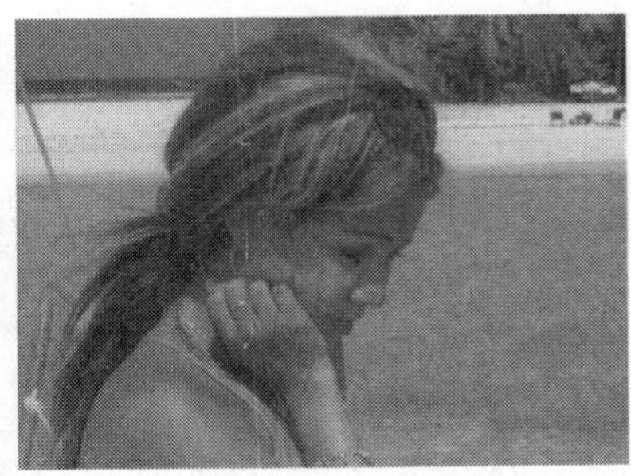

Nombre ______________________ Fecha ______________

REALIDADES en VIDEO

LECCIÓN 8

En este episodio, Valeria quiere sorprender a sus amigos, en especial a Tony (Antonio) y les va a preparar un plato típico. Con Valeria y Alejandra, vamos a visitar un mercado al aire libre en Puerto Rico para comprar los ingredientes de la comida.

¿Dónde está Valeria? ¿Qué está haciendo?

Expresiones

Las siguientes expresiones están en el video:

hacer unos mandados	*do some errands*
¡Yo que sé!	*What do I know about it?*
¿Estás loco(a)?	*Are you crazy?*
¡No seas inútil!	*Don't be helpless!*
¡No seas tonto(a)!	*Don't be silly!*

ANTES DE VER REALIDADES

1. Discute con los compañeros de clase:
   a. ¿Te gusta cocinar? ¿Preparas platos típicos de otros países? ¿Qué tipo de comida te gusta cocinar: española, mexicana, francesa, italiana, china, americana?
   b. ¿Piensas que Valeria sabe cocinar? Si Valeria quiere sorprender a Antonio cocinado un plato típico de su país (el de Antonio), ¿qué tipo de comida va a preparar? ¿Conoces algunos platos típicos de este país? ¿Cuáles son?

Nombre ______________________________ Fecha ______________

Después de ver REALIDADES

1. Lean las siguientes situaciones y decidan qué **expresiones** de la lista anterior (página 358) pueden usar.

   Modelo: Hoy no puedo salir porque tengo muchas cosas que hacer.
   Tengo muchos mandados.

   a. Vas a cenar con tu amigo(a) y él (ella) quiere pagar toda la cuenta.

   ____

   b. Tu amigo(a) quiere pasar toda la noche estudiando y no quiere dormir antes del examen que tiene.

   ____

   c. Tu compañero(a) de casa quiere preparar una cena francesa para sorprender a su novia(o), pero tú no sabes nada de la comida francesa.

   ____

   d. Tu compañero(a) de clase no sabe como usar el programa de Excel, y tú le enseñas pero no entiende; entonces pierdes *(lose)* la paciencia y dices:

   ____

2. Ahora que sabemos lo que hicieron Valeria y Alejandra, completa el siguiente relato usando los verbos en el pretérito:

   Valeria ____________ (decidir) sorprender a sus amigos y en especial a Antonio y les ____________ (preparar) un plato típico mexicano. Alejandra ____________ (ayudar) a Valeria en la cocina y las dos muchachas ____________ (leer) una receta muy interesante: chiles rellenos. Ellas ____________ (hacer) la lista de ingredientes y ____________ (ir) al mercado libre a comprar estos ingredientes. Cuando ellas ____________ (regresar) a casa, Valeria ____________ (cocinar) la comida y Alejandra ____________ (poner *[to set]*) la mesa.

¿Dónde están Valeria y Alejandra?

3. ¿Cuáles son los ingredientes para preparar los chiles rellenos? Ahora sabemos cuales son los ingredientes para cocinar este plato mexicano. Marca con una X los ingredientes necesarios:

¿Qué compran Valeria y Alejandro?

_____________ arroz blanco guisado

_____________ chiles poblanos

_____________ pollo

_____________ salsa verde

_____________ crema

_____________ aceite

_____________ cebollitas de cambray

_____________ papas

_____________ tomates o jitomates

_____________ sal

_____________ pimienta

_____________ queso

Tu propia REALIDAD

Discute con tus compañeros:

a. ¿Te gustaría preparar este plato mexicano? ¿Qué otro plato te gustaría cocinar? ¿Te gusta cocinar para tus amigos? ¿Cuándo les cocinas?

b. ¿Dónde haces las compras de frutas y vegetales, en el supermercado o en una tienda especializada? ¿Te gusta comprar en el "farmer's market"? ¿Puedes comparar un mercado al aire libre hispano con el "farmer's market"?

En la Lección 10, vamos a saber como le quedaron los Chiles Rellenos a Valeria y si ella pudo sorprender a sus amigos con la comida...

Nombre ______________________ Fecha ______________

REALIDADES en VIDEO

LECCIÓN 9

En este episodio, es el cumpleaños de Valeria pero nadie le escribió un mensaje electrónico y nadie la llamó para felicitarla. Por eso ella está un poco triste. Entonces, Valeria y Alejandra recuerdan como celebraban sus cumpleaños cuando eran niñas.

¿De qué hablan Valeria y Alejandra?

Expresiones

Las siguientes expresiones están en el video:

¿Te pasa algo?	*Is something the matter with you?*
No lo tomes tan a pecho.	*Don't take it to heart/so hard.*
Cambiemos de tema (cambiar de tema)	*Let's change the subject.*
¿Pero qué caras son ésas...? ¿Quién murió?	*But why the long faces . . .? Who died?*
No exageres...	*Don't exaggerate . . .*

ANTES DE VER REALIDADES

1. Discute con los compañeros de clase:
   a. ¿Cómo celebraste tu último cumpleaños? ¿Lo celebraste con tu familia y amigos? ¿Dónde lo celebraste? ¿Tuviste un pastel (en México), un bizcocho (en Colombia), una torta (en Venezuela), una tarta (en Argentina) de cumpleaños?
   b. ¿Cómo celebrabas tu cumpleaños cuando eras niño(a)? ¿Dónde vivías? ¿Con quién lo celebrabas?

Nombre ______________________________ Fecha ______________

Después de ver REALIDADES

1. ¿Recuerdas por qué las siguientes personas dijeron las siguientes **expresiones** en este episodio? Comenta con tus compañeros de clase.
   a. Alejandra a Valeria: "¿Te pasa algo?"
   b. Alejandra a Valeria: "No lo tomes tan a pecho"
   c. Alejandra a Valeria: "Cambiemos de tema"
   d. Sofía a Alejandra y a Valeria: "¿Pero qué caras son ésas...? ¿Quién murió?"
   e. Valeria a Alejandra: "No exageres"

2. Ahora sabemos como Valeria y Alejandra celebraban sus cumpleaños. Completa el relato con el imperfecto de los verbos que están en el cuadro:

ser	celebrar	disfrutar
llevar	preparar	gustar
hacer	divertir(se)	regalar

Valeria ______________ más de su cumpleaños cuando ______________ niña. Su papá le ______________ un ramos de flores y su mamá y hermanas le ______________ su comida favorita. Sus padres siempre le ______________ una fiesta muy grande con todos sus amigos y primos.

En cambio, Alejandra ______________ su cumpleaños con sus compañeros de escuela. Su mamá les ______________ un bizcocho, refrescos y helados a la escuela. A Alejandra le ______________ mucho su fiesta y se ______________ mucho con sus compañeros de clase.

3. ¿Por qué estaba Valeria muy triste el día de su cumpleaños? Lee las siguientes oraciones y escribe lo que sucedió realmente...

Modelo: ¿Quién llamó a Valeria? Sus padres o sus amigos.
Ni sus padres ni sus amigos llamaron a Valeria.

a. Valeria recibió muchos mensajes de sus amigos.

____

b. Todos los amigos de Valeria la llamaron para felicitarla.

____

c. Sus compañeros de casa le regalaron algo ese día.

____

d. Ellos también la invitaron a cenar ese día.

____

Nombre ______________________ Fecha ______________

Tu propia REALIDAD

Discute con tus compañeros:

a. ¿Cómo te gustaría celebrar tu próximo cumpleaños? ¿Te gustan las fiestas sorpresas? ¿Les haces fiestas sorpresas de cumpleaños a tus amigos?

b. ¿Qué haces cuando olvidas *(forget)* el cumpleaños de tu mejor amigo(a) o de algún pariente?

c. ¿Qué pudieron regalarle los amigos de la hacienda a Valeria el día de su cumpleaños?

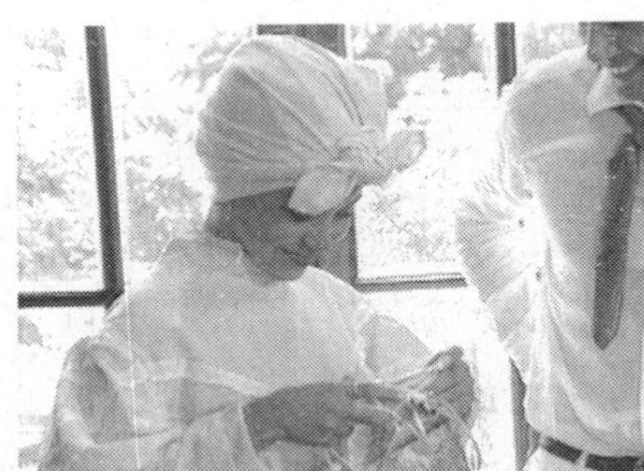

Nombre ____________________ Fecha ____________

REALIDADES en VIDEO

LECCIÓN 10

En este episodio, nosotros y los muchachos de la **Hacienda Vista Alegre** *vamos a saber si Valeria sabe cocinar o no. ¿Para quién va a ser la sorpresa?*

¿Qué plato típico está preparando Valeria? ¿Recuerdas algunos de los ingredientes de este plato?

¿Qué están haciendo Valeria y Alejandra en el mercado?

Expresiones

Las siguientes expresiones están en el video:

¡Buen provecho!	*Have a good meal!*
¡Provecho!	*Have a good meal! (In Mexico)*
Fue un detalle muy dulce de tu parte.	*It was a very nice gesture from you.*
Se hace lo que se puede.	*One does what one can.*

ANTES DE VER REALIDADES

1. Recuerda y discute con tus compañeros de clase:
   a. ¿De dónde es el plato típico que Valeria preparó? ¿Para quién preparó ese plato? ¿Cuáles eran algunos de los ingredientes de este plato?
   b. Usando las **expresiones,** discutan cuándo se debe usar: "Buen provecho", "Fue un detalle muy dulce de tu parte" y "Se hace lo que se puede".

Nombre ______________________ Fecha ____________

Después de ver REALIDADES

1. Recuerdan que Alejandra ayudó a Valeria a comprar los ingredientes. Ahora Alejandra le va a leer a Valeria lo que tiene que hacer para preparar los chiles rellenos. Completa la receta usando el mandato informal (la forma de "tú") de los verbos en paréntesis.

   Modelo: **Escucha** (escuchar) y **sigue** (seguir) bien las instrucciones, Valeria.

   a. ____________ (preparar) el arroz guisado.
   b. ____________ (cortar) los chiles por la mitad.
   c. ____________ (poner) la crema, las cebollitas y la sal juntas en la batidora *(blender)*.
   d. ____________ (bañar) los chiles con el jugo de tomatillos o tomates.
   e. ____________ (poner) luego la crema por encima.
   f. ____________ (colocar) el queso al final.
   g. ____________ (cocinar) los chiles en el horno por diez minutos a 190° C.
   h. ¡No ____________ (quemar) los chiles rellenos, por favor!

2. Bueno, al final la pobre Valeria que no sabe cocinar mucho, quemó *(burnt)* los chiles. Todos tienen hambre así que Javier hace reservaciones en el restaurante donde Sofía trabaja. Compara la comida del restaurante con la comida de Valeria.

   Modelo: La comida de Valeria es **más** económica **que** la comida del restaurante.

   a. La comida del restaurante está ____________ quemada ____________ la de Valeria.
   b. Los chiles son ____________ típicos ____________ las fajitas.
   c. La comida de Valeria es ____________ costosa *(expensive)* ____________ la del restaurante.
   d. Los chiles rellenos son un plato ____________ costoso ____________ los tacos.
   e. Sofía es ____________ como mesera ____________ Valeria como cocinera.

Nombre ______________________ Fecha ______________

TU PROPIA REALIDAD

Discute con tus compañeros:

a. ¿Te gustaría probar *(to try)* los chiles rellenos? ¿Qué plato mexicano te gustaría probar?

b. ¿Te gustaría tener tu propio restaurante? ¿Te gustaría ser chef de cocina? ¿Qué tipo de comida te gustaría cocinar en tu restaurante?

c. ¿Qué te parece la idea de Javier de hacer reservaciones en el restaurante donde trabaja Sofía?

Nombre ______________________________ Fecha ______________

REALIDADES en VIDEO

LECCIÓN 11

En este episodio, los muchachos irán a la playa y Sofía necesita sandalias y ropa nueva. Alejandra la ayuda y además le presta (lends) *ropa para ir a la playa. Las dos hablan de la moda, aunque a Sofía no le interesa mucho la moda.*

Describan la ropa de Antonio.

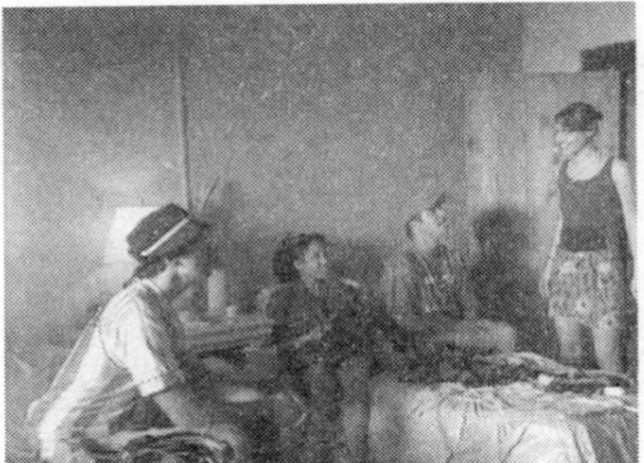

Describan la ropa de Sofía y de Javier.

Expresiones

Las siguientes expresiones están en el video:

mi locura	*my fascination; craziness (good sense)*
Eso no resuelve mi problema.	*That does not solve my problem.*
Ya pasó de moda.	*It's out of style.*
Está de moda. (estar de moda)	*It's in style. (to be fashionable)*
playeras de algodón	*cotton beach cover-ups*
disfrazarse	*to dress up*

ANTES DE VER REALIDADES

1. Usando las **expresiones** de la lista, discute con tus compañeros:
   a. ¿Te interesa la moda? ¿Te pones ropa que ya pasó de moda? ¿Te gusta ir de compras frecuentemente para estar de moda? ¿Cuál es tu locura: la ropa, los zapatos o los accesorios? ¿Usas playeras de algodón? ¿Cuándo y en dónde las usas?
   b. ¿Te gusta disfrazarte? ¿Te disfrazas para el 'Día de las brujas' *(Halloween)*? ¿Existe el 'Día de las brujas' en Latinoamérica? ¿En qué otras fiestas las personas se disfrazan en Latinoamérica?

Nombre ______________________________ Fecha ______________

Después de ver Realidades

1. Sofía tendrá que ir de compras con Alejandra. Completa el siguiente relato de las actividades que ellas tendrán que hacer el próximo fin de semana. Usa los verbos del cuadro en el futuro.

necesitar	visitar	comprar
ir	tener	pedir
probarse	pensar	pagar

El próximo fin de semana, Sofía ______________ con Alejandra de compras porque el grupo ______________ la playa en San Juan. Sofía ______________ comprarse una sandalias nuevas, ______________ que probarse un traje de baño nuevo con más colores porque el que tiene ahora es negro, ______________ unos vaqueros a la moda y se ______________ unas playeras de algodón más modernas. Sofía le ______________ a Alejandra su opinión y luego ______________ con la tarjeta de crédito. Al regreso a casa, sus amigos ______________ que ella está muy bonita y a la moda.

2. Escribe lo que tú crees que los muchachos quieren que hagan las otras personas. Recuerda que cuando tenemos (1) el verbo **querer,** (2) dos personas haciendo la acción y (3) la segunda parte de la oración unida por el *que* se usa el segundo verbo en ***el subjuntivo.***

Modelo: **Alejandra quiere** *que* **Sofía *se vista*** a la moda.

a. Alejandra quiere que Sofía ______________ (ir) de compras.

b. Sofía quiere que Alejandra la ______________ (ayudar) a comprar sandalias.

c. Alejandra quiere que Sofía ______________ (ponerse) ropa colorida.

d. Antonio quiere que Sofía ______________ (comprar) ropa de moda.

e. Javier quiere que Sofía y Alejandra ______________ (vestirse) rápido para poder disfrutar del día de playa.

Nombre ______________________ Fecha ______________

Tu propia REALIDAD

Discute con tus compañeros:

a. ¿Cuál es tu ropa o prenda de vestir favorita? ¿Te gusta vestirte elegantemente o casualmente? ¿Adónde vas con ropa elegante / casual? ¿Te interesa la moda?

b. ¿Te gustaría ser diseñador(a) de modas? ¿Qué tipo de ropa te gustaría diseñar?

c. ¿Crees que Alejandra y Valeria se preocupan demasiado por estar de moda?

Nombre ______________________ Fecha ______________

REALIDADES en VIDEO

LECCIÓN 12

En este episodio, los muchachos recibieron una carta donde les recuerda que ya es tiempo de regresar a casa. En la carta, se les pide que hagan un último proyecto juntos, y además veremos cómo se sienten ellos al pensar en regresar a sus países.

¿Qué están discutiendo las muchachas? ¿Qué tipo de proyecto harán?

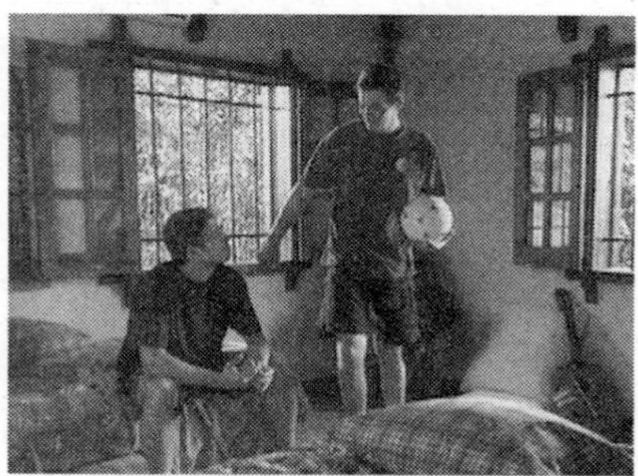

¿Cómo se sienten los muchachos al tener que regresar a sus países?

Expresiones

Las siguientes expresiones están en el video:

tener que alejarme	*have to say good-bye*
Me rompe el corazón.	*My heart is broken.*
Voy a extrañar esta casa y a ustedes.	*I'm going to miss this house and all of you.*
estar pasando por un buen / mal momento	*going through a good/bad period of life*

ANTES DE VER REALIDADES

1. Discute y haz predicciones de lo que harán nuestros amigos de la **Hacienda Vista Alegre:**
   a. ¿Qué tipo de proyecto harán? ¿Estarán contentos o tristes de hacer este proyecto? ¿Cómo se sentirán los muchachos y las muchachas? ¿Quiénes estarán más tristes porque regresan a casa? ¿Por qué?
   b. En el pasado, ¿hiciste algún proyecto especial con tus compañeros de casa, de cuarto o de clase? ¿Qué tipo de proyecto hicieron? ¿Fue una buena o una mala experiencia?
2. Usando las **expresiones** de la lista, discute con tus compañeros:
   a. ¿En qué situación se te rompe o se te rompió el corazón?
   b. ¿Cuándo es necesario tener que alejarse de algo o de alguien?
   c. ¿Extrañas a alguna persona o algún lugar en especial? ¿Por qué?
   d. ¿Estás pasando por un buen / mal momento ahora? Explícales a tus compañeros.

Nombre ______________________ Fecha ______________

Después de ver REALIDADES

1. Todos los amigos de la **Hacienda Vista Alegre** saben que tienen que irse por diferentes razones. Completa las siguientes ideas...

   ¡Ojo! Recuerda que estas expresiones impersonales necesitan que el verbo esté en ***presente del subjuntivo.***

   Modelo: Es importante que Valeria ***regrese*** a Venezuela.

   a. Es necesario que Antonio ______________________

   b. Es una lástima que Alejandra ______________________

   c. Es importante que Sofía ______________________

   d. Es lógico que Javier ______________________

   e. Es mejor que Valeria ______________________

   f. Es imposible que Antonio le pida a Valeria que ______________________

2. En el Testimonio de Javier, él dice que:

   "Antonio debe viajar a los Estados Unidos y dejar de ver a Valeria. Pero es admirable.... Sacrifica una relación personal por una meta profesional. Es admirable también Sofía. Es valiente y decidida."

Discute con tus compañeros, si es admirable o no el sacrificio de Antonio y si Sofía es valiente y decidida. ¿Qué harías tú *(would you do)* en su lugar?

Nota Cultural: Antonio le dice a Javier que en su universidad lo llaman *Rivera* por el pintor mexicano *Diego Rivera.* Diego Rivera nació en Guanajuato, México, en 1886. Cuando tenía 20 años hizo su primera exposición en la Ciudad de México y se estableció como un gran pintor. Sus obras más impresionantes son los murales por sus temas y sus dimensiones. Entre sus temas están los trabajadores, la Revolución Mexicana (1910–1920), la Revolución Rusa (1917–1921), la historia de México y la cultura popular mexicana como se muestra en el siguiente mural.

***El día de los muertos* (1924) by Diego Rivera. Ministerio de Educación, México.**

Nombre ______________________________ Fecha ______________

Tu propia REALIDAD

Discute con tus compañeros:

a. ¿Qué proyecto te gustaría hacer con tus compañeros de la clase de español? En grupos de cuatro personas hagan un proyecto que represente la clase de español y lo que significa para ustedes.

b. ¿Crees que al pintar un cuadro, los amigos de la hacienda podrán explicar su amistad y diversidad de culturas? ¿Qué otro tipo de proyecto pueden hacer los muchachos para explicar sus culturas?

REALIDADES en VIDEO

LECCIÓN 13

Los muchachos decidieron que van a pintar un cuadro y ahora, en este episodio, discuten el tema del cuadro. Luego, Alejandra les dice a sus amigos lo que piensa hacer cuando regrese a Colombia y Sofía discute las ideas para su libro.

¿Cuál debe ser el tema de este cuadro?

Expresiones

Las siguientes expresiones están en el video:

montar una exposición	*to have an exhibition*
cumplir esa meta	*to reach that goal*
¡Qué buena idea!	*What a great idea!*
el folleto	*pamphlet*
la portada	*the cover of a book*
la contraportada	*the back cover of a book*
Estamos muy orgullosos de ti.	*We are very proud of you.*

ANTES DE VER REALIDADES

1. Discute y haz predicciones de lo que pintarán los amigos de la hacienda:
   a. ¿Qué temas deben pintar en este cuadro? ¿Cómo pueden representar su amistad y la diversidad de culturas en el cuadro? ¿Podrán hacer un buen trabajo?
   b. ¿Eres pintor(a)? ¿Te gusta pintar o te gusta visitar galerías de pintura? ¿Qué tipo de arte te gusta más?

2. Usando las **expresiones** de la lista anterior (página 373), discute con tus compañeros:
   a. ¿Cumples todas las metas que te propones? ¿Últimamente cumpliste con tus metas?
   b. ¿Estás orgulloso(a) de algo que haces ahora o que hiciste anteriormente? ¿Hay alguien que está orgulloso(a) de ti? ¿Quién y por qué?

DESPUÉS DE VER REALIDADES

1. ¿Qué metas quieren cumplir los amigos de la **Hacienda Vista Alegre**? Completa las ideas.

   ¡Ojo! Recuerda que las expresiones que implican duda y algunas palabras que expresan tiempo necesitan que el verbo esté en ***presente del subjuntivo.***

   Modelo: Sofía les dice a sus amigos: **"Antes de que *comencemos*, necesitan saber que pinto como una niña de tres años."**

   a. Cuando Alejandra ______________ (regresar) a Colombia montará una exposición de fotografía.
   b. Tan pronto como Antonio ______________ (ir) a Texas terminará sus estudios de negocios.
   c. Cuando Sofía ______________ (escribir) su libro será famosa entre sus amigos.
   d. Valeria duda de que Antonio ______________ (querer) que ella lo visite en Texas.
   e. Javier no está seguro de que ______________ (poder) cumplir su meta.
   f. Alejandra cree que sus fotos ______________ (ser) muy buenas.

2. En el testimonio de Alejandra, ella dice:

   "Cuando regrese a Colombia quiero montar una exposición de fotografía en el Museo de Arte. Siempre quise hacerlo, pero nunca me quedaba tiempo con la Escuela de Danza. Pero ahora, es importante que cumpla esa meta. Estoy lista para hacerlo."

Discute con tus compañeros si siempre o nunca cumples tus metas. Explica y da ejemplos de situaciones.

Nombre ______________________________ Fecha ______________

TU PROPIA REALIDAD

Discute con tus compañeros:

a. ¿Cuáles son tus metas al terminar este trimestre o semestre? ¿Cuáles son tus metas al terminar este período en la universidad?

b. En tu opinión, ¿qué temas culturales importantes debe incluir Sofía en su libro? ¿Cómo debe ser la portada y la contraportada? Diseña una portada para el libro de Sofía con tus compañeros.

c. ¿Te gustaría ser escritor(a)? ¿Te gustaría escribir un libro? ¿Cuál sería el tema de tu libro? ¿Qué tendría la portada y la contraportada?

Nombre ______________________ Fecha ______________

REALIDADES en VIDEO

LECCIÓN 14

En este episodio, los muchachos están muy contentos con su proyecto final y lo que pintaron en el cuadro. Al final cada uno discute lo que siente y lo que aprendió de vivir con cuatro personas extrañas en una misma casa por un mes.

¿Estarán contentos los muchachos con lo que están haciendo?

Expresiones

Las siguientes expresiones están en el video:

¿Se van a separar?	*Are you going to break up?*
hacerse de noche	*to get late*
un momento clave	*an important moment*
Fue como un reto.	*It was a challenge.*
una sonrisa a mi cara	*a smile on my face*

ANTES DE VER REALIDADES

1. Discute con los compañeros:
   a. ¿Cómo crees que se sienten los amigos? ¿Cómo se sienten Antonio y Valeria? ¿Crees que se van a separar?
   b. ¿Qué crees que pasará entre Valeria y Antonio? ¿Crees que Sofía terminará su libro sobre Puerto Rico? ¿Crees que Javier viajará por Latinoamérica?
2. Usando las **expresiones** de la lista, discute con los compañeros:
   a. Un momento clave en tu vida
   b. Un reto que te pones actualmente o que te pusiste anteriormente
   c. ¿Cuándo se te hace de noche? ¿Qué actividades distraen tu atención y por eso se te hace tarde?

Nombre ______________________________ Fecha ______________

Después de ver REALIDADES

1. Ya sabemos que los amigos aprendieron mucho los unos de los otros. ¿Qué pasaría si ellos no vivieran en Puerto Rico por un mes? Completa las siguientes ideas: con el imperfecto del subjuntivo **(-ron, -ra, -ras, -ramos, -rais, -ran)** o con el condicional **(-ía, -ías, -ía, -íamos, -íais, -ían)**

   Modelo: Si Valeria no **viviera** (vivir) en Venezuela, viviría en Texas.

   a. Si Javier no ______________ (conocer) a Sofía, no sería valiente.

   b. Si Sofía ______________ (trabajar) en España, no escribiría sobre la cultura de Puerto Rico.

   c. Si Antonio no ______________ (estudiar) en Texas, se quedaría en Puerto Rico.

   d. Si Valeria no terminara su carrera en Italia, la ______________ (terminar) en Texas.

   e. Si Sofía no encontrara un trabajo como mesera, no ______________ (poder) alquilar un apartamento.

   f. Si Alejandra no regresara a Colombia, no ______________ (montar) su exposición de fotografía.

2. En el Testimonio de Sofía, ella dice:

   "Este mes es un momento clave en nuestras vidas. Y estoy segura de que todos lo recordaremos para siempre."

Discute con los compañeros: ¿Por qué fue un momento clave en las vidas de los muchachos? ¿Cómo cambiaron ellos sicológicamente y socialmente?

Tu propia REALIDAD

Discute con los compañeros:

a. ¿Cuál es el reto más difícil de tu vida?

b. ¿Qué deberían hacer Valeria y Antonio? ¿Qué crees tú que decidirá Valeria? ¿Por qué?

c. ¿Te gustó el cuadro que pintaron los muchachos? ¿Qué figuras geométricas tiene el cuadro? ¿Qué crees que representan? ¿Crees que los muchachos seguirán siendo amigos después de regresar a casa?

d. ¿Te gustaría tener una experiencia como la que vivieron estos muchachos en otro país?

Nombre ______________________________ Fecha ______________

REALIDADES en VIDEO

LECCIÓN 15

En esta última lección, vamos a analizar algunas escenas que fueron importantes en la vida de los muchachos en la **Hacienda Vista Alegre.** *¿Qué harían ustedes si estuvieran en el lugar de los muchachos?*

Expresiones

Las siguientes expresiones están presentes en los videos:

¿De verdad?	*Really?*
¡Qué curioso(a) eres!	*You are so curious!*
hacer fila	*wait in line*
¡Me fascina!	*I love it!*
pedir trabajo	*to ask for a job*
(No) me atrevo (atreverse)	*I (don't) dare to do (something) (to dare to)*
¿Qué te pasa?	*What's happening with you?*
estar listo	*to be ready*
Quedamos en... (quedar en)	*We agree on... (to agree on...)*
¡Qué buena idea!	*What a great idea!*

¿Te gustaría vivir con un grupo de personas que no conoces por un mes? ¿Con cuál de estos amigos te gustaría vivir y por qué?

Recuerdas que Valeria no quería salir del baño y todos los muchachos estaban haciendo fila para entrar porque tenían que salir de casa a las nueve de la mañana y ya eran las 8:35.

¿Qué harías o qué le dirías a tu compañero(a) si uno de ellos no tuviera consideración *(consideration)* con las otras personas?

Nombre ____________________________ Fecha ______________

Recuerdas que Sofía tiene un plan para cuando termine el proyecto de la **Hacienda Vista Alegre.** ¿Cuál es la meta de Sofía? ¿Cuál es el plan de Sofía? ¿Qué necesita hacer ella? ¿Qué harías tú si fueras Sofía?

¿Recuerdas cuál es la profesión de Javier? ¿Qué quiere hacer Javier de verdad? ¿Se atreverá Javier a hablar con su padre y explicarle lo que él realmente quiere hacer? ¿Qué harías tú si fueras Javier?

Recuerdas que nadie se acordó de la pobre Valeria el día de su cumpleaños y Sofía no tuvo paciencia con ella tampoco. ¿Cómo celebraba Alejandra su cumpleaños en Colombia y cómo celebraba Valeria su cumpleaños en Venezuela? ¿Si vivieras en esta casa, cómo celebrarías el cumpleaños de Valeria? ¿Cómo celebrabas tu cumpleaños cuando tenías 10 o 12 años? ¿Cómo celebrarás tu próximo cumpleaños?

Nombre ______________________________ Fecha ____________

Recuerdas la escena entre Antonio y Valeria en la cocina. ¿Qué le preguntó Antonio a Valeria? ¿Qué harías tú si fueras Antonio? ¿Qué harías tú si fueras Valeria?

Recuerdas que los muchachos quedaron en pintar un cuadro. ¿Qué pintarías tú si fueras uno de los chicos(as)? ¿Qué otro proyecto harías tú? ¿Qué te parece buena idea hacer?